# BLACK BROADWAY

## AFRICAN AMERICANS ON THE GREAT WHITE WAY

## STEWART F. LANE

### FOREWORD BY KENNY LEON

SQUAREONE PUBLISHERS

Cover Designer: Jeannie Tudor
In-House Editor: Joanne Abrams
Typesetter: Jeannie Tudor


**Square One Publishers**
Garden City Park, NY 11040
(516) 535-2010
www.squareonepublishers.com




**Library of Congress Cataloging-in-Publication Data**

Lane, Stewart F.
  Black Broadway : African Americans on the great white way / Stewart F. Lane.
    pages cm
  Includes bibliographical references.
  ISBN 978-0-7570-0388-2 (hardback)
  1. African Americans in the performing arts--New York (State)--New
York—History—20th century. 2. African American theater—New York (State)—New
York—History—20th century. 3. American drama—African American
authors—History and criticism. 4. Broadway (New York, N.Y.)—History. I.
Title.
  PN2270.A35L36 2015
  792.089'96073—dc23
               2014006513

Printed and bound in India by Nutech Print Services


10  9  8  7  6  5  4  3  2  1

# Contents

*This book is dedicated to my family—*
*my wife, Bonnie, and my children,*
*Eliana, Harlyn, Leah, Leonard, and Franklin—*
*who have always been there for me*
*and allowed me time to pursue all things theater.*

# Acknowledgments

I have been fortunate to have many people guide me throughout my life. I would like to thank my long-time friends and partners James M. Nederlander and James L. Nederlander for their counsel and trust. I also thank Kenny Leon for his friendship and for continuing to bring quality shows to the Broadway stage, and Susan Weaving, who brought us together. I am grateful to Sheldon Epps, Artistic Director of the Pasadena Playhouse. And I thank the Boston University College of Fine Arts for the vital role it plays in supporting American theater through training and education.

In regard to this book, it has been both a great pleasure and a great labor to put together the words and photos that form *Black Broadway*. Like most undertakings, it was not accomplished alone, and I owe a debt of gratitude to the many people who helped me along the way by generously providing invaluable information and illustrations.

Part of what makes *Black Broadway* so fascinating is its wealth of stories about African-American entertainers. I am grateful to all of these performers for their immeasurable contributions to the field, and I would especially like to thank James Earl Jones and Leslie Uggams, who graciously shared their personal stories and offered insights into the world of the theater.

The New York Public Library made an invaluable contribution to this book by allowing us to explore and use the library's photo collections. First and foremost, I owe a debt of gratitude to Thomas Lisanti, Manager of Permissions and Reproduction Services at the NYPL. Tom guided us through the Library's vast resources and helped us find hundreds of magnificent photos. I also thank Jeremy Megraw, Photograph Librarian of the New York Public Library for the Performing Arts, and Tammi Lawson, Assistant Curator of the Art and Artifacts Division of the Schomburg Center for Research in Black Culture. Without these dedicated professionals, this book would not have been possible.

In several cases, we had to seek special permission to reprint the beautiful photos we located in our search. The following organizations and individuals have been immeasurably helpful in this regard: the Folger Shakespeare Library, George Mason University, the Harriet Beecher Stowe Center, the Harvard Theatre Collection, the Yale

School of Drama/Yale Repertory Theatre, the Harmon Foundation of the National Archives, Michal Daniel, Marsha Hudson, James Kriegsmann, Jr., Joan Marcus, and Gabriel and Avivah Pinski. Special thanks are due to photographer Lisa Pacino, who generously provided not only great photos, but also precious time and information.

*Black Broadway* has been made more colorful and lively by the vibrant *Playbill* cover images that grace its pages. For these, I am grateful to my friend Philip S. Birsh, president and chief executive of Playbill, who kindly allowed us to reprint the photos in this book. I also thank Andrew Ku, director of Playbill.com, who provided us with the images.

Even before the first word of this project was written, Rudy Shur, the head of Square One Publishers, believed that this was a story worth telling. I thank

Rudy for his confidence, his encouragement, and most important, for guiding *Black Broadway* from start to finish. I also thank Richard Mintzer, who performed the initial research for the project and put me in touch with Square One. And I am grateful to Square One's Executive Editor, Joanne Abrams, for her meticulous editing and coordination of text and images, and Square One's Art Director, Jeannie Tudor, who helped transform hundreds of photos into a unique record of African-American history. I also thank Square One editors Marie Caratozzolo, Anthony Pomes, and Miye Bromberg for their assistance in locating graphics, securing reprint permission, and helping to ensure the quality of the book.

Finally, and most important, I thank my wife, Bonnie Comley, and our beautiful children, whose support and encouragement always inspires me.

# Foreword

## by Kenny Leon

Growing up in Florida in the early 1960s, I could never have imagined the world of Broadway. But it existed. Many miles away, American history was unfolding on stage as theater. Far away from my front porch in Florida, where I would sit with my grandmother laughing and discussing life's mysteries, art was imitating life. Does my story, growing up poor in North Florida with my grandmother and later in Central Florida with my mother, stepfather, and four siblings, count as one of America's stories? Of course. I would find out in my later years that everyone's life belongs on a raised stage as the broader community sits in the dark to be reminded of life's commonalities.

I was introduced to play acting in the Southern Baptist church and later to formal acting through the government-sponsored Upward Bound Program. But my world view would be changed for the better when I attended college in Atlanta, Georgia as a political science major. It was there that I met folks like Samuel L. Jackson, LaTanya Richardson, and Bill Nunn. These classmates dreamed of being professional actors—they wanted to tell stories to the world that would have an impact. It is during this time that I combined my thirst for political change with my newly developed eyes for theater and forged a purpose for life and a passion for making a difference.

As I continued on life's journey, I found myself acting on stage and in television; directing plays, musicals, and films; and running one of America's leading non-profit regional theaters. Through these experiences, I discovered life's challenges, including society's holes and lack of diversity. This book fills in these gaps; this book presents it all. We need all of our stories like we need all of history—not just *his* story. The powerful truths in these pages remind this poor boy from Miccosukee Road in Tallahassee, Florida that I, too, have contributed to and belong on Broadway.

This book is a celebration of nearly 200 years of African-American theater history in the United States, illustrating its contributions to American art and culture, including contributions to Broadway, Main Street, and the way in which theater has evolved. It is also a unique tribute to the

*Kenny Leon* is an award-winning director of plays, musicals, and films, including the original Broadway productions of *Gem of the Ocean* (2004), *Radio Golf* (2007), *Stick Fly* (2011), and *The Mountaintop* (2011); the 2010 revival of *Fences*; and the 2014 revival of *A Raisin in the Sun*, which won Tony Awards for the Best Revival of a Play, the Best Performance by an Actress in a Featured Role (Sophie Okonedo), and the Best Direction of a Play (Kenny Leon). Mr. Leon is also cofounder and Artistic Director of one of America's leading non-profit regional theaters, True Colors Theatre Company.

many African-American actors, directors, playwrights, and others who have contributed to the fabric of American theater, most of whom are pictured in these pages.

While the emphasis of this work is on providing a thoughtful account of developments in African-American theater history, it contains much that will be of interest to those seeking a broader understanding of all of American history. Since Dutch traders brought the first African slaves to Jamestown in 1619, the discourse of race has been and continues to be a pervasive force in shaping the ethos of America's social, economic, and political evolution. Historically, African-American theater has not only personified racial discourse but has paralleled the cultural development of perceptions of race through performance and writing. Such portrayal is two-dimensional. There's the early characterization of African Americans by whites simply as minstrels. In contrast, at least as early as the 1820s, African-American playwrights depicted a more realistic portrait of black life. Performances were not limited to portrayals of black life but included more universal art such as Shakespearean plays.

The history of African-American theater is the story of human resilience. It is a story that has been previously documented, but not as thoroughly explored as now. With the artful use of historical details, this book chronicles the progress of African-American theater from the 1700s to the contemporary stage. The reader is further rewarded with a more thorough understanding of the injustice, appalling racial violence, and adversity faced by those devoted to their artistic craft. In addition, the book emphasizes the boldness of creativity, perseverance, and tenacity exhibited by those same individuals.

As an artist, director, patron, and champion of the arts, I firmly believe that understanding the contributions of African-American culture to the stage is not only important but also necessary. In the words of Oscar Wilde, "Life imitates art far more than art imitates life." The moral progress of American society has been and continues to be shaped by the past. One cannot really know American theater without knowing African-American theater. Only through an appreciation of the history of African-American theater can we sustain an open and tolerant "Broadway" community and society throughout America.

# Preface

During the 1960s, when I was attending high school in the suburbs of New York, I was the resident "theater geek." I was fascinated by drama and was the "go to" guy for theater projects. On one occasion, a classmate approached me about putting on a production of Martin Duberman's *In White America*, a documentary drama that tells the story of black people in the United States. Working on the show was a marvelous experience. It brought together a diverse group of students, and all of us learned and grew as we explored different aspects of African-American history. *In White America* proved to me the power of theater to provoke discussion and social change. Here was theater sharing both what was and what could be—including a more integrated and tolerant nation.

Both my interest in the theater and my awareness of social issues had taken root, and looking back, it was inevitable that both would flourish. Certainly, it was an exciting time to be young, for the decade of the sixties was marked by sweeping social changes, including the civil rights movement and the beginning of black power. Through strikes, marches, and rallies, African Americans were demanding (and beginning to win) greater equality. The theater—which has always mirrored society—reflected these changes by offering more plays that dealt with important black issues, as well as a greater number of talented African-American performers. *In White America* was just one of the many significant works that resulted from this social revolution. During my life, I would become aware of many more.

In college, I pursued a degree in the fine arts, and afterwards, I began working as an actor. Although I would never stop performing, over time, I became involved in other facets of the theater, as well, including screenwriting and producing. This gave me an amazing opportunity to participate in a range of productions, first in regional theater and then on Broadway. It also allowed me to work with a wide array of performers, including many talented people of color. Just a few examples of the plays in which I've been involved are *Thoroughly Modern Millie* (2003) and *Stormy Weather* (2009), both starring Leslie Uggams; *The Best Man* (2012), starring James Earl Jones; and the all-black revival of *A Streetcar Named*

*Desire* (2012), starring Blair Underwood and Nicole Ari Parker. As I got to know not just the actors but also behind-the-scenes people like pioneering black producers Stephen Bryd and Alia Jones-Harvey, my appreciation of African-American involvement in the entertainment field grew and deepened. My theater career had begun during a time of increasing social progress and tolerance, but I knew that life in America hadn't always offered opportunities to all people. Blacks had trodden a long, rocky road to reach Broadway, and I was becoming increasingly interested in learning about the struggle and sharing what I'd learned with others.

This book chronicles the progress that African Americans have made in the theater, and particularly, on Broadway. It begins by taking a brief look at the history of American theater, and then examines how early black artists reached the stage, first in minstrel shows and later in the highly popular entertainment known as vaudeville. By the 1900s, when Broadway was in its infancy, talented black composers and writers were already writing musicals, and their works were being performed by black actors and actresses. Black dramas took a little longer to make an appearance, but progress was being made. Change came slowly, with setbacks along the way, but in each decade, more black voices were heard, more stories of African-American life were told, and more people of color found a means of expression on the Great White Way. Just as important, black audiences, who had long been barred from major theaters, ultimately joined the throngs of New York theatergoers.

To do justice to the rich history of African Americans on Broadway would, of course, require several volumes. At the cost of leaving some individuals and shows out, I have provided a narrative that explores the hardships and triumphs of some of the most significant people involved in black theater along with vibrant images that provide a window to the world of entertainment.

It is my hope that, through words and photos, *Black Broadway* introduces you to the remarkable people and events that helped weave the tapestry of American theater, enabling you to see how we arrived where we are today.

# Introduction

In 1821, Alexander Brown, a free black, took a bold course of action. Using money he had earned as a ship's steward, Brown founded the African Grove Theatre, the first known theater established by and for African Americans in New York City. Finally, people of color were able to perform in plays of their own choosing. Finally, they were able to attend dramatic performances.

Because of the intense racism of the time, the African Grove had to move frequently from one area of the city to another, and in 1923, it was forced to close. But an important first step had been taken. Black people had, for a brief time, taken the stage. Their history in the American theater had begun.

Through text and photos, *Black Broadway* tells the story of the long road that people of color have taken from the first modest productions at the African Grove to the grand stages of Broadway. Chapter 1 discusses the birth of American theater and examines how black people began to make their way in the field of entertainment. It looks at the era of the minstrel show, which, while demean-

ing to blacks, gave them the opportunity to ply their trade and develop their skills as performers. It also introduces the talented African-American composers, lyricists, playwrights, and actors who produced the first black musicals to grace the stages of Manhattan.

At the dawn of the twentieth century, New York City received a flood of southern blacks in search of greater social and economic equality. Although these immigrants did not find the equal opportunities they sought, they did discover a growing metropolis that boasted not only a newly established theater district but also a popular form of entertainment known as vaudeville. Chapter 2 first explores the important role that African-American entertainers played in vaudeville. It then looks at turn-of-the-century African-American musicals and shares the initial attempts made by the black community to produce drama that represented their experience in America.

For most of the nation, the 1920s was a time of economic prosperity and high spirits. For African

Americans, it also marked the birth of a social and artistic movement best known as the Harlem Renaissance. Chapter 3 discusses this blossoming of black culture and looks at the groundbreaking dramas and musicals that enabled people of color to play their part on the Broadway stage during the Roaring Twenties.

Although the Great Depression had a devastating effect on all aspects of American life, including entertainment, New York continued to offer productions throughout this bleak period of our history. Chapter 4 provides a window to the theater of the time. It looks at a number of significant dramas, including a captivating all-black production of Shakespeare's *Macbeth* that was funded by the Federal Government's Negro Theater Project. It also explores musicals that stirred controversy, inspired praise, and launched the careers of great black performers.

By the 1950s, Americans had largely bounced back from both the Depression and World War II, and the country's rising spirits were reflected in its theater. Chapter 5 first presents an array of fabulous musicals performed by great African-American actors and actresses. It then looks at the dramas of the fifties, including a landmark production that not only dealt with serious racial issues but also demonstrated that plays written by black artists could enthrall theatergoers of all races.

Chapter 6 focuses on the turbulent sixties—a time of enormous social change in America and tremendous experimentation in the world of the theater. Long-standing conventions were being questioned, old barriers were being torn down, and African-American performers were being featured in greater numbers than ever before. This chapter explores the noteworthy productions born of this unique period of history.

Despite economic recession, the seventies and eighties would produce an astounding variety of musicals, including all-black revivals of traditionally white plays and revues that honored legendary African-American songwriters. Unfortunately, Broadway was far less hospitable to black dramas, but off-Broadway filled the gap, with the Public Theater and other venues offering opportunities to both black writers and black performers. This period also saw the emergence of August Wilson, an African-American playwright who would chronicle black history through a series of brilliant plays. In Chapter 7, you'll learn of both the struggles and the triumphs of these decades.

The 1990s began with a much-needed revitalization of the theater district. Now theatergoers could better enjoy the fruits of Broadway, including a host of plays that featured black performers. As the nineties gave birth to a new millennium, a quiet revolution began to take place as African-American producers joined the theater community. Black playwrights, composers, and performers had long been part of the Great White Way, but black producers had been few and far between. As this began to change, new opportunities would arise for actors of color, and—just as important—African-American audiences would take an increasing interest in what Broadway had to offer.

Change comes slowly and often painfully in any area of society. For decades, African Americans have struggled to become part of Broadway, and while the fight continues, many battles have been won and significant changes have been made. It is my hope that *Black Broadway* serves as a guide to the many people who have blazed a trail to the Great White Way and made it more accessible to everyone—black and white—who seeks to entertain and enlighten us through the performing arts.

"If there is no struggle, there is no progress."
–Frederick Douglass

"Human progress is neither automatic nor inevitable. . . .
Every step toward the goal of justice requires
sacrifice, suffering, and struggle; the tireless exertions
and passionate concern of dedicated individuals."
–Martin Luther King, Jr.

"There's nothing that can match Broadway
for stature and dignity."
–Sammy Davis, Jr.

# STARRING
## IN ORDER OF APPEARANCE

William Alexander Brown

James Hewlett

Ira Aldridge

William Henry Lane

Thomas Dilward

James Bland

Dora Dean

Charles E. Johnson

Sam Lucas

Sissieretta Jones

Will Marion Cook

Paul Laurence Dunbar

Ernest Hogan

Bert Williams

George Walker

Abbie Mitchell

Bob Cole

William Johnson

# 1.

# African-American Theater Through the Nineteenth Century

Long before the 1900s, when Broadway became known as the Great White Way, the many talented African-American performers who struggled to gain the recognition they deserved found the New York theater district to be just that—white. It took time and determination for African Americans to tear down racial barriers, but those performers, composers, and writers who firmly believed in self-expression, in freedom, and in developing their own artistic potential found ways to bring their talents to the stage in productions that helped shape American theater.

## EARLY AMERICAN THEATER

The American theater was likely born in the 1700s, but for a long time, productions were held in any available space—not in formal theaters—or in small theaters that remained in use for only a few seasons before closing. Records exist of plays being staged in the 1700s in various American cities, including Williamsburg, Virginia; Charleston, South Carolina; Boston, Massachusetts; and New York.

In 1798, the Park Theatre, with a capacity of 2,000 people, was built opposite City Hall in New York City. Although it was Manhattan's first world-class theater, it was facing financial hardship by the time a fire destroyed it in 1848.

At the start of the nineteenth century, the nation's most populous city and cultural and financial center was not New York, but Philadelphia. It

While colonists in the South loved the theater, many northern states—including Massachusetts, Pennsylvania, and Rhode Island—issued laws against play-acting on religious and moral grounds. Nevertheless, throughout the 1700s, stage performances were given in the North, especially in larger towns and cities, where theater-banning laws were largely ignored.

Slavery began in New Netherland in 1626, when the Dutch West India Company brought eleven African slaves to New Amsterdam, an area that would later be renamed New York. The first slave auction was held in New Amsterdam in 1655, and by 1703, more than 42 percent of the city's households included slaves.

During the Revolutionary War, the British actively recruited slaves belonging to Patriot masters, promising them freedom if they fought for the Crown. Because British troops occupied New York City from 1776 to the end of the war, thousands of slaves fled to that area, seeking refuge. By 1780, 10,000 blacks made their home in New York.

was there that the Walnut Street Theatre was completed in 1809. Theatrical productions began in 1812 with Richard Sheridan's Restoration comedy *The Rivals*, whose opening night was attended by Thomas Jefferson. Often referred to as simply the Walnut, this theater—with a capacity of over 1,000 people—still stands today, making it the nation's oldest continuing theater and a National Historic Landmark.

In the early 1800s, American theater was largely influenced by performers and plays that hailed from Great Britain. After the War of Independence, a good number of talented English actors decided to make their home in the New World, and with them came the plays of their homeland. The most popular shows of the time were Shakespearean tragedies, farces, Restoration comedies, and melodramas. By the 1820s, even though many shows were still imported from Great Britain, American-born playwrights and actors began to have an influence, and theater presentations started to reflect life in the New World.

For several decades, the *stock company* or *repertory company*—a system that originated in England—was popular in major cities such as Philadelphia, New York, and Boston. Each company employed a troupe of actors who would regularly perform in a specific theater, presenting a different play from the group's repertoire each night. But not all performers were employed by stock companies. "Star" actors and actresses would usually go on tour, attracting enthusiastic crowds both nationally and internationally. While lead actors in stock companies were paid less than $100 a week, the most admired touring performers would earn as much as $500 for a ten-day engagement,

As the Industrial Revolution drew more people to cities, a larger audience became available. It now became common for popular shows to run for an extended period of time—as long as a hundred performances or more. Gradually, stock companies were forced out of business as actors were hired for the full run of a play. At the same time, the increased number of spectators led to the building of more theaters throughout the country. In the early nineteenth century, as a growing number of theaters were constructed in New York City, the center of the theater world shifted from Philadelphia to lower Manhattan.

Although theaters were proliferating in Manhattan, the African Americans of New York did not find the same opportunity to perform that was enjoyed by white actors and actresses. Most theaters were off-limits to both black performers and black theatergoers, and those people who were determined to present entertainment by and for an African-American audience had to use whatever makeshift theater space was available. But all that would change—for a short time, at least—because of an enterprising man named William Alexander Brown.

Between 1790 and 1800, the population of New York soared from 33,000 to 60,000, making the city the largest in America, with Philadelphia a distant second. As more theaters were constructed to meet the metropolis's growing need for entertainment, New York also became the cultural center of the New World.

In 1785, some of New York's most influential residents—including future governor John Jay— founded the New York Manumission Society to protect African Americans who sought to be liberated from slavery or had already been freed. The society's first effort was to stop the common practice of kidnapping black New Yorkers and selling them into slavery in other states.

Born into slavery around 1787, Sojourner Truth escaped to freedom in 1826, eventually becoming a noted abolitionist as well as an advocate for women's rights and prison reform. Truth was considered a radical because she criticized the abolition community for focusing on the rights of black men while failing to seek rights for black women.

# THE AFRICAN GROVE THEATRE

William Alexander Brown was a free black man who worked as a ship steward. In 1816, after retiring from his job on a Liverpool line, Brown took the money he had saved over the years and purchased a two-story home at 48 Thomas Street in lower Manhattan. This alone was an accomplishment, as there were few black homeowners in the city at that time, but Brown had an additional goal in mind. Recognizing that there was a lack of entertainment venues for urban black audiences, Brown filled the void by staging poetry readings and dramatic performances in his home's large tea garden. He also served ice cream and cold drinks, since blacks were not allowed in the city's popular ice cream gardens. Within a short time, Brown had a regular following of other black residents.

Often, the performances staged at Brown's home were attended by his friend James Hewlett. An aspiring actor, Hewlett was enthusiastic about the backyard theater and inspired Brown to go a step further. So in 1821, Brown purchased a spacious house at the corner of Bleecker Street and Mercer Street, in the neighborhood that was then called "Little Africa," and built a 300-seat theater on the second floor. On September 21, the African Grove Theatre—sometimes known as the African Company—opened with a performance of Shakespeare's *Richard III*, with James Hewlett in the title role. Limited space, few performers, and makeshift costumes necessitated that some of the scenes be condensed or eliminated, and light-hearted songs and dances were added, but the production nevertheless featured much of the original play. By performing a Shakespearean work, Brown felt that the company could gain respectability while presenting familiar content and characters to the audience, since all schools at the time—including free black schools—taught Shakespeare. A review of the opening night by George Odell in the *National Advocate* read:

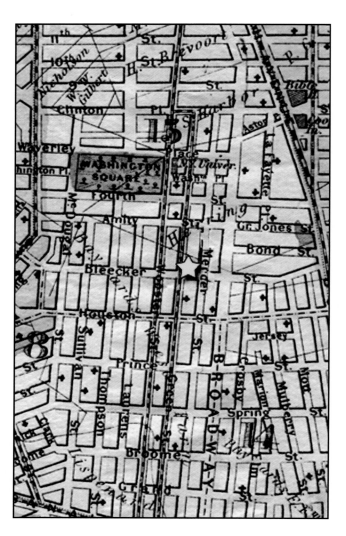

This map shows the site of William Brown's African Grove Theatre in 1821, when the 300-seat playhouse was located in lower Manhattan, at the corner of Bleecker Street and Mercer Street. Due to harassment by white patrons and resulting police raids, the company would move several times before its demise in 1823.

> Negroes resolved to get up a play, and used the upper apartments of the African Grove for a performance of *Richard III*. A dapper, wooly haired waiter at the City Hotel personated the royal Plantagenet in robes made up from discarded merino curtains of the ballroom. Owing to the smallness of the company King Henry and the Duchess were played by one person, and Lady Anne and Catesby, by another. Lady Anne, in Act III, sang quite incongruously.

In 1796, the African Free School—the first formal educational institution for blacks in America—was opened in New York City by the New York Manumission Society. Six additional African Free Schools would eventually open, and in 1834, after educating thousands of children, all of them would be incorporated into the public school system.

As early as the Dutch colonial period, former slaves settled in what is now Greenwich Village, New York, forming a black community. Over the years, as freed blacks migrated to New York from the South, the neighborhood grew until, by the mid-1800s, it was known as "Little Africa" and was one of the largest black neighborhoods in the city.

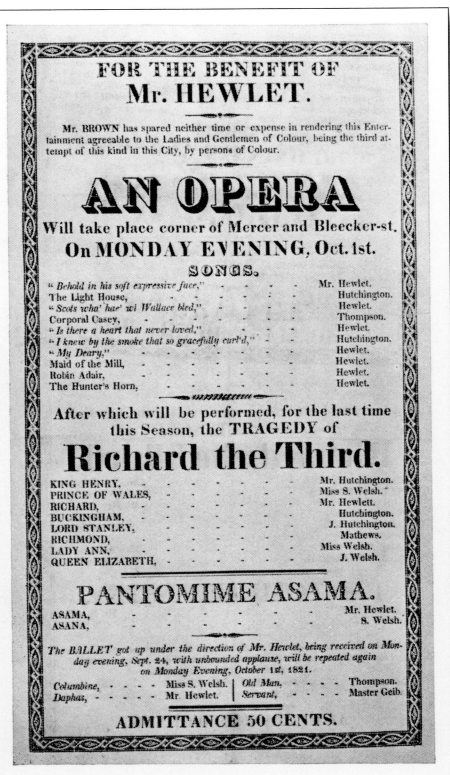

## FOR THE BENEFIT OF
## Mr. HEWLET.

Mr. BROWN has spared neither time or expense in rendering this Entertainment agreeable to the Ladies and Gentlemen of Colour, being the third attempt of this kind in this City, by persons of Colour.

# AN OPERA

## Will take place corner of Mercer and Bleecker-st.
## On MONDAY EVENING, Oct. 1st.
### SONGS.

| | |
|---|---|
| "Behold in his soft expressive face," | Mr. Hewlet. |
| The Light House, | Hutchington. |
| "Scots wha' hae' wi Wallace bled," | Hewlet. |
| Corporal Casey, | Thompson. |
| "Is there a heart that never loved," | Hewlet. |
| "I knew by the smoke that so gracefully curl'd," | Hutchington. |
| "My Deary," | Hewlet. |
| Maid of the Mill, | Hewlet. |
| Robin Adair, | Hewlet. |
| The Hunter's Horn, | Hewlet. |

After which will be performed, for the last time this Season, the TRAGEDY of

# Richard the Third.

| | |
|---|---|
| KING HENRY, | Mr. Hutchington. |
| PRINCE OF WALES, | Miss S. Welsh. |
| RICHARD, | Mr. Hewlett. |
| BUCKINGHAM, | Hutchington. |
| LORD STANLEY, | J. Hutchington. |
| RICHMOND, | Mathews. |
| LADY ANN, | Miss Welsh. |
| QUEEN ELIZABETH, | J. Welsh. |

## PANTOMIME ASAMA.

| | |
|---|---|
| ASAMA, | Mr. Hewlet. |
| ASANA, | S. Welsh. |

The BALLET got up under the direction of Mr. Hewlet, being received on Monday evening, Sept. 24, with unbounded applause, will be repeated again on Monday Evening, October 1st, 1821.

| | | | |
|---|---|---|---|
| Columbine, | Miss S. Welsh. | Old Man, | Thompson. |
| Daphas, | Mr. Hewlet. | Servant, | Master Geib. |

## ADMITTANCE 50 CENTS.

PLAYBILL, NEGRO THEATRE, 1821

According to this October 1821 African Grove playbill, William Brown provided varied entertainments—including an opera, a pantomime, and a performance of *Richard III*—for "Ladies and Gentlemen of Colour." Like other theater groups of the time, the Grove frequently offered the plays of William Shakespeare, for the Bard was the most popular playwright in America throughout the nineteenth century. Productions of *Richard III*, *Othello*, and other Shakespearean works attracted large and enthusiastic audiences drawn from different socioeconomic and ethnic groups.

The Act Prohibiting Importation of Slaves, passed by Congress in 1807, ended legal transatlantic slave trade in the United States. However, this legislation did nothing to impede the buying and selling of slaves within the South. There, the children of slaves became slaves, ensuring an ever-growing population of enslaved African-American laborers and servants.

In an effort to preserve the political balance between free and slave states, the Missouri Compromise of 1820 admitted Maine as a free state and Missouri as a slave state. In 1854, the Kansas-Nebraska Act repealed the Compromise by allowing white settlers in the Kansas and Nebraska territories to determine whether they would allow slavery within each territory.

Although liberties were taken with the play, this marked the first time that black performers would stage a drama on a legitimate American stage. After opening night, the small company of actors mounted productions that ranged from Shakespeare to farce to pantomime, and other actors joined the troupe—most notably, Ira Aldridge, who was to later achieve fame in Europe. (See the inset on page 9.) At first, the plays were performed in front of predominantly black audiences. But William Brown realized that for the Grove to succeed, he would also need to reach out to white theatergoers. This was not difficult, since there was a growing curiosity about black actors portraying Shakespearean characters. Some whites, in fact, were already attending the shows. In a reversal of what was commonplace at that time, Brown built a section in the back of the theater reserved for a white audience. Unfortunately, the whites in attendance would mock the performers and become rowdy, making it necessary for the police to be summoned and shut down the productions.

So great was Ira Aldridge's fame that his image can be found in photographs, etchings, and paintings. Here, the actor wears two of the medals he was awarded during his European tours.

Because of complaints about noise and frequent police raids, the Grove relocated several times, moving to small theaters on Houston Street and lower Broadway, near Prince Street. Each of these locations was fraught with danger, as raucous white audience members verbally harassed the actors. After being physically assaulted on one occasion, Brown supposedly posted a sign that read, "Whites Do Not Know How to Behave at Entertainments Designed for Ladies and Gentlemen of Colour."

Brown suspected that, in addition to the usual discrimination against African Americans, the disruptive behavior was a strategy devised by Stephen Price. Owner of the Park Theatre, Price did not want any local competition, especially by blacks. Determined to make his presence felt, Brown rented a theater next to the Park and staged a performance of *Richard III*—the same play that Price was presenting that evening. Price responded to the "stunt" by hiring several local rowdies to stage a riot during the African Grove's opening performance. During the commotion, actors were beaten up, the chandelier was cut down, and many of the costumes were destroyed. The police were called in, and rather than arresting the troublemakers, they took the black actors into custody. A judge later prohibited Brown's performers from staging any more works of Shakespeare. This would, of course, force the company to perform other material.

On September 21, 1821, New York's African Grove Theatre opened with an all-black performance of Shakespeare's *Richard III*. This marked the first time that African-American performers would stage a drama on a legitimate American stage. Although it was regularly harassed by the white community and suffered financial problems, as well, the African Grove would continue to offer entertainment until 1823.

Although slavery is generally thought of as being a phenomenon of the southern states, the enslavement of African Americans was legal in New York State until 1827. But slavery did not entirely disappear from New York even after 1827, as for many years, nonresidents and part-time residents could bring their slaves into the state on a temporary basis.

# Principal Actors of the African Grove Theatre

The two principal actors of the African Grove Theatre were James Hewlett and Ira Aldridge. Both would leave indelible marks on African-American history, and one would become known throughout Europe.

An immigrant from the West Indies, James Hewlett became the first black actor to star on the stage of the Grove, and possibly, the first African American to perform Shakespeare. He began learning his craft in the balcony of the Park Theatre—one of the few places in Manhattan open to black audience members. Hewlett would remain with the Grove for most of the theater's existence before heading off to do his own one-man shows. Taking a page from the book of British comic actor Charles Matthews, who mocked Hewlett and other black actors during his tour of the United States, Hewlett decided to impersonate famous white actors of the era. But rather than ridiculing them, Hewlett worked hard to accurately imitate their performances as Hamlet, Richard III, and other Shakespearean characters.

Through his impressions and his own interpretations of serious roles, Hewlett would sustain himself as a successful actor during the 1820s. He would rent out large New York City theaters and sell advance tickets in an attempt to limit the number of rowdy drunks who could buy last-minute tickets and disrupt his performances. This did not completely solve the problem, but Hewlett was ready with responses for those who harassed him.

By the 1830s, however, Hewlett's star power had faded, and he left New York. He was last seen performing *Othello* in Trinidad in 1839, and he died a year later. At a time when there were few black actors, Hewlett took great pride in his craft and often advertised himself as "Shakespeare's proud representative."

Ira Aldridge was born in Maryland, and, as a teenager, apprenticed under James Hewlett at the Grove. Aldridge participated in some of the performances at the Grove, but soon realized that he could not achieve success in the United States because of the widespread discrimination against African Americans. Employed as a ship's steward, he worked his passage to England, where he found far greater opportunity. Beginning in the mid-1820s, Aldridge performed in London, Liverpool, Edinburgh, Bristol, and Bath, portraying characters in *Othello, King Lear, Macbeth,* and *The Merchant of Venice.* In 1852, he embarked on a series of European tours that would last until the end of his life, in 1867. He died while on tour in Poland, having received honors that included the Prussian Gold Medal for Arts and Sciences from King Frederick. Aldridge was the first black actor to attain success on the international stage.

This depiction of James Hewlett was commissioned by the actor himself between 1827 and 1828, years after the African Grove had closed. Hewlett is said to have sold prints of the portrait at his one-man performances.

Although Ira Aldridge received his start at New York's African Grove Theatre, he would find far greater opportunity and success in Europe. In this engraving, Aldridge portrays Othello, one of the many roles that won him international acclaim.

Located across from City Hall, the Park Theatre was built in 1798 and became Manhattan's first world-class playhouse. Despite the Park's popularity, owner Stephen Price most likely viewed the struggling African Grove Theatre as competition, and once staged a riot during the black company's performance of *Richard III*.

Brown was determined to keep his theater alive, and in addition to producing the plays, he began writing. In 1823, two years after the founding of the Grove Theater, the company presented Brown's work *The Drama of King Shotaway* at a new location, just north of Greenwich Village. The first play written and produced by an African American, it was based on the true story of Joseph Chatoyer, a Garifuna chief who, in 1795, led a black Carib revolt against the British colonial government on the island of Saint Vincent. Starring James Hewlett, the production was well received but short-lived. That same year, financial problems, ongoing battles with the law, and regular harassment by white patrons led to the demise of the African Grove Theatre.

Although the African Grove existed for only a few years, it remains significant as a groundbreaking step in the history of black American theater. Brown, Hewlett, and Aldridge were committed to getting black performers heard and seen on the legitimate stage. In that, they succeeded, and in the years to come, both Hewlett and Aldridge would forge new careers as performers.

Founded on March 16, 1827, *Freedom's Journal* was the first United States newspaper owned and operated by African Americans. Established in New York City by a group of free black men, including Samuel E. Cornish and John B. Russwurm, the paper was intended to counter the racist commentary offered by mainstream journalists.

On January 1, 1831, William Lloyd Garrison, a leading voice of the growing abolitionist movement, distributed the first issue of *The Liberator*, a weekly paper that advocated the emancipation of slaves. Published for over thirty years—until the Thirteenth Amendment went into effect—the paper reached thousands of people worldwide.

# THE ERA OF THE MINSTREL SHOW

At one time, the minstrel show was America's most popular form of stage entertainment. A savage parody of African Americans, strangely, it attracted white and black audience members alike, and even provided work for many black performers at a time when legitimate theater was closed to them.

## The History of the Minstrel Show

From the 1790s onward, blackface acts were common features of traveling shows and circuses. However, this form of entertainment was brought to a new level in the 1820s, when white performer Thomas Dartmouth "Daddy" Rice darkened his face with burnt cork and portrayed a stereotypical black character named Jim Crow. Dressed in tattered garments, Rice performed highly exaggerated dance steps and—using a heavy African-American dialect—sang the song "Jump Jim Crow," supposedly modeling his character after a disabled black street singer who had made up the lyrics:

> Come listen all you galls and boys I's jist from Tuckyhoe,
> I'm going to sing a little song, my name's Jim Crow,
> Weel about and turn about and do jis so,
> Eb'ry time I weel about and jump Jim Crow.
>
> —1820s sheet music

Thomas Dartmouth Rice (left) created the stereotypical black character Jim Crow in the 1820s and portrayed him for many years. So popular was Rice's act that the name "Jim Crow" became not only a derogatory term for a black man but also a byword for the laws that enforced racial segregation in the South.

Although not born into a wealthy family, Thomas Rice became affluent and famous through his signature Jim Crow act. The portrait on the right (ca. 1837) shows that, when not on stage, Rice dressed to display his wealth and success.

Mr T. RICE
as
THE ORIGINAL JIM CROW
New York Publ. by E. RILEY, No 29 Chatham St.

TCS 82 (T.D. Rice), Harvard Theatre Collection, Houghton Library, Harvard University.

Rice and his parody of a black man became immensely popular—so popular that "Jim Crow" became not only a derogatory term for a black man but, eventually, a byword for laws that enforced strict racial segregation. Soon after Rice began his shows, minstrel troupes in blackface began staging carefully constructed three-act performances that combined songs, dances, comic banter, and comedy sketches, many of which presumably portrayed the daily life of slaves on southern plantations. Stock characters included, among others, the country bumpkin Jim Crow, established by Rice; Zip Coon, a smooth-talking free black who was lazy and rather dim-witted, and "put on airs" by donning an extravagant but foolish-looking hat and coat; and Mr. Tambo, a black musician.

By the late 1830s, minstrel shows were drawing significant crowds, in part because of the economic depression of 1837 to 1844, which made sophisticated theater too expensive to either stage or attend. As a result, the rowdy, low-brow, significantly cheaper minstrel show moved into many established theaters.

Like most blackface troupes, Dan Emmett's Virginia Minstrels featured crude, stereotypical depictions of African Americans. This clearly appealed to American audiences, as the group was a smash hit from the start. But when the Minstrels toured England in the spring of 1843, the reception was less positive, and by midsummer, the group had disbanded.

One highly successful minstrel troupe was the Virginia Minstrels, who launched their career at New York's popular Bowery Amphitheatre in February 1843. Led by Dan Emmett, who later wrote the song "Dixie," the four minstrels—all white men sporting blackface with accentuated red lips—would sing, dance, and perform comedy in the guise of American slaves and free blacks. They accompanied their numbers with banjo, tambourine, and bone castanets. The Minstrels went on to become one of the most successful acts of their era, traveling the country to sold-out houses.

Although most minstrel troupes presented gross stereotypes of African Americans, some groups did strive to be more "refined." For instance, in the 1840s, the Ethiopian Serenaders—all white men performing in blackface—attempted to appeal to a higher-class audience by avoiding offensive stereotypes; eliminating bawdy material; and offering more music, even including pieces from popular opera. The troupe, however, found more success in England than in the United States, where audiences seemed to crave ribald humor.

By the 1850s, minstrel shows were the hottest tickets in major cities throughout the country. In New York alone, there were ten minstrel houses. White theatergoers—most of whom had little contact with African Americans and were ignorant of the harsh realities of slavery—often thought that the shows accurately depicted black people. Surprisingly, despite the degrading performances, African Americans were also in attendance. They became such a significant part of the audience that some theater owners who typically did not allow blacks in their establishments were prompted to bend or change their rules.

In the early 1830s, the already established system of helping slaves escape to the North was dubbed the Underground Railroad. Made up of numerous individuals, most of whom were black, the Railroad assisted about 100,000 African Americans between 1810 and 1850. One of the most well-known participants was Harriet Tubman, who was herself an escaped slave.

On September 3, 1838, carrying false identification papers, Frederick Douglass escaped from slavery and travelled for twenty-four hours by rail and boat before reaching safety at the New York City home of an abolitionist. Dedicated to ending the enslavement of his people, Douglass would become a highly influential social reformer, orator, writer, and statesman.

Despite its exotic name, the group known as the Ethiopian Serenaders was composed of white men performing in blackface. When the company tried to avoid the offensive stereotypes common in other minstrel shows, American audiences found the act too tame, and the Serenaders moved to England, where they were better appreciated. This sheet music cover (ca. 1843), while it mentions the group's true name, bills it as the Boston Minstrels.

It's not clear why the African Americans of the era turned out to see shows that lampooned the way black people walked, talked, sang, danced, and struggled to survive. Some historians believe that they laughed at the absurdity of the caricatures, while others think they were attracted by those songs and dances that had developed from their culture. Whatever the reason, many blacks were regular attendees.

Perhaps less surprising is the participation of black players in the shows themselves. For many years, although black performers were forbidden by law to take the stage with whites in many states, some minstrel companies secretly employed African Americans. They, too, had to wear blackface and exaggerate the size of their lips to present the now widely accepted caricature of plantation slaves and free blacks. As state laws changed, all-black minstrel companies began to tour both the United States and Great Britain. For many black performers, the minstrel show was their first professional outlet.

One of the first black performers to be featured in white minstrel shows was William Henry Lane. Appearing in the 1840s, Lane excelled in the rhythmically complex hand-clapping, knee-slapping style of dance known as Juba, earning himself the title "Master Juba." So proficient at his craft was Lane that, outside of the minstrel shows, he was often challenged to dance competitions against white dancers—and would always win. Despite his superior skills, he would acquiesce to his minstrel-show role by dressing in rags and darkening his face with coal. (To learn more about Lane, see the inset on page 15.)

Another African American who worked in white minstrel shows prior to the Civil War was Thomas Dilward, a dwarf who stood less than three feet tall. At first considered a novelty, Dilward proved to be proficient in singing, dancing, and playing the violin. Throughout the 1850s, he was a hot ticket, and several white troupes competed for his skills. In the 1860s, he would perform in a number of black minstrel shows.

In addition to pulling white performers into battle—which allowed more black performers to take the stage—the Civil War had other effects on the minstrel show. Initially, the shows satirized both the North and the South, but as war reached the northern states, criticism of the Confederacy became more common. The shows also began to reflect the nation's grief by presenting heartrending songs and sketches.

When the Civil War began in 1861, and especially after a conscription act was passed by the US Congress in 1863, many white performers were drawn into battle, and the number of black minstrel shows increased. One of the ways in which white promoters sold these shows was to extol their supposed authenticity. Audiences could view actual black performers as they sang, danced, and played music rooted in their African-American heritage. Of course, while displaying their skills, these performers also engaged in self-deprecating humor, aware that this was what audiences were paying to see. While the black minstrel troupes, mostly in blackface, caricatured themselves with jokes and plantation skits, they drew many rave reviews—even from white critics.

As mentioned, most white theatergoers were drawn to the black minstrel shows by pure curiosity, since most white people had never seen black

As a means of pacifying slave-state politicians, and thereby strengthening the Union, the Fugitive Slave Act was passed in 1850. Nicknamed the "Bloodhound Law," the act required escaped slaves to be returned to their masters. As a result, many slaves who had sought refuge in the northern United States were forced to flee to Canada.

An emotional portrayal of the cruelty of slavery, *Uncle Tom's Cabin or Life Among the Lowly* by Harriet Beecher Stowe was published in installments from 1851 to 1852, and was then offered in book form. The novel—along with Stowe's public stand on social issues—helped energize anti-slavery forces throughout the northern states.

# William Henry Lane, the Father of Tap Dance

During an era in which African Americans were seldom permitted to perform on a public stage, William Henry Lane was one of the few men of color who not only appeared alongside white dancers, but drew large, enthusiastic crowds wherever he went.

Born in Providence, Rhode Island around 1825, Lane learned about the Irish jig and the Irish reel from a dance hall and saloon entertainer known as "Uncle" Jim Lowe, and began performing in the Five Points District of New York when he was only ten. Mingling European and African rhythms, by the 1840s, Lane had created a unique style of dancing that involved lightning-fast, complex, syncopated rhythms. In the African tradition, he accompanied his dazzling physical feats with laughter and song. One critic wrote that Lane was able to "tie his legs into such knots, and fling them about so recklessly, or make his feet twinkle until you lose sight of them altogether in his energy." He is credited as being a highly influential figure in the history of American tap dance.

Like actor Ira Aldridge, Lane would eventually move to London, where racial discrimination was much less prominent. By the mid-1840s, he was receiving top billing with a white minstrel troupe called Pell's Ethiopian Serenaders.

William Henry Lane is thought to have died in London at the young age of twenty-seven. During his short lifetime, he made a lasting mark not only on African-American history, but also on the wider world of entertainment.

**William Henry Lane combined European and African rhythms to create a unique style of *Juba*—a dance form originally brought to the United States by West African slaves. Called "Master Juba" during his lifetime, Lane is now considered the father of tap dance.**

In 1853, the first known piece of fiction written by an African American was published. Based on the relationship between President Thomas Jefferson and his slave mistress, Sally Hemings, *Clotel*, a novel written by escaped slave and abolitionist William Wells Brown, explored the hardships endured by two enslaved mixed-race women.

On March 6, 1857, the Supreme Court issued the *Dred Scott v. Sandford* decision, declaring that slaves are not citizens of the United States and therefore cannot sue in Federal Courts. Ultimately, the decision was overturned by the Thirteenth and Fourteenth Amendments to the Constitution.

people on stage, and some had little familiarity with African Americans in their daily lives. The promoters, white and black, likened the appeal to the type of prurient curiosity that brought crowds to the circus sideshows. Advertisements focused on the spectacle of seeing blacks not playing roles, but behaving naturally. One promoter wrote, "See the Darky as he is at home." Shocking as it reads today, such an ad would draw a large crowd. But not all white people believed the promoters' claims. From the beginning of the minstrel show era, a number of educated Americans were highly critical of the players' distortion of black people and black culture.

Once inside the theater, despite the caricatures that typified minstrel shows, white northern audiences did get a taste of black culture. Minstrel show music featured the banjo, tambourine, and bones—all of which were characteristic of black music—and many of the songs and lyrics were adapted from slave spirituals and other forms of African-American cultural expression. Dance was a significant part of these shows. The cakewalk, the most notable dance on the minstrel circuit, had originated in the South, where black slaves mocked the dancing of their white masters by perform-

In the late 1800s and early 1900s, the cakewalk became a craze not only in American ballrooms, but in Europe, as well. This colorful French poster depicts Europe's "a la mode" (fashionable) dance.

Despite the 1807 prohibition against importing slaves to the United States, the last known ship to bring slaves to the country arrived at Mobile, Alabama in 1859. Captain William Foster and shipyard owner Timothy Meaher were unable to sell their human cargo, and eventually, the slaves were freed and able to establish their own community, Africatown.

Issued by President Abraham Lincoln on January 1, 1863, the Emancipation Proclamation declared the freedom of slaves in the Confederate states. By immediately liberating from 20,000 to 50,000 slaves and preventing the South from using them as laborers, this act helped the Union move towards victory.

ing exaggerated bows, curtsies, and high-stepping struts. Ironically, slave owners, believing that this was the native dance of the slaves, adopted it as a means of mocking African Americans. Cakewalk competitions actually became part of white plantation life, with the winners receiving a slice of cake as a prize. Northern white audiences, who knew nothing of plantation activities, were intrigued by what appeared to be a window into another world.

Even with the growing number of black minstrel shows, white troupes cornered the market until after the Civil War. At that point, most white performers moved to the vaudeville stage. With the tastes of northeastern theatergoers changing, the black minstrel troupes gradually moved out of large eastern cities to the stages of the South, the Midwest, and the West. There, they unintentionally spread the racial stereotypes that minstrelsy had developed. It would be many years before the country completely lost interest in blackface performing and minstrel-inspired acts.

## The Influence of the Minstrel Show

Minstrel shows not only directly misinformed several generations of Americans, but also had a profound effect on American thought and culture for decades to come. The highly negative stereotypes of blacks in America persisted throughout the years of vaudeville and became so ingrained in white America that they would not be shaken loose for many decades.

White composer Stephen C. Foster took a compassionate approach to the writing of minstrel songs, attempting to avoid the destructive racial stereotypes and "offensive words" that were all too common at the time. Foster's "Camptown Races," "My Old Kentucky Home," and "Oh! Susanna" are still sung today.

Yet, minstrel shows made positive contributions, as well. The dances performed on minstrel stages—especially those offered by black performers—had a lasting impact on American dance. Although the cakewalk died out in the early twentieth century, its influence was evident in later popular dances such as the Charleston and the Lindy Hop. And, of course, the dance style created by William Henry Lane would eventually evolve into tap dance, a uniquely American form of art.

The minstrel show also brought America many musical standards, including "Camptown Races," "My Old Kentucky Home," and "Oh! Susanna," all written by white composer Stephen Foster. Foster once said that his minstrel songs were intended to inspire compassion and to avoid the "trashy and really offensive words" that too often characterized the minstrel stage. Considered "America's First Composer," Foster was to write over two hundred works and eventually won a place in the Songwriter's Hall of Fame. Many of his songs are still performed today.

On January 31, 1865, the US House of Representatives passed the Thirteenth Amendment to the United States Constitution, formally abolishing slavery throughout the nation. The amendment read, "Neither slavery nor involuntary servitude . . . shall exist within the United States, or any place subject to their jurisdiction."

Passed by Congress, and lasting from 1865 to 1877, Reconstruction was designed to reorganize the southern states so that they could be readmitted to the Union, as well as to define the place of freed blacks. This period led to bitterness on the part of the South, which passed codes designed to limit the economic and civil rights of African Americans.

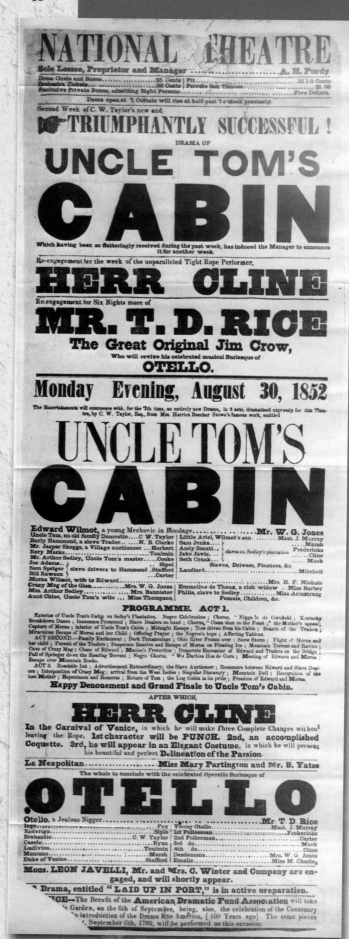

# Uncle Tom's Cabin & American Theater

The second best-selling book of the nineteenth century—following only the Bible in popularity—was the 1852 anti-slavery novel *Uncle Tom's Cabin or Life Among the Lowly*. Penned by New England abolitionist Harriet Beecher Stowe, this book is said to have helped lay the groundwork for the Civil War through its sympathetic portrayal of African-American slaves. In its first year alone, it sold hundreds of thousands of copies in the United States. Yet most Americans of the time learned Uncle Tom's story not by reading Stowe's novel but by attending one of the many plays based on her work.

The first adaptation of Stowe's work was performed—months before the release of the book—on January 5, 1852, at the Baltimore Museum, and the second, in August of that year at Purdy's National Theatre in New York. Both were very short dramas that omitted a good part of the novel's plot, and they were not well received. The first important dramatic interpretation of *Uncle Tom's Cabin*, written by George L. Aiken, opened in Troy, New York on September 27, 1852. This adaptation, which was truer to the novel, was a huge hit. Very soon, several versions appeared in nearby theaters, and productions were also mounted in London, Paris, and Berlin. And the public's zeal for the play did not fade with the end of the Civil War and the abolition of slavery. By the late 1870s, nearly fifty companies were performing various versions of the story—often called "Tom Shows"—across the United States. The story was so appealing that plays based on Stowe's novel were still being staged at the start of the twentieth century.

Unfortunately, because the copyright laws of the time gave Stowe no control over dramatic presentations of her works, the plays varied greatly in quality and content. After attending an 1853 production of the George L. Aiken adaptation, William Lloyd Garrison, editor of the anti-slavery newspaper *The Liberator*, wrote, "If the shrewdest abolitionist among us had prepared a drama with a view to make the strongest anti-slavery impression, he could

C.W. Taylor's stage version of *Uncle Tom's Cabin* appeared at Purdy's National Theatre in New York in August 1852, less than a year after the publication of Harriet Beecher Stowe's novel. A short piece designed to fill a gap in the program, it received poor reviews and ran for only eleven performances.

scarcely have done the work better. . . . It was a sight worth seeing those ragged, coatless men and boys . . . cheering the strongest and sublimest antislavery sentiments." But not all adaptations were designed to have that effect. Also in 1853, P.T. Barnum offered a version by H.J. Conway that began with a plantation scene depicting slave life as happy and free from care. The remainder of the play omitted the tragic consequences of bondage and diluted the anti-slavery statements. An article printed at the time—not surprisingly, in a newspaper owned by Barnum—assured potential theatergoers that Barnum's offering presented "not a single word calculated to offend those whose opinions on this topic [slavery] favor its non-agitation." In fact, many Tom Shows were little more than minstrel shows.

In terms of the Tom Shows' lasting effect on American theater, it is important to note the way they presented Stowe's characters. In the novel, Uncle Tom is brave, forgiving, and willing to endure indignities in order to save his fellow slaves. Harriet Beecher Stowe was a devout Christian, and Uncle Tom is the model of Christian humility. But nowadays, when most people hear the name "Uncle Tom," they think of a submissive, rather childlike creature who is without dignity. This is largely due to the stage plays, which exaggerated certain aspects of the characters, reducing them to stereotypes. Almost always portrayed by white actors rather than African-American performers, these characters included the affectionate "mammy"; the scruffy "pickaninny" children; and the docile, long-suffering Uncle Tom. Although Stowe's novel undoubtedly fueled America's anti-slavery movement, the stereotypes perpetuated by the Tom Shows were to haunt African-American performers well into the twentieth century, on both the stage and the silver screen. These days, *Uncle Tom's Cabin* is rarely performed because American audiences, by and large, no longer welcome its racist portrayals of African Americans.

The best-known stage version of Stowe's novel began as a four-act play written by George Aiken. Premiering in Troy, New York in September 27, 1852, and featuring the famous Howard company of actors, it was so popular that it was expanded to six acts and moved to New York's National Theatre—the same theater where Taylor's version had failed—in July of 1853. It was a great success.

NATIONAL THEATRE

Formerly the CHATHAM, Chatham-street, near Roosevelt

Sole Lessee, Proprietor, and Manager........................A. H. Purdy
Treasurer....................................................Mr. William Hancock

Dress Circle and Boxes...........25 Cents | Pit...........................121-2 Cents
Orchestra Tickets..................50 Cents | Private Box Tickets..........One Dollar
Exclusive Private Boxes admitting Eight Persons.............................Five Dollars

Doors open at a quarter past 7 o'clock.    Curtain will rise at 8 precisely

SECOND WEEK OF THE GREAT DRAMA

The immense success attending the first weeks representation of the great UNCLE TOM'S CABIN, has induced the Manager to engage the following artists for another week.

THE YOUTHFUL WONDER,

LITTLE CORDELIA HOWARD

Generally called the Child of Nature, together with

MR. G. C. HOWARD
MR. G. C. GERMON,
MR. C. K. FOX,
MRS. E. FOX,
AND
MRS. G. C. HOWARD
Formerly Miss Caroline Fox.

Who will appear in conjunction with

THE FULL NATIONAL COMPANY

This Tuesday Evening, July 26th

In the New Dramatic Version of

UNCLE TOM'S CABIN

Or, Life among the Lowly.

DRAMATISED FROM

MRS. HARRIET BEECHER STOWE'S

World renowned work by G. L. Aiken Esq. expressly for Mr. G. C. Howard, and produced at his Museum in Troy, where it was played over one Hundred nights to crowded houses, with that

Unbounded Applause, Unprecedented in the history of the stage; it is

IN SIX ACTS

Eight Tableaus & Thirty Scenes,

EMBRACING THE WHOLE WORK,

In which will be introduced the Songs composed and written by G. C. Howard,

TO LITTLE EVA IN HEAVEN, and
UNCLE TOM'S RELIGION.

Published and for sale at Firth and Pond's, and all the principal Music Stores in New York.

LITTLE CORDELIA HOWARD,

In her Original Character of EVA, as performed by her over ONE HUNDRED NIGHTS.

MRS. G. C. HOWARD,

In her original Character of TOPSY, as played by her over One Hundred Nights.

MR. G. C. GERMON,

In his original Character of UNCLE TOM, as played by him over One Hundred Nights.

Uncle Tom, the faithful Slave.......................Mr. G. C. Germon
St. Claire, the Southern Gentleman......................G. C. Howard
Gumption Cute, the Yankee..............................C. K. Fox
Phenias Fletcher, the Kentuckian....G. W. L. Fox; Sambo, the Slave of Legree............Mack
George Harris, a fugitive...........Siple; Jumbo, the Slave Driver............McDonnell
Legree, the Pirate Slave dealer......N. B. Clarke; Alf Mann, the Slave purchaser..........Henderson
Mr. Wilson, the Quaker..............Toulmin; Skegga, the Auctioneer..............Thompson
Deacon Perry, the Deacon............Lingard; Adolph, the Master's man..............Mitchell
Marks, the Lawyer..................Herbert; Waiter, the smart man..............Cline
Old Shelby, the insolvent Planter.....Rose; Doctor, the last Visitor..............Smith
George Shelby, the son..............H. Stone; Harry, the child of the fugitive......Mast. Murray
Tom Loker, the Slave hunter..........G. Lingard; Slaves, Planters, Citizens, &c.
Haley, the Slave Trader..............Lamb

EVA, the Flower of the South.......................LITTLE CORDELIA HOWARD
Topsy, the Girl that never was Born.......................Mrs. G. C. Howard
Aunt Ophelia, the Vermonter.......................Mrs. E. Fox
Eliza, the fugitive wife..........Mrs. W. G. Jones; Marie St. Claire, the victim of custom..Miss Landers
Cassy, the distracted............Mrs. Bannister; Chloe, the wife of Uncle Tom........Mrs. Lingard
Emeline, the Quadroon Slave........Miss Barber; Female Slaves, &c.

The Play is beautifully interspersed with Singing and Dancing.

Song, Old Folks at Home, words and Music by E. P. Christy, Esq.......Uncle Tom
Dance and Song.......................................................Topsy
To Little Eva in Heaven, words and Music by G. C. Howard.......by.....St Clare
Uncle Tom's Religion, words and Music by G. C. Howard........by.....Uncle Tom

TABLEAUS IN THE DRAMA.

1st.  THE ESCAPE OF ELIZA.
2nd.  THE TRAPPERS ENTRAPPED.
3rd.  THE FREEMAN'S DEFENCE.
4th.  DEATH OF LITTLE EVA.
5th.  THE LAST OF St. CLARE.
6th.  TOPSY BUTTING THE YANKEE.
7th.  CASSY HELPING UNCLE TOM.
8th.  DEATH OF UNCLE TOM.

NO TICE.—The Ladies and Gentlemen will please remain seated until the Curtain Descends th... every effect may be given to the Last Grand Tableaus. Owing to the great

Considered America's first prominent black composer of popular music, James Bland wrote "In the Evening by the Moonlight," "Oh, Dem Golden Slippers," and "Carry Me Back to Old Virginny," as well as other important minstrel tunes.

Another important songwriter of the era was James Bland, who is considered to be America's first prominent black composer of popular music. Bland attended Howard University in Washington, DC, where he studied liberal arts. Upon graduation, the young man's ambition was to become a stage performer, but he was initially turned down by several minstrel groups, which favored white men in blackface. Eventually, Bland was to work with several minstrel troupes, and, as a member of the Callender-Haverly Minstrels, would even perform for Queen Victoria and the Prince of Wales. Today, he is best remembered for his many noteworthy minstrel compositions, which include "In the Evening by the Moonlight," "Oh, Dem Golden Slippers," and "Carry Me Back to Old Virginny," the last of which, with revised lyrics, was Virginia's state song from 1940 to 1997.

Perhaps most important, minstrel shows opened the door to African-American performers. Although the black actors, singers, and dancers who participated in these shows had to present stereotypes of their own race, their work not only provided them with an opportunity to hone their skills but also helped them gain entry into emerging forms of American entertainment such as burlesque.

Written in 1878 by James Bland, the minstrel song "Carry Me Back to Old Virginny" reflected the struggles of newly freed slaves. With revised lyrics, it became the state song of Virginia in 1940 and remained so until 1997.

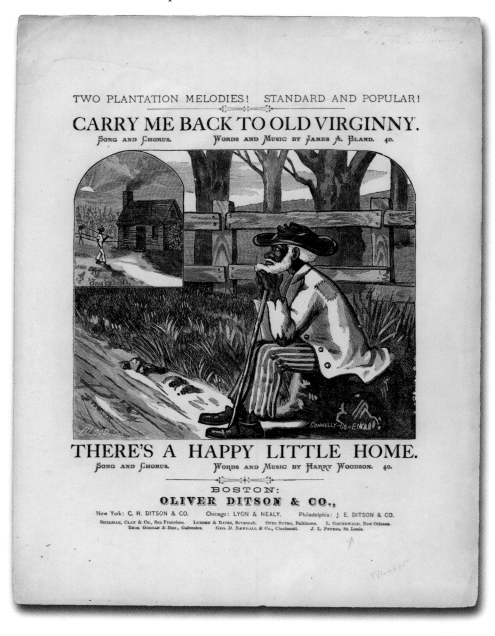

# FROM BURLESQUE TO BROADWAY

The second half of the nineteenth century witnessed a growing diversity of stage shows. A new form of entertainment—burlesque—began to capture the attention of New Yorkers, and would eventually spread across the nation. In fact, variety shows of all types were popular, and the first American musical comedies began to take shape, presenting audiences with a range of lively diversions. Eager to compose, to write, to produce, and to perform, talented African Americans found new opportunities in theaters throughout Manhattan and beyond.

In the late 1860s, burlesque came to New York City in the form of a British import—Lydia Thompson and her mythological spoof *Ixion*. An undeniably bawdy form of entertainment, burlesque capitalized on America's prurient interests. From racy jokes, skits, songs and dances—all delivered with plenty of innuendo—to under-dressed young women, the source of burlesque's drawing power was far from subtle. It was also the first medium that significantly brought women to the stage.

Burlesque was similar to minstrelsy in that it was a variety show, but instead of deriding black people, as the minstrel show did, burlesque usually spoofed traditional theatrical productions as well as the social habits of the upper classes. Many people now associate burlesque with female strippers, but that was true only during its declining years. When this entertainment form was at its best, the genre was rich with popular music and comedy, although it was certainly geared for adults—especially adult men—rather than families, and was most popular with the lower and working class audiences.

Lydia Thompson's show was a major hit in New York City, grossing over $370,000 by the end of the first season. Pretty soon, burlesque was flourishing in New York City—and elsewhere in the country, as well. Two national circuits of burlesque thrived, and Manhattan had several resident companies, such as Minsky's at the Winter Garden Theatre. The more that burlesque was criticized for being "indecent," the more people flocked to see it. Whether offered in theaters, cabarets, music halls, or clubs, burlesque was attracting larger and larger audiences, and performers and managers everywhere scrambled to form troupes.

Sam T. Jack, a white burlesque manager, was known as much for his nerve as for his ambition. In 1889, eager to produce something that no one had ever seen before, Jack created *Sam T. Jack's Creole Show*—later to be known as simply *The Creole Show*. This entertainment was unique in that although it was designed for white people, all of its performers were African American, and *none* was wearing blackface. Included in the show was a chorus line of sixteen beautiful women. Also performing was the

Hailing from London, actress-comedian-producer Lydia Thompson brought her spoof *Ixion* to New York City during the 1868-1869 theatrical season. A combination of satire, parody, song, dance, racy jokes, and saucy costumes, Thompson's hit show launched the American age of burlesque.

In 1865, the Ku Klux Klan was founded in Pulaski, Tennessee by Confederate Army veterans. A vigilante group, the KKK tried to assert white supremacy through the use of terrorism—threats, violence, and murder—aimed against freed African Americans and their allies. The group began to fade out in the 1870s, but would flourish again in the 1920s.

Founded in 1865, Shaw University is the oldest HBCU—historically black college and university—created in the South. Established by Henry Martin Tupper, Shaw graduated its first college class in 1878 and its first class of medical doctors in 1886. It would not, however, elect its first black president (Dr. William Stuart Nelson) until 1931.

Beginning in the late nineteenth century, the elegant cakewalk was featured in African-American Broadway shows and became the first black dance widely accepted by white society.

dance team of Dora Dean and Charles E. Johnson. The premier cakewalk dancers of their time, the elegantly dressed Dean and Johnson would eventually be known as the "King and Queen of Colored Aristocracy." Another well-known cast member was actor, comic, singer, and songwriter Sam Lucas, who had already made the transition from the minstrel stage to the legitimate stage by becoming the first black man to perform the title role in *Uncle Tom's Cabin*. As the featured entertainers, Lucas, Dean, and Johnson led *The Creole Show* to Broadway.

With its long-legged chorus girls, smart urban comedy, fashionable costumes, and star appeal, *The Creole Show* was a huge hit in New York City

Written by Walter Smart and George Williams, the 1895 song "No Coon Can Come Too Black for Me" was created for the black touring musical *The Octoroons*. This sheet music cover shows the dancing team of Charles E. Johnson and Dora Dean, and the top bears a dedication to "The Two Real Coons," Bert Williams and George Walker.

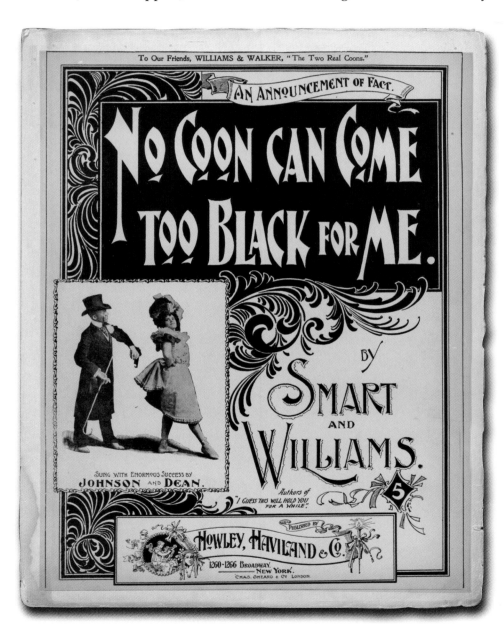

Adopted in July 1868, the Fourteenth Amendment granted citizenship to "all persons born or naturalized in the United States"—including freed slaves. It also asserted that no state could reduce the "privileges and immunities" of citizens, and that no person could be denied "life, liberty or property without due process of the law."

In 1869, Howard University became the first African-American law school in the United States. The school served an important need, as political and social changes were making it crucial to train lawyers who could assist African Americans in securing and protecting the rights established by the Thirteenth Amendment.

and also generated great fanfare when it toured the country. Upon returning to Manhattan, the show ran for five seasons at Broadway's Standard Theatre at Greeley Square and Thirty-Third Street.

In 1895, *The Creole Show's* booking agent, John W. Isham, produced a touring musical called *The Octoroons*. Described as a musical farce, the show had the three-act format of a minstrel show and featured songs such as "No Coon Can Come Too Black for Me." Like *The Creole Show*, *The Octoroons* included a chorus line of talented African-American beauties. When the travelling production arrived in New York City, the town had a brief taste of a true black musical.

The early success of *The Creole Show* and *The Octoroons* opened the door to other black variety acts, including Black Patti's Troubadours, which hit the stages of New York City in 1896. The show—which featured more than forty African-American comedians, acrobats, singers, and other entertainers—was the brainchild of Matilda Sissieretta Joyner Jones. Born in 1869 in Virginia, Jones was an immensely talented soprano. When in 1892, Jones sang in New York's Madison Square Garden, a reviewer compared her to Italian opera singer Adelina Patti, and—to Jones' dismay—he referred to the new singer as "the Black Patti." Jones' displeasure with her new name did not prevent her from forming a blackface group called Black Patti's Troubadors, which she led from 1895 to 1916. The troupe toured throughout the United States and abroad, presenting minstrel shows and musical skits. Although Jones found the minstrel acts demeaning, she was able to use the show's finale to sing spirituals and operatic arias. During the twenty or so years in which Patti's Troubadors toured, it was a training ground for literally hundreds of African-American performers, many of whom would go on to work in vaudeville. And through her own performances, Jones set the standard for the many female vocalists who would eventually rise to prominence.

As Black Patti's Troubadours attracted audiences throughout the world, two groundbreaking plays were staged in New York theaters. The produc-

Performer Matilda Sissieretta Joyner Jones was known not only for her remarkable soprano voice and commanding presence, but also for adorning her elaborate gowns with the medals and awards she had received from admirers, such as the President of Haiti. The press often called her "the Black Patti"—a reference to white opera singer Adelina Patti.

In the years after the American Civil War, Congress debated the rights of the millions of African Americans who had been freed by the Thirteenth Amendment. Because former Confederate states often took steps to disenfranchise blacks, in 1870, the Fifteenth Amendment—the last of the Reconstruction Amendments—was formally adopted, giving black males the right to vote.

Booker T. Washington opened Tuskegee University in Tuskegee, Alabama on July 4, 1881. Initially called Tuskegee Normal and Industrial Institute, this was one of the first schools to provide higher education for black Americans. Although early classes were held in Butler Chapel AME Zion Church, the campus was soon relocated to an abandoned plantation.

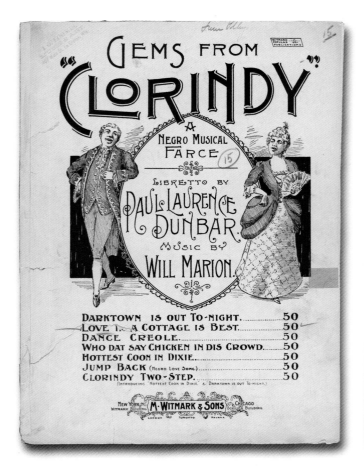

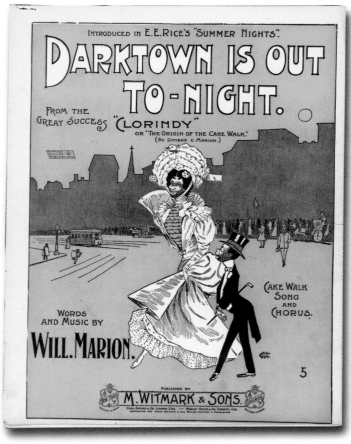

Billed as "an original Negro operetta," *Clorindy* opened on July 5, 1898 at the Casino Theatre "roof garden" in New York City. Its success was so great that it launched the career of composer Will Marion Cook.

tion of one of these plays was partly the result of a new innovation—the theater roof garden. Previously, the city was often too hot for summer shows, so some theaters began to open "roof gardens" where they could present entertainment outdoors. The Casino Theatre was the first venue specifically built with a roof garden for summer performances, and it was there that the first musical entirely produced and performed by African Americans opened in 1898.

*Clorindy, or The Origin of the Cakewalk* introduced the ragtime music of composer and performer Will Marion Cook—sometimes billed as Will Marion—coupled with the lyrics of Paul Laurence Dunbar. A one-act musical billed as "an original Negro operetta," *Clorindy* had a cast of twenty-six African Americans headed by Ernest Hogan, a veteran stage performer and songwriter. The cast also featured the vaudeville team of Bert Williams and George Walker, as well as up-and-coming soprano Abbie Mitchell.

Edward E. Rice, musical composer and manager of the Casino, had agreed to present *Clorindy* as a rooftop "afterpiece" to Rice's own play *Summer Nights,* which was being staged indoors. As legend has it, *Clorindy* opened on July 5, 1898 to an audience of roughly fifty people, but as the

Written by Edward A. Johnson, an ex-slave who became an educator and attorney, *A School History of the Negro Race in America* was published in 1890. It was intended to counteract the lack of information about African Americans in the textbooks of the time and, in Johnson's words, to correct "the sin of omission and commission on the part of white authors."

George W. Johnson—a former slave and New York City street performer—became the first African-American recording artist in 1890. Only a few years after Thomas Edison invented his "talking machine," Johnson recorded a version of a racist minstrel song called "The Whistling Coon" for the Metropolitan Phonograph Company.

# Will Marion Cook
# Composer, Teacher, and Mentor

Will Marion Cook was born on January 27, 1869 to middle-class parents in Washington, DC. His father, John Hartwell Cook, graduated from Howard University Law School and later became the school's first dean.

Will Cook began studying classical music in his early teens. He would hone his skills at the Berlin Hochschule fur Musik in Germany, where he worked with renowned violinist Joseph Joachim, a student of Johannes Brahms. Upon returning to the United States in the 1890s, Cook began composing classical music while playing the violin, but he was unable to find work in the world of white classical music.

After switching his focus to the composition and performance of ragtime, Cook enjoyed his first success in 1898, with the original musical *Clorindy, or The Origin of the Cakewalk.* (For details, see page 24.) Following the show's triumphant debut, Cook wrote, "I was so delirious that I drank a glass of water, thought it wine and got glorious drunk. Negroes at last were on Broadway, and there to stay. . . . We were artists and we were going a long way."

Cook had every reason to celebrate, because his landmark operetta marked the beginning of a highly successful career. He would go on to compose the scores for a number of musicals, including *Uncle Eph's Christmas, In Dahomey,* and *The Southerners,* all of which were produced on Broadway. *The Southerners,* which premiered on May 23, 1904, was especially significant. Although all characters with speaking parts were played by white actors in blackface, they were supported by African-American singers and dancers, making this the first Broadway musical to feature a racially integrated cast. Among the black performers was Abbie Mitchell, whom Cook had married a year after the debut of *Clorindy.*

Highly talented, Cook's ambitions extended far beyond Broadway. He also achieved success as a choral and orchestral conductor, and in 1912, he led his 150-voice chorus in a performance of *Swing Along!* at New York's Carnegie Hall. Six years later, he began the all-black Southern Syncopated Orchestra, which toured Europe with Abbie Mitchell as lead singer.

Cook also served as teacher and mentor to many young African-American musicians. His most famous student was a young composer and performer named Edward Kennedy "Duke" Ellington, whom Cook famously advised, "Let your inner self break through and guide you. Don't try to be anybody but yourself." Cook certainly followed that advice through his own long, varied, and very successful career.

Classically trained, Will Marion Cook turned to the composition of ragtime when he was unable to find work in the world of white classical music. Eventually, he would achieve success not only as a composer of black musicals but also as a choral and orchestral conductor.

In 1895, W.E.B. DuBois became the first African American to receive a PhD from prestigious Harvard University. A social activist who believed in using art to combat the myth of racial inferiority and promote black pride, DuBois would later encourage African Americans to produce theater "by us, for us, near us, and about us."

In 1896, the U.S. Supreme Court upheld the right of states to maintain racially segregated facilities that were "separate but equal." This landmark decision (*Plessy v. Ferguson*) provided constitutional consent for the adoption of Jim Crow segregation laws throughout the South—until the decision was overruled by 1954's *Brown v. Board of Education.*

With songs by composer Bob Cole and lyricist William Johnson, *A Trip to Coontown* was the first full-length musical comedy that was written, directed, and performed solely by African Americans. A spoof of the white musical *A Trip to Chinatown*, *Coontown* was also notable for challenging racial stereotypes.

music was heard by the audience leaving the theater below, many came upstairs searching for the source of the magnificent choral singing. The show was a triumph, with the performers receiving a ten-minute ovation at the end of the evening. *Clorindy* was so successful that it launched the song-writing career of Will Marion Cook. (For more about Cook, see the inset on page 25.)

That same year, yet another black play appeared on Broadway. A spoof of *A Trip to Chinatown*—an all-white musical comedy produced in 1891—*A Trip to Coontown* was written by composer-actor Bob Cole and lyricist-actor William Johnson. Cole and Johnson's play had the distinction of being the first full-length musical comedy written, directed, and performed exclusively by African Americans. In addition, although *Coontown* was largely inspired by minstrel show routines, Cole challenged the typical racial stereotypes by playing Willie Wayside, an inebriated hobo, in *whiteface*. Meanwhile, Johnson portrayed the humorous con artist Jimmy Flimflammer without presenting the usual minstrel-style caricature.

A *Trip to Coontown* was a hit. After an initial run of just eight well-received performances, it headed out on a short tour. It then returned to Manhattan for a second sold-out run at the prestigious Grand Opera House. After another tour, the play had its third and final run at the Casino Theatre's roof garden, where Will Marion Cook's production of *Clorindy* had made its mark. Within the next few years, Bob Cole would go on to compose several more black musicals with J. Rosamond Johnson and James Weldon Johnson. (See page 46.)

*A Trip to Coontown* was applauded by audiences and critics alike. After its April 1898 premiere at the Third Avenue Theatre, a reviewer for *The Sun* wrote that the musical was "one of the most artistic farce comedy shows that New York has seen in a long time."

## THE LEGACY OF THE NINETEENTH CENTURY

Although the nineteenth century had seen the end of slavery, it had not seen equality for African Americans in the theater or in any other aspect of American life. Nevertheless, a great deal of progress had been made. A new generation of black men and women had found a place on stage—albeit, a stage that still helped perpetuate the racial stereotypes that had been popularized by minstrelsy and the Tom Shows. Audiences, both black and white, had applauded the energetic, innovative dancing of William Henry Lane; the elegance of Dora Dean and Charles E. Johnson; and the vocal abilities of Sissieretta "Black Patti" Jones and Abbie Mitchell. Groundbreaking musicals—*The Creole Show*, *Clorindy*, and *A Trip to Coontown*—had enjoyed enormous success. Will Marion Cook had begun to demonstrate the many ways in which he would contribute to the country's musical heritage, and Bob Cole had launched his successful career as a composer of black musicals. African Americans had taken the stage, and, as Cook himself predicted, they were there to stay.

In September 1896, former slave George Washington Carver was appointed the director of the Agricultural Department at Alabama's Tuskegee Institute. Carver's groundbreaking work led to advances in the farming of sweet potatoes, soybeans, and—most important—peanuts. It was his research on peanuts that catapulted Carver to fame.

*Clorindy, or The Origin of the Cakewalk*— the first musical entirely produced and performed by African Americans—opened on July 5, 1898 at the roof garden of New York's Casino Theatre. That same year, *A Trip to Coontown* became the first full-length musical comedy written, directed, and performed exclusively by African Americans.

# STARRING IN ORDER OF APPEARANCE

Bert Williams

George Walker

The Whitman Sisters

Will Marion Cook

Paul Laurence Dunbar

Lottie Williams

Aida Overton Walker

Hattie McIntosh

Abbie Mitchell

Jesse A. Shipp

Alex Rogers

Tom Lemonier

Cecil Mack

Chris Smith

Bob Cole

J. Rosamond Johnson

James Weldon Johnson

Joe Jordan

Scott Joplin

Ernest Hogan

Will Vodery

Angelina Weld Grimké

# 2.

## The Turn of the Century

In the 1870s, incandescent lights began to replace gas lights on New York stages—an innovation that made theatergoing both safer and more pleasurable. Then, in the 1890s, Broadway became one of the first streets to be fully illuminated by electric light, inspiring visitors to call it "the Great White Way."

During the 1800s, New York City had grown by leaps and bounds, becoming the epicenter of the new country. As immigrants poured into the city, largely settling in lower New York, the legitimate theater had begun its movement northward to keep its distance from crowded immigrant neighborhoods. Although it had originally been located in the City Hall area, over the years it had made its way first to Union Square and then to Herald and Madison Squares. Then, in the late 1800s, a line of theaters began to move north along Broadway. The Broadway theater district was established early in the twentieth century, when the building of the subway system, the opening of the Times building, and the installation of electric lights—which would eventually inspire the term "Great White Way"—made the area on and around Forty-Second Street a prime location for entertainment venues. Within the first five years alone of the new century, the Victoria, New Amsterdam, and Republic Theaters were all completed in the heart of this new district. But entertainment was certainly not limited to that locale. Burlesque and vaudeville flourished in all of the city's boroughs. There was also a so-called "subway circuit" of theaters—in both Manhattan and the other boroughs—that hosted shows when they began touring after their Broadway runs. During this period, too, smaller playhouses began to emerge in downtown New York.

With so many theaters open throughout the city, there were opportunities for many kinds of performers. Although what historians term the "Great Migration" of African Americans would not begin for a few years,

Starting in the 1880s and ending with the migration to Harlem, black artists found a creative environment in an area of Manhattan that became known as Black Bohemia. Situated in the West fifties and sixties, Black Bohemia was, for a time, the home of Bert Williams, George Walker, and many other African-American musicians, writers, and entertainers.

In 1900, Booker T. Washington published his first autobiography, *The Story of My Life and Work*, largely for black readers. At the same time, with a more diverse audience in mind, Washington published *Up From Slavery*, a serialized account of his life detailing how he had risen from slavery to success as a black educator. It was a bestseller.

between 1890 and 1914, New York City experienced a flood of southern blacks searching for greater social and economic equality. What they found, instead, was a city in which discrimination was actually on the rise and jobs were usually limited to work as laborers or servants. Yet even in this atmosphere of racial prejudice, many talented African Americans were able to find work in the city's entertainment industry. And, in time, through their successes, they would help shape the ever-changing world of theater.

## VAUDEVILLE

As the legitimate theater settled into its new home on Broadway, one of America's longest-lasting and most celebrated forms of entertainment was at its peak. This, of course, was vaudeville. From the 1880s until the early 1930s, vaudeville was the craze both in New York City and throughout the nation. Although it borrowed from previous genres, including the minstrel show, burlesque, and the circus, vaudeville was different. It offered diversity the likes of which Americans had never seen, and—unlike burlesque— it barred bawdy material as well as alcohol. With the goal of providing entertainment that was suitable and appealing to both genders and all ages, vaudeville featured singers (both classical and popular), dancers, comedians, magicians, clowns, acrobats, animal acts, jugglers, athletes, lecturing celebrities, and practically anyone else who could entertain while maintaining respectability.

Vaudeville became a national showcase for talent. The who's who of legendary vaudeville is long and diverse, and includes Fred Astaire, Ethel Barrymore, Count Bassie, Jack Benny, Milton Berle, Eubie Blake, Fanny Brice, Cab Calloway, Ella Fitzgerald, W.C. Fields, Judy Garland, Harry

From the 1880s through the early 1930s—and from the small-town stage to the grandest New York theater— vaudeville was the most popular form of entertainment in America.

As New York City spread north, midtown Manhattan became the center of activity, and Times Square, shown here, became the center of the theater district.

# The Theaters of Old New York

The early settlements of Manhattan were on the island's southern tip, near New York Harbor, and for many years, most of the city's population lived and worked in that area. But very slowly—as the population grew and increased the demands for housing, employment, and entertainment—the city began to spread north. In the early 1800s, land speculator John Jacob Astor began to buy large tracts of land in midtown Manhattan, and by the end of the century, a new center of city life was being established there. In the first few years of the twentieth century, the opening of the Times Square building, the construction of a subway system that had several lines converging at Times Square, and the installation of electric lights would spur the development of the Great White Way near Forty-Second Street and Broadway, a street whose name would become synonymous with New York theater.

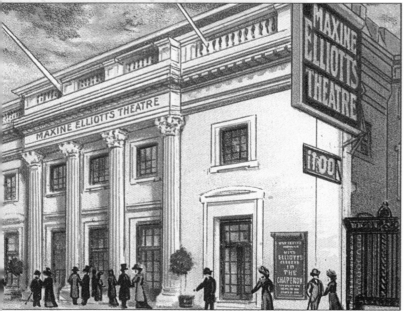

People attended shows more often at the turn of the century than they do today, and entrepreneurs were quick to construct theaters that could serve the public in style. Within only a few years—between 1898 and 1904—theater impresario Oscar Hammerstein I opened the Victoria Theatre, the Theatre Republic, and the Lew M. Fields Theatre, all in midtown Manhattan. In 1903, the Lyceum was completed. In 1905, the Hippodrome opened and thrilled theatergoers with its state-of-the-art technology, including a rising glass water tank, and a seating capacity of 5,200, which made it the largest theater in the world. In 1911, the American Horse Exchange was converted into the Winter Garden Theatre. But perhaps the most impressive entertainment venue of all was the New Amsterdam Theatre. Opening in 1903, the New Amsterdam was an eleven-story building, and although it did not have the seating capacity of the Hippodrome, it was extraordinary in other ways. Lavishly decorated, it was known as the "House Beautiful," and for many years, it would be the home of the equally extravagant Ziegfeld Follies. Like a number of other theaters of that era, the New Amsterdam boasted a rooftop garden, where performances could be held when the summer heat made indoor shows uncomfortable.

By 1920, Manhattan had over fifty theaters, and most of them were located in the Times Square-Broadway area. In years to come, the city's population would continue to expand northward, but Broadway would remain Manhattan's theater district.

Houdini, Bob Hope, Gypsy Rose Lee, and many more entertainers of the era. Baseball players such as Babe Ruth and Ty Cobb spent time on the vaudeville stage, as did temperance leader Carrie Nation and evangelist Aimee Semple McPherson. Even Helen Keller and her teacher, Anne Sullivan, engaged in the phenomenon that was vaudeville.

Because this form of entertainment was so popular, vaudeville circuits developed, with each circuit including a group of houses controlled by a single manager. This not only made it easier for individual theaters to maintain a roster of new acts but also served to regulate the salaries of performers so that the house always had the advantage. One of the largest and most famous of these organizations was the Orpheum Circuit. Operating from 1886 to 1927, when it merged with another large circuit, the Orpheum included about forty-five houses located in thirty-six cities across the country. By the late 1890s, the circuits had houses in nearly every sizeable location in the United States. Travel from one theater to another was carefully arranged by a slew of managers, booking agents, and theater owners, helping to ensure that audiences were never disappointed. The schedule was exhausting for the performers, who sometimes worked forty or more weeks a year, but top acts made upwards of $3,000 annually, which was impressive at the turn of the century.

Theater managers exercised strict control over the people they hired. Vaudeville performers were not allowed to talk directly to audience members or to present religious or off-color material, and any performer who failed to follow a manager's rules was handed a blue envelope of directions to omit or replace the offensive language. Thus, the term "blue material" came to mean material that was risqué.

Although turn-of-the-century America was permeated by racial prejudice, a good many African Americans did find jobs in vaudeville. Joe Laurie, a vaudeville comedian, once said, "Talent has no color," and it's true that vaudeville show lineups often included whites, blacks, Asians, and Jewish performers on a single stage. Nevertheless, acceptance on the vaudeville stage often came at a steep price, and the price was self-respect. Black performers were routinely paid less than white performers and had no say regarding the way their acts were booked. Two strong black acts were often teamed up so they wouldn't take up two separate spots in the lineup. Moreover, not unlike minstrel show performers, vaudevillians—African Americans included—were expected to wear blackface and continue to play stereotypical black characters, such as the subservient Uncle Tom. Finally, there were theaters, especially in the South, that did not permit black people to perform.

Racial prejudice also reared its head when it came to the theaters' treatment of black patrons. Many playhouses did not allow black people in the

Although vaudeville was by no means free of the racial prejudice of the time, this popular form of entertainment was a fusion of many different cultural traditions, from the Yiddish theater to the English Music Hall to the minstrel show. And for many white theatergoers, vaudeville provided their first exposure to African Americans.

In 1901, popular African-American entertainers Bert Williams and George Walker made their first recordings for the Victor Talking Machine Company. Until 1909, when the Fisk University Jubilee Singers recorded for Victor, the vaudeville team was among the only black recording artists who were advertised by a national company.

History was made on October 16, 1901, when President Theodore Roosevelt invited black educator Booker T. Washington to dine with the president's family at the White House. While a number of black leaders had attended meetings at the White House, none had been invited to a meal, and news of this precedent-setting social occasion shocked the nation.

audience, while some relegated African Americans to the balcony only. Those theater owners who permitted blacks in other sections restricted them to aisle seats so that they wouldn't have to squeeze past white patrons. This policy lasted into the 1940s.

Because racial issues limited not only black people's access to entertainment but also the theaters in which black performers could work, a circuit of theaters and nightclubs emerged that featured African-American entertainers and catered to black audiences. These venues were found in most major cities, including New York, Washington, and Philadelphia in the Northeast; Richmond, Atlanta, and New Orleans in the South; and Chicago and Kansas City to the West. The network of black theaters—which included not only formal playhouses but also smaller venues such as high school auditoriums—came to be known as the Chitlin' Circuit after the traditional southern African-American food. In a way, the theaters could be compared to the more than two hundred all-black baseball teams that sprang up from the 1880s forward because of the racial barriers erected in the white leagues.

In 1909, in an effort to manage the Chitlin' Circuit, a group of white theater owners formed the Theater Owners Booking Agency, or TOBA, to arrange the tours of black performers. Starting with thirty-one theaters, TOBA eventually expanded to include more than one hundred venues. TOBA theaters did not pay as well as white theaters, and TOBA bookings generally involved poor touring and working conditions, making life so difficult for performers that the agency's initials were sometimes said to stand for "tough on black actors" or "tough on black asses." But the black vaudeville circuit did succeed in providing work for many African Americans and making it possible for black people to attend shows without being treated as second-class citizens. In the highly segregated South, TOBA houses were the only ones that regularly accepted black audiences.

The list of black performers who got their start on the TOBA circuit is impressive. A few of the best-known entertainers include singers Bessie Smith and Ethel Waters; musicians Fats Waller, Louis Armstrong, Eubie Blake, and Duke Ellington; dancers Bill "Bojangles" Robinson and Josephine Baker; and actress Hattie McDaniel. Sammy Davis, Jr. began working on the circuit when he was just four years old. Major vaudeville acts such as Williams and Walker (discussed on page 37) were in demand on the white vaudeville circuits, but many other black performers relied on TOBA for steady work. Some entertainers who were accepted on white stages actually preferred playing to African-American audiences, believing that these theatergoers better appreciated and understood their material. Bert Williams, Ethel Waters, Ma Rainey, and Bessie Smith were among those who sometimes took cuts in pay to bring their entertainment to other people of color.

Although the Theater Owners Booking Agency (TOBA) was well known for its poor treatment of the black performers it managed, many entertainers—from Josephine Baker to Ethel Waters—got their start on the TOBA circuit, and some performers preferred the black circuit to the white because they felt that their work was better appreciated by their own people.

The all-black 1903 musical comedy *In Dahomey* was both groundbreaking and successful. When it went on tour abroad, it became the first play in the United Kingdom to be written and performed by African Americans. It was also the first black musical to have its score published. And when its receipts were tallied, it provided investors with a 400-hundred-percent return.

In 1903, W.E.B. DuBois' landmark book *The Souls of Black Folks*—a founding work in the literature of black protest—was published. A collection of essays, DuBois' work polarized African-American leaders into two groups: those who believed in Booker T. Washington's strategy of accommodation to whites, and those who supported more aggressive action.

The team of Bert Williams (left) and George Walker (right) was a success both on the vaudeville stage and in musicals. Their act was based on standard minstrel routines, and Williams even performed in blackface.

One of the most notable black vaudeville acts—an act that was in high demand on the white vaudeville circuit and was received well throughout the United States—was Williams and Walker. George Walker was born around 1873 in Kansas, and began his career in a troupe of black minstrels before working his way to California. Bert Williams was born in the West Indies around 1874, and eventually moved to California, where he performed in a range of venues. When the two men met in 1893 in San Francisco, they decided to team up. After appearing in various shows, Williams and Walker, billing themselves as "The Two Real Coons," developed an act based on standard minstrel routines. Dressed as a dandy, Walker told the jokes, while Williams, dressed in mismatched clothing, was the straight man. After several years of struggling, the two captured the public's attention with their cakewalk, and doors began opening. Soon, their skits, songs, and comedic dances were in great demand, and they not only toured the vaudeville circuit as major stars but also appeared in New York City's top venues. Williams and Walker even recorded some of their comedy routines for the Victor Talking Machine Company, making them among the first African-American recording artists. (For more information about Bert Williams, see the inset on page 38.)

Another very successful black vaudeville act was the Whitman Sisters. The sisters—which included Mabel, Essie, Alberta, and "Baby" Alice—received formal musical training at the New England Conservatory of Music, and they were all accomplished musicians. In 1899, the three eldest of the group formed the Whitman Sisters Comedy Company, which played to both black and white audiences in leading southern vaudeville houses. In 1904, when the group adopted the name Whitman Sisters New Orleans Troubadours, Mabel became one of the first African-American women to manage her own company. All four sisters were top performers, and between them, they created

In 1893, when this sheet music was published, Williams and Walker already had a highly popular stage act. A few years later, in 1901, the team would begin making recordings for the Victor Talking Machine Company.

A black civil rights organization established in 1905 by W.E.B. DuBois, the Niagra Movement was named after the falls where the first meeting was held. The original plan was to assemble on the American side of the falls, but when racially prejudiced hotel managers denied the group accommodations, it moved to the Canadian side.

A former slave from Georgia, Alonzo Franklin Herndon was a model of entrepreneurial spirit. In 1905, Herndon—already the owner of several barber shops—established the Atlanta Life Insurance Company, and by the late 1920s, he had become Atlanta's wealthiest African American. Throughout his life, Herndon remained committed to advancing black business and social progress.

# Bert Williams
# From Vaudeville to the Broadway Stage

Egbert Austin "Bert" Williams was one of the most significant vaudeville stars of the early twentieth century. But he was not simply a star of vaudeville, for his talents extended to the Broadway stage—including the Ziegfeld Follies—and even to early sound recordings and moving pictures.

Born in Antigua, West Indies, on November 12, 1874, Williams lived in New York City for a time before his family moved to Riverside, California. There, Williams graduated from high school and made plans to become a civil engineer, but his father's death forced him to abandon his dreams of further education. So the young man first became a barker for traveling medicine shows; then, a singer in bars; and then, a minstrel show performer. While on tour in 1893, he met George Walker, and the two formed the team Williams and Walker. Vaudeville's variety format allowed the team to showcase their many talents. Williams and Walker presented song-and-dance numbers, sang humorous songs, and performed comic skits. Even in these early days of performing, Williams was noted for his skills in "stage business" and his flair for comedy. Comic actor and fellow vaudevillian W.C. Fields later described Williams as "The funniest man I ever saw—and the saddest man I ever knew."

In 1896 and 1897, Williams and Walker headlined the Koster & Bial's Music Hall—a prominent New York vaudeville house—for thirty-six weeks. Together, they also appeared in several successful musical comedies, including *Sons of Ham* (1900), *In Dahomey* (1903), and *Abyssinia* (1906), which had a score co-written by Williams. (See page 40 for more information on the team's Broadway achievements.)

Beginning in 1901, Williams and Walker made several recordings of their comedy routines and songs with the Victor Talking Machine Company. Again, Williams' contributions were especially noteworthy, for while Walker's voice was thin on the playback, Williams' voice was strong. "Good Morning, Carrie," written and performed by Williams, was one of the biggest hits of 1901. Later, when appearing in the 1906 show *Abyssinia*, Williams recorded "Nobody," which became his signature theme. It has been estimated that sales of the

recording far exceeded 100,000, which was high for that time.

In 1910, a year before Walker passed away, Williams joined the Ziegfeld Follies, becoming the only African American on the bill. There, he often played the "Jonah Man," a hard-luck character that was based on a minstrel show standard, but that Williams fleshed out into a full human being. Audiences applauded both the performer's humor and his considerable acting abilities, and Williams was to return to the Follies—always as a featured star—for many years. (See page 48 for more about the Follies.)

Williams' stage success led to more recordings, this time with Columbia Records. There, he cut seventeen titles, including at least one hit, "Play That Barbershop Chord." Critics and fans alike loved Williams' warm personality and unique half-spoken singing style, and many consider him to be one of the finest recording stars of the time.

Williams became the first black comedian to appear in movies when he debuted in *Darktown Jubilee* in 1914. He acted in other movies, as well, and continued to star in stage productions. In fact, he was on tour with *Under the Bamboo Tree* when he died in 1922.

Throughout Williams' career, although he was a headliner who was welcome on nearly any stage in the country—including Ziegfeld's otherwise "white" stage—he faced racial discrimination everywhere he went. During performances, he was forced to wear the obligatory blackface of the era. Routinely, he was denied simple privileges, such as the freedom to ride in the same hotel elevator that was used by white guests. After one such incident, he said to a friend, "It wouldn't be so bad . . . if I didn't hear the applause still ringing in my ears."

Yet Bert Williams' pioneering achievements—on stage, on screen, and in the recording studio—did not go unnoticed or unappreciated. At his funeral, more than five thousand people filed past his casket, and many more were turned away. African-American leader Booker T. Washington once observed, "Bert Williams has done more for the race than I have. He has smiled his way into people's hearts. I have been obliged to fight my way."

Although both George Walker and Bert Williams were in huge ▶ demand, it was Williams who was to achieve the greater success in show business, appearing on some of the best vaudeville circuits, on the stage of the prestigious Ziegfeld Follies, and even on the silver screen.

the acts, composed the music, made the costumes, handled the bookings, and kept the books. Their fast-paced shows—which included dozens of other black performers, as well—offered songs, dances, and comedy skits. A combination of devoted fans and TOBA helped ensure that the Whitman Sisters became one of the most popular, longest-running, and best-paid companies on the black vaudeville circuit. Even when vaudeville began to wane in popularity, the sisters performed in churches and theaters throughout the country. And many of the performers they trained went on to have successful careers in entertainment.

Changing public tastes, the introduction of motion pictures, and the Great Depression would eventually cause vaudeville to disappear from the scene. But even when vaudeville was at its height of popularity, many black performers, composers, and writers—including George Walker and Bert Williams—were already attracting attention on the Broadway stage.

## MUSICAL THEATER

Black performers, writers, and producers had gained their first foothold on Broadway in the late 1800s with productions such as *Clorindy, or The Origin of the Cakewalk* and *A Trip to Coontown*. Their success on Broadway continued throughout the first decade of the twentieth century.

## Williams and Walker

**Bert Williams and George Walker spent the latter part of 1902 planning *In Dahomey*, the grandest African-American musical attempted to date. A collaborative effort involving numerous composers and lyricists, the show was a great success.**

Even as Bert Williams and George Walker enjoyed popularity on the vaudeville stage, the team's goal was to produce and perform in their own Broadway musical. After a number of small productions—*A Lucky Coon* (1898), *The Policy Player* (1899), and *Sons of Ham* (1900)—the pair joined other talented African Americans to produce a full-length musical comedy. *In Dahomey* was truly a collaborative effort, and over the years, as it went on tour, many composers and lyricists became involved. But Will Marion Cook, the fine composer of *Clorindy* fame, was responsible for most of the musical compositions, and a lion's share of the lyrics was written by Paul Laurence Dunbar. The play told the story of a group of African Americans who, after finding a pot of gold, move to Africa and become rulers of Dahomey. The cast starred Bert Williams and George Walker, and also included Lottie Williams (Williams' wife), Aida Overton Walker (Walker's wife), and Hattie McIntosh.

*In Dahomey* opened on February 18, 1903 at the New York Theatre. In addition to the usual opening-night jitters, the cast and crew feared that the production would incite racial riots outside the theater. Fortunately, the show premiered without a hitch and ran for fifty-three performances,

In 1907, Harvard University graduate Alain Locke became the first African American to be awarded a Rhodes Scholarship. Because of his race, Locke was unable to gain admission to several of Oxford's colleges, but he eventually was accepted by Hertford College. Later, Locke became chair of Howard University's Department of Philosophy.

On December 4, 1909, James H. Anderson produced the first edition of New York's *Amsterdam News*, one of fifty black newspapers in the country at the time. As a mouthpiece for one of the nation's largest African-American communities, the *News* would champion numerous civil rights causes over the years.

which was considered excellent at that time. The musical then began a seven-month tour of England. After opening at London's Shaftesbury Theatre, it travelled throughout the country. The show was so well-received in Great Britain that, by royal command, it was staged at Buckingham Palace on the occasion of the Prince of Wales' birthday celebration. After being lauded as "the most popular musical show in London," *In Dahomey* returned to New York, where it was a hit at the Grand Opera House. Following this, it went on a ten-month tour of the United States.

By any measure, *In Dahomey* was a great success. When the receipts were finally tallied, the producers enjoyed a 400-hundred-percent return on their investments. This confirmed that an all-black show could make money. The play was also groundbreaking in many ways. During its tour, it became the first play in the United Kingdom's long theatrical history to be written and performed by African Americans. It was also the first black musical to have its score published—although it was published in the UK rather than the US. Another distinctive feature of *In Dahomey* was that it masterfully combined different types of lyrics as well as the many musical genres that were being enjoyed at the turn of the century. Some songs used black dialect, while others featured mainstream English. The Viennese high-operetta style of music characterized some pieces, while other num-

The 1903 musical comedy *In Dahomey* was an artistic and financial triumph both in the United States and in England. This photo shows *In Dahomey* stars (from left to right) Hattie McIntosh, George Walker, Aida Overton Walker, Bert Williams, and Lottie Williams.

# Abbie Mitchell and Aida Overton Walker

With her beautiful soprano voice and regal bearing, Abbie Mitchell performed in dozens of plays and concerts both in the United States and abroad. When she was not on stage, Mitchell devoted much of her time to training young black singers, and in 1931, she became the head of the vocal department at Tuskegee Institute.

Along with the many talented African-American men who performed, composed, and wrote for the theater at the turn of the twentieth century, many African-American women were also enjoying success on the stage. The best known of these great ladies were Abbie Mitchell and Aida Overton Walker.

Abbie Mitchell was born on the Lower East Side of New York City on September 25, 1884. The daughter of a German-Jewish father and an African-American mother, she began studying voice at a young age and was considered a child prodigy. A soprano, her voice was described as being natural and pure, and her bearing, regal.

Mitchell's first role was in Will Marion Cook and Paul Laurence Dunbar's groundbreaking musical *Clorindy, or The Origin of the Cakewalk.* The play opened in 1898, and that same year, Mitchell married Cook. She was only fourteen years old.

After Mitchell's success in *Clorindy*, the immensely talented young woman was a featured performer at parties given by the Astors, the Vanderbilts, and other prominent New York families. Cook, eager to capitalize on his wife's popularity, wrote another musical—*Jes Lak White Folks*—to showcase her talents. Mitchell also had a major role in her husband's 1903 groundbreaking musical *In Dahomey.* Her rendition of "Brownskin Baby Mine," one of the play's many notable songs, helped make it a hit of the era. And when the show toured Great Britain and was staged at Buckingham Palace, Mitchell gave a command performance for the royal family.

During her long career, Mitchell appeared in a variety of productions—musicals as well as straight plays—and sang the works of many composers. In 1908, for instance, she was the lead soprano in Bob Cole's *Red Moon.* And once again, she was to give a command performance—this time, for Czar Nicholas II of Russia. When racial boundaries tightened in the second decade of the twentieth century, preventing black performers from appearing in many Broadway theaters, Mitchell toured with Black Patti's Troubadours, appeared on the London stage, and worked in other venues. In 1931, she would return to New York City, where she would share the stage with Helen Hayes in a Town Hall production of *Coquette.* She would also return to Broadway, where she played in shows as diverse as *Porgy and Bess, Dr. Jekyll and Mr. Hyde,* and *Othello.* Eventually,

# Leading Ladies at the Turn of the Century

she became a voice teacher at the Tuskegee Institute. Mitchell died in 1960.

Born four years before Mitchell, on Valentine's Day of 1880, Aida Overton Walker studied music in New York City. At only fifteen years of age, she joined John W. Isham's *The Octoroons*, a major black touring show, and then became a member of Black Patti's Troubadours. Shortly afterwards, she met performer George Walker, and the two were married. A quadruple threat, Aida was not just an actress, singer, and dancer, but also a gifted choreographer who created innovative dances for her husband's vaudeville team, Williams and Walker. She also won important roles in black musicals such as *Sons of Ham* (1900), *In Dahomey* (1902), *Abyssinia* (1906), and *Bandana Land* (1908). While touring with *In Dahomey* in 1903, a command performance at Buckingham Palace transformed the talented artist into an international star. Showing amazing versatility, she even took over her husband's role (while continuing to play her own) in *Bandana Land* when ill health forced him to drop out of the production in 1908.

Aida Walker temporarily retired from stage work to care for her ailing husband. Shortly after George Walker's death in 1911, she signed a contact with an all-black traveling show. But in 1912, appearing on the same bill as Harry Houdini and Mae West, Aida Overton Walker once again danced her way into the hearts of New Yorkers. This time, high atop the new roof garden of the Victoria Theatre, she was Salome performing the Dance of the Seven Veils. Noted theater critic Robert Speare was quite impressed, writing that Walker "fully lives up to expectations and gives a graceful and interesting version of the dance."

This was to be the entertainer's last major performance, for while she was still relatively young, she began to develop health problems that limited her ability to perform. She died in 1914 at only thirty-four years of age. Yet Aida Overton Walker had made her mark on the American stage. She is considered the best African-American dancer of her time, with a style that was "clean" and "refined." She is also regarded as the first black female choreographer, with original dances that were intended to break away from minstrel-show tradition and offer a new and more positive view of black people in America.

During her relatively short lifetime, Aida Overton Walker enjoyed success as an actress, singer, choreographer, and dancer. The wife of George Walker, she created many innovative dances for the Williams and Walker team and appeared with Walker on stage. After her husband's death in 1911, Aida struck out on her own and was in great demand.

44

Williams and Walker's *Bandana Land* proved to be another hit for the talented team. Sadly, while on tour with the show in 1908, George Walker became ill and was forced to drop out of the production. His wife, the talented Aida Overton Walker, took over his role while continuing to play her own.

A departure from the standard back-to-Africa formula, 1908's *Bandana Land* was set entirely in the United States. The score was a collaborative effort, combining the works of several black artists.

bers were written as popular songs, and the finale employed the newly popular ragtime syncopation. (See the inset on page 50 to learn more about ragtime.)

In 1906, Williams and Walker starred in another Broadway musical. Featuring music by Bert Williams and Will Marion Cook, and a book and lyrics by Jesse A. Shipp and Alex Rogers, *Abyssinia*—another African-themed show—premiered at the Majestic Theatre. The show proved to be a hit. One of the songs from the score, the doleful "Nobody," would become Bert Williams' signature theme.

The next musical that Williams and Walkers starred in was 1908's *Bandana Land*. Instead of using the usual back-to-Africa theme, this show was set in the United States. The score incorporated works by a number of African Americans, including Tom Lemonier, Cecil Mack, and Chris Smith. *Bandana Land*, too, opened at the Majestic and proved to be a hit. But while on tour with the show in 1909, George Walker became ill and had to drop out of the production. He died in 1911, making this the last musical in which Williams and Walker would appear.

In 1912, Aida Walker's interpretation of Salome's Dance of the Seven Veils, performed ▶ at New York's Victoria Theatre, downplayed the sensual aspects of the dance and emphasized its dramatic elements. This was very intentional, as Walker was determined to show the world that black female artists were as dignified as they were talented.

## Bob Cole and the Johnson Brothers

A performer, playwright, and composer, Bob Cole was an influential figure in the development of black musicals. He is known for his contributions to *A Trip to Coontown* (1898), *The Shoo-Fly Regiment* (1907), and *The Red Moon* (1909), as well as for the 1902 hit song "Under the Bamboo Tree."

In a bold move, the authors of 1907's *Shoo-Fly Regiment* avoided minstrel stereotyping, instead offering black characters that were intelligent, educated, and highly patriotic. Although some white reviewers complained that blacks should "continue to write shows of a minstrel nature," the play was well received and had a long run.

As important as the Williams and Walker's shows were, theirs were not the only black musicals that played in New York theaters in the early 1900s. Another great team was that of Bob Cole, J. Rosamond Johnson, and James Weldon Johnson.

Bob Cole was initially signed as a comic in *The Creole Show*, where, in short order, he became one of the featured stars as well as a songwriter. Following this, he joined Black Patti's Troubadours, where he met another composer-performer named William Johnson. Seeking higher pay, Cole left the Troubadours, and shortly thereafter, Johnson followed. In 1898, Cole and Johnson teamed up to write the songs for *A Trip to Coontown*, the first full-length all-black musical comedy. (See page 27 for more about *Coontown*.) But after *Coontown*, Cole broke off his working relationship with Billy Johnson and joined forces with brothers J. Rosamond Johnson and James Weldon Johnson.

Bob Cole had always been serious about his craft and meticulous about every detail of his productions. At this point in his career—perhaps because of his own increasingly progressive attitude towards social issues, or perhaps because of his association with the college-educated, politically active Johnson brothers—he wanted to cut loose from minstrel-show stereotypes and degrading "coon songs." He and the Johnsons set about producing Broadway musicals with more sophisticated music and lyrics. To raise money for their shows, Cole and J. Rosamond Johnson performed on big-time vaudeville circuits, although they refused to appear in blackface. Their intention was not only to stage fine productions but also to replace black stereotypes with a more dignified view of African Americans. A prolific team, Cole and the Johnson brothers would write over two hundred songs, the most famous of which was 1902's "Under the Bamboo Tree," which sold over 400,000 copies of sheet music.

In 1907, Cole, Johnson, and Johnson produced their first Broadway musical, *The Shoo-Fly Regiment*. With music by J. Rosamond Johnson, lyrics by James W. Johnson, and a book by Bob Cole, the musical was unusual for the time because it did not rely on minstrel themes or characters. Instead, it told the story of a highly patriotic Tuskegee Institute graduate who—against the wishes of his girlfriend—gives up his dream of teaching and enlists in the Spanish-American War. After a successful combat mission and some complications, he returns to his girl and marries her. With the exception of the Tuskegee Institute, the play could have been about white people. The male characters were educated and brave, not lazy or foolish, and the romantic aspect of the story was treated seriously rather than comically. This was new, because it had always been assumed that white audiences would find an earnest romance offensive when the characters were black.

With the goal of ending racial discrimination and segregation, the National Association for the Advancement of Colored People (NAACP) was founded in 1909. Originally headed by black activist W.E.B. DuBois and several prominent white civil rights leaders, the NAACP directed its first efforts toward ending the lynching of black Americans.

*The Crisis* was launched in 1910 as the official publication of the National Association for the Advancement of Colored People. Edited by W.E.B. DuBois, the magazine presented a militant voice in the battle for black civil rights. By 1918, *The Crisis* had more than 100,000 readers, and it is still being published today.

In 1906, *The Shoo-Fly Regiment* began a long pre-New York tour that took the production first to theaters on the East Coast and then throughout the West. The tour ended in 1907, and on June 3 of that year, the play opened at New York's Grand Opera House. Following this, it moved to the Bijou Theatre, where it ran for several months. The company then embarked on another tour of the United States. All told, the play ran for about two years.

*The Shoo-Fly Regiment* met with mostly favorable responses. Some white critics, though, were unable to accept black people in anything but stereotypical roles. One critic wrote that blacks should "continue to write shows of a minstrel nature and leave modern musicals to white authors."

Cole, Johnson, and Johnson's next musical was *The Red Moon*, which was written in collaboration with musician Joe Jordan. The team based the plot on the actual education program for African Americans and Native Americans established at the Hampton Institute in Virginia. The play tells of a Native American chief who abducts his half-black, half-American Indian daughter after she graduates from the Swamptown (Hampton) school. Following only a short stay on the reservation, the chief's daughter finds that she doesn't like her new home. Fortunately, two African-American men not only rescue her but also help reconcile the chief with his wife, and ultimately, the grateful girl marries one of her champions. The play's all-black cast included Bob Cole and J. Rosamond Johnson, as well as stars Aida Overton Walker and Abbie Mitchell.

*The Red Moon* opened in May of 1909 at New York's Majestic Theatre, where it ran for thirty-two performances. It then toured the country for nearly a year. This play broke away from minstrel traditions not only by presenting a serious romantic theme, but also by portraying positive rela-

*The Red Moon* (1909) once again broke from minstrel tradition by offering a serious romantic theme and black characters that defied the racial stereotypes of the time. The play was also noteworthy for including characters of both African-American and Native American backgrounds.

Bob Cole (left), James Weldon Johnson (center), and John Rosamond Johnson (right) combined their formidable talents to create shows that, while entertaining, did not sacrifice the dignity of African Americans for audience appeal.

Although the writing team of Bob Cole, James Weldon Johnson, and John Rosamond Johnson showed great promise, Bob Cole died in 1911, bringing an end to the highly successful partnership.

tionships between people of different races. Reviewers and audiences did not love the book, but they adored the songs, which one critic called "ambitious and always pleasing to hear." Certainly, the writing team of Cole, Johnson, and Johnson showed great promise. Unfortunately, *The Red Moon* was to be their last Broadway production, for in 1911, after a period of illness and depression, Bob Cole committed suicide, bringing an end to a highly successful period of collaboration.

## The Ziegfeld Follies

It's fascinating to explore musicals that, like *The Shoo-Fly Regiment*, were written and performed entirely by African Americans. But it's important to remember that talented black artists—including performers, writers, and musicians—also contributed to white productions like the celebrated Ziegfeld Follies.

Inspired by the Folies Bergères of Paris, the elaborate productions of the Ziegfeld Follies were the creation of legendary showman Florenz Ziegfeld. The Follies' revues—which were something between higher-class vaudeville shows and later Broadway musicals—featured topical comedy routines, popular songs, and beautiful girls. In a span of twenty-four years, there were thirty-two Follies, making them the longest-running series of musical productions in Broadway history.

The Ziegfeld Follies were most definitely white. Certainly, there was never an African-American Ziegfeld girl, and no black people were allowed in the audience. Yet Florenz Ziegfeld, who always hired the best performers, composers, and writers he could find, did employ black artists when he knew that their talents would draw ever-greater audiences.

In 1910, a year before George Walker passed away, Ziegfeld asked Bert Williams to star in the Follies. Because of his long experience in vaudeville, Williams was used to being the only African American on the bill. He was also probably used to white performers' refusing to share the bill with him—in part, because he was black, and in part, because they could not match his comedy material. But Ziegfeld would not allow such rebellion in his own troupe. Legend has it that when several cast members delivered an ultimatum, threatening to leave the show unless Williams was fired, Ziegfeld replied, "I can replace every one of you, except [Williams]."

The pay offered by the Follies was lower than Williams could command on the vaudeville stage, but less travel was involved, and the Broadway-based Follies were higher in prestige than even the best shows that vaudeville had to offer. Because Williams was black, his arrangement with Ziegfeld was unusual: He would not have to interact with the white showgirls, nor would he have to accompany the show when it travelled to the South.

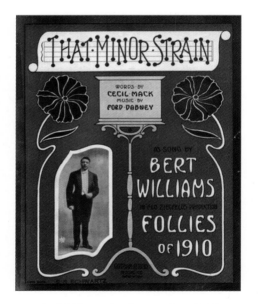

In 1910, vaudeville star Bert Williams appeared in the otherwise all-white Follies for the first time. He would continue to be featured in Florenz Ziegfeld's extravaganzas nearly every year from 1910 through 1919.

In December 1910, Baltimore, Maryland enacted the first citywide law in the country to mandate segregation of each residential block. This ordinance would be followed by similar ones in other American cities, including Richmond, Virginia; Dallas, Texas; Greensboro, North Carolina; Oklahoma City, Oklahoma; Louisville, Kentucky; and St. Louis, Missouri.

In 1911, at a time when few educational and professional opportunities were available to African Americans, Dr. Solomon Carter Fuller—the first black psychiatrist in America—performed groundbreaking studies on the brain. His paper on Alzheimer's disease, published in what would become the *American Journal of Psychiatry*, provided early insights into the cause of the disorder.

# Black Bohemia

At a time when each new wave of immigrants to the United States faced discrimination, the African Americans who resettled from the South to New York perhaps had the roughest experience of all due to racial prejudice. Only a very narrow range of jobs was available to them, so most men did manual labor or took service jobs as waiters and porters, while women were confined to domestic work. But their struggles often paid off in terms of greater opportunities for their children, and little by little, many black New Yorkers were no longer confined to manual labor. As their prosperity increased, some were able to move to a slightly better area on the West Side of Manhattan. The buildings weren't new and the neighborhood wasn't especially safe, but it was an improvement over the tenements in which the blacks had first lived. Soon, grocers, tailors, restaurants, and a variety of entertainment venues were established to serve this growing urban community.

By the 1890s, Black Bohemia, as it became known, was firmly established in the area of the West fifties and sixties that white New Yorkers called San Juan Hill or the Tenderloin. Although it was originally settled mostly by people in sports, who were the first African Americans to escape manual occupations, Black Bohemia soon became a sanctuary for those in the arts, as well, attracting celebrities like Bert Williams and George Walker. At its center was the Marshall Hotel, which was a magnet for black performers, musicians, and writers. J. Rosamond Johnson and brother James Weldon Johnson lived there full time, and other performers—including white entertainers from nearby Broadway—would crowd its dining room and bar. Vaudevillian Tom Fletcher later recalled that the hotel was often "filled with members of both races, all in proper evening attire, mingling and having a good time."

Black Bohemia existed for a relatively short period of time. In 1904, African-American families began moving out of the area into a newer, still sparsely settled neighborhood known as Harlem. This later resettlement would pave the way for the Harlem Renaissance of the 1920s.

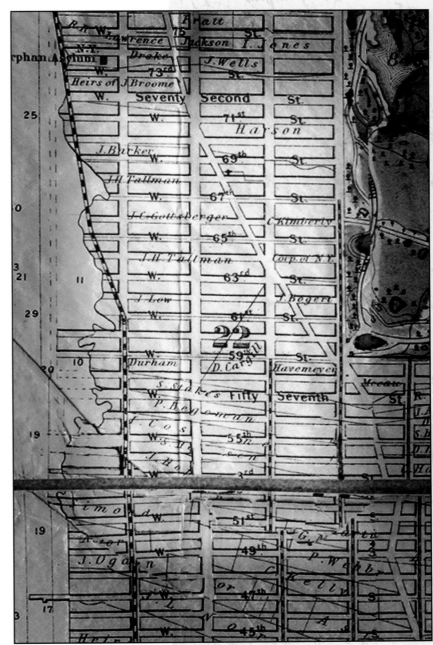

Black Bohemia was a lively African-American community from the 1890s until 1904, when black families began relocating to Harlem.

As a presidential candidate in 1912, Woodrow Wilson promised African Americans "absolute fair dealing." But after taking office, Wilson began segregating federal workplaces. From the Post Office to the offices of cabinet members, black workers were segregated, downgraded, or fired. This remained the norm until Franklin Roosevelt's administration.

In 1914, Jamaican-born Marcus Garvey launched the Universal Negro Improvement Association (UNIA). UNIA's goal was to unite black people and "establish a country and absolute government of their own" in Africa. Although some blacks were inspired by Garvey's "Back to Africa" movement, others disliked his separatist philosophy.

# Ragtime and Black Theater

It was up-tempo and lively, and it was the rage between the 1890s and the first two decades of the 1900s. It was ragtime, and its history is inextricably entwined with that of black musicians.

Ragtime had its roots in the folk music of African Americans, which then evolved into the cakewalks and "coon songs" of the minstrel show. The term *ragtime* is thought to be derived from the term "ragged time," which refers to the use of *syncopation*—the stressing of musical beats that are normally not accented. The distinctive rhythm of syncopation is at the very heart of all ragtime music.

Scott Joplin is known as the "King of Ragtime," and his legendary "Maple Leaf Rag" (1899) is believed to have sold a million copies of sheet music during the composer's lifetime. Joplin's piece "The Entertainer: A Rag Time Two Step" was a hit, as well, with the *St. Louis Globe-Democrat* calling it "the best and most euphonious" of Joplin's compositions to date. But all of the black musicians discussed in this chapter wrote and performed ragtime pieces. When Bert Williams and George Walker first brought their vaudeville act to New York in the late 1890s, the pit musicians had trouble handling the syncopated rhythms of their musical numbers. By the early 1900s, though, ragtime was everywhere, including the vaudeville stage and Broadway, and a more mature form of ragtime had evolved, with greater depth and sophistication. At the start, rag was scored just for piano, but eventually, rag would be scored for dance bands and brass bands. The finale of *In Dahomey* (1903), composed by Will Marion Cook, featured ragtime syncopation. The musicals of Bob Cole, J. Rosamond Johnson, and James Weldon Johnson were rich with ragtime songs. And, of course, many black musical groups of the time—like Joe Jordan and Ernest Hogan's Memphis Students—brought ragtime music to other venues and audiences. But African Americans did not have a monopoly on the ragtime genre. The 1893 Chicago World's Fair exposed white Americans to ragtime en masse, with about 27 million people passing through the gates of the fair during one season. In 1911, Irving Berlin's first truly popular song was "Alexander's Ragtime Band." The Turkey Trot and Grizzly Bear dance crazes, which swept the North in 1910, also helped foster a love of syncopated tunes. Ragtime was everywhere—in sheet music, piano rolls, phonograph records, and even music boxes.

Like many musical trends, the ragtime rage eventually came to an end. When Scott Joplin died in 1917, ragtime music was already evolving into jazz. But ragtime never truly disappeared. When the 1973 movie *The Sting* used Joplin's "The Entertainer" as theme music, it created a resurgence of interest in this all-American form of music, and ragtime is still being composed and performed today.

Broadway star Bert Williams became the first black comedian to appear in motion pictures when he debuted in 1914's *Darktown Jubilee*. A screening of the black film in Brooklyn elicited boos and jeers from the white audience, and *Darktown Jubilee* was soon taken out of circulation. But that didn't stop Williams from making more pioneering films.

In 1915, when D.W. Griffith's racist film *The Birth of a Nation* premiered, the NAACP fought unsuccessfully to get the film banned. More successful was the Ku Klux Klan, which used the pro-Klan film to launch a massive recruiting campaign that would bring in millions of new members, especially in the Midwest and West.

Although Williams was only a modest success in the 1910 Follies, after he began developing his own comedy routines—which many comedians had to do because Ziegfeld was so focused on "glorifying the American girl"—his acts were enthusiastically received. Williams also commissioned Will Vodery, an African-American composer, to write some of his songs. Ziegfeld must have been highly impressed by Vodery's work, because from 1913 through the late 1920s, the gifted musician was to arrange numerous musical scores for the Follies.

During his time on the Ziegfeld stage, Williams found an excellent partner in Australian-born white comedian Leon Errol. Errol and Williams shared several talents, including a skill in pantomime and a great comedic sense, and together, they wrote and performed many successful routines. A sketch in which Williams played a railway redcap and Errol portrayed a drunken tourist is considered to be one of the funniest in the history of the Follies. Their performances may have been the first stage pairing of African-American and white entertainers. Always a crowd-pleaser, whether alone or part of a team, Bert Williams continued to be featured on the Ziegfeld stage for nearly every year from 1910 through 1919.

Another black artist who was associated with the Follies—although for only a brief time—was Joe Jordan. Born in Cincinnati, Ohio in 1882, Jordan grew up in St. Louis, Missouri and received formal musical training at the Lincoln Institute in Jefferson City, Missouri. Over the years, Jordan showed great talent as both a musician and a composer, and played a major role in creating a number of innovative groups. In 1900, for instance, he teamed up with three other musicians to form a quartet in which all four men sang and played piano at the same time. Then in 1905, Jordan collaborated with Ernest Hogan, one of the originators of ragtime, to form the Memphis Students, a seventeen-piece ragtime orchestra. Although the musicians were neither students nor from Memphis, the group was unique. Playing instruments, singing, and dancing, they were, in the words of James Weldon Johnson, "the first modern jazz band ever heard on a New York stage." Jordan also worked on the Broadway stage when, in 1909, he collaborated with Bob Cole and the Johnson brothers on the groundbreaking musical *The Red Moon*.

In 1910, Jordan teamed up with Will Marion Cook to write the song "Lovie Joe," which was presented to Ziegfeld star Fanny Brice. Although Florenz Ziegfeld liked the song, the show's producer, Abe Erlanger, detested the piece, saying that it "sounded like burlesque," and wanted it removed from the Follies' lineup. Ziegfeld and Erlanger argued, and finally, they reached a compromise: "Lovie Joe" would not be performed on the Broadway stage, but would be included when the Follies travelled to Atlantic City, New Jersey.

Bert Williams was the first African American to become a star comedian on Broadway as a single act and the only black performer on the Ziegfeld Follies bill from 1910 to 1919. *Theatre Magazine* called him "a vastly funnier man than any white comedian now on the American stage."

Beginning around 1915 and continuing for many decades, the Great Migration was the relocation of more than 6 million African Americans from the rural South to the cities of the North, the Midwest, and the West. In search of greater economic opportunity and social equality, people of color would build a new place for themselves in urban America.

Carter G. Woodson, sometimes called the Father of Negro History, founded the Association for the Study of Negro Life and History (ASNLH) in 1915. A year later, ASNLH launched the *Journal of Negro History*—now the *Journal of African American History*—the first scholarly publication dedicated to studying black life in America.

# Why Did Black Performers Wear So Many Hats?

One of the themes that seem constant in the history of early black entertainment is the astounding versatility of the artists involved. The Whitman Sisters not only sang, danced, played musical instruments, and performed comedy skits, but also booked their own acts, made their own costumes, and more. Bob Cole composed music, wrote lyrics and librettos, produced, directed, and acted. In addition to being an accomplished actress, singer, and dancer, Aida Overton Walker was an extraordinary choreographer. Why did each of these people do so many jobs?

These were exceptionally talented individuals, of course, but their diverse skills were also a matter of necessity due to the racism of the times. It simply was not possible to hire white comedy writers, bookkeepers, choreographers, and other specialists. Instead, within each project, the participants would perform all the work that was necessary to produce the show. Resourceful, they would often collaborate with other African Americans who had the skills they needed, but they would not reach outside the black community.

An artist of astounding versatility, Joe Jordan was a gifted pianist, composer, songwriter, orchestrator, and conductor. Jordan wrote more than six hundred songs, and many—like "Lovie Joe"— became nationwide hits.

Fortunately, Brice recognized the song's worth and, against her employers' wishes, she performed Jordan's piece in her inimitable comic style. The audience responded with applause so thunderous that the singer was forced to give eight encores. "Lovie Joe" was added to Brice's act, and Erlanger, who had vehemently fought against using the song, claimed to have clapped so enthusiastically that he broke the straw hat he was holding in his hands.

Although the audience's enjoyment of Fanny Brice's performance was whole-hearted, Jordan's was bittersweet. Because African Americans were denied seats in the theater, he had to stand in an adjoining alley, straining to hear his own song being performed. He is said to have wept when he heard the crowd's response.

Joe Jordan was to go on to enjoy successful tours of Europe, act as financial manager and assistant director of Will Marion Cook's New York Syncopated Orchestra, and, in 1921, finally make it inside a Broadway theater to become the musical director of Eubie Blake's *Shuffle Along*. During his career, he would even direct symphonies in Carnegie Hall. But in 1910, the talented Joe Jordan—although he was permitted to write material for the Ziegfeld Follies—was not allowed to sit in the audience of Ziegfeld's theater simply because he was a black man.

In 1916, the NAACP's Drama Committee staged a landmark black drama entitled *Rachel*. Written by African-American Angelina Weld Grimké, the play was, in the words of the NAACP, "the first attempt to use the stage for race propaganda in order to enlighten the American people relative to the lamentable condition of . . . colored citizens."

On July 28, 1917, close to 10,000 black Americans and their supporters marched down Manhattan's Fifth Avenue in a silent parade designed to protest lynchings and anti-black violence. Organized by the NAACP, this demonstration—often called the Silent Protest—is considered to be the first major civil rights demonstration of the twentieth century.

## THE SEEDS OF
## AFRICAN-AMERICAN DRAMA

Through minstrelsy, burlesque, vaudeville, and a scattering of Broadway musicals, Americans had seen black entertainers perform song, dance, and comedy. But at the turn of the twentieth century, the idea that black people should create their own dramas about the African-American experience was only in its infancy.

In 1904, W.E.B. DuBois, who would eventually help found the National Association for the Advancement of Colored People, dreamed of a "new theatre" that would teach black people about their own history and make white people aware that African Americans were full human beings. In 1915, with the debut of D.W. Griffith's highly racist film *The Birth of a Nation,* DuBois' desire for black drama became more urgent. Now, the NAACP actively sought original dramatic material that would counter the film's

For many years, white theatergoers demanded that African-American entertainers appear only in musical comedies, usually playing stereotypical black characters. But at the turn of the century, black activists like W.E.B. DuBois began demanding dramatic works that would represent, enlighten, and inspire people of color.

In 1904, W.E.B. DuBois, eventual co-founder of the NAACP, dreamed of an African-American theater that was "by us, for us, near us, and about us." After the 1915 release of the racist film *Birth of a Nation,* DuBois' plea for socially significant black drama grew more insistent.

degrading depictions of blacks and glorification of the Ku Klux Klan. The result was *Rachel* by African-American playwright Angelina Weld Grimké.

Born on February 27, 1880, Angelina Grimké was the daughter of Archibald Grimké, a black lawyer who was to become an executive director of the NAACP, and Sarah Stanley, a white woman from a middle-class family. Angelina was educated in private schools and became a teacher of English in Washington, DC, as well as a writer of poetry, fiction, and plays. The first play she completed, *Rachel*, has the distinction of being the first black drama that was meant to be staged rather than read aloud.

Grimké's work told the story of a young black southern woman who loses her desire to have a child after her father and brother are lynched. The playwright chose the theme of motherhood because she hoped that it would make white women understand the brutal effects that prejudice was having on African-American families. The NAACP made no pretense about its goal in producing the drama, for the program clearly stated, "This is the first attempt to use the stage for race propaganda in order to enlighten the American people relative to the lamentable condition of ten million colored citizens in this free republic."

In 1916, the NAACP's Drama Committee staged two performances of *Rachel* in a school in Washington, DC, and in 1917, single performances were given in a playhouse in Lower Manhattan and a church in Cambridge, Massachusetts. Grimké's blunt way of depicting the results of racial prejudice met with both supporters and detractors. Some critics felt that a more "artistic approach to the matter" would have been preferable. But even though the play was produced on a small scale and did not meet with universal acclaim, an important first step had been taken. Meaningful black drama had been brought to the American stage, and inevitably, more productions would follow.

Born in Boston, Massachusetts to a biracial family, Angelina Weld Grimké wrote her anti-lynching play *Rachel* (staged in 1916) in response to W.E.B. DuBois' request for black drama. Grimké also penned short stories and poetry.

Long treated as second-class citizens, African Americans saw World War I as a chance to win the respect of their white countrymen. Even before May 1917, when Congress passed the Selective Service Act requiring male citizens to register for the draft, black men from all over the nation enthusiastically joined the war effort. About 370,000 were to serve.

On February 17, 1919, 3,000 veterans of the 369th Infantry Regiment—also known as the Harlem Hellfighters—paraded in triumph up the streets of Manhattan as crowds cheered. One of World War I's few black combat regiments, the 369th had earned the prestigious Croix de Guerre from the French army under which it served.

Bird's-Eye View of Lower New York,

At the turn of the twentieth century, New York City's entertainment industry grew apace with the thriving metropolis.

## A LOOK BACK AT TURN-OF-THE-CENTURY BLACK THEATER

As New York City grew and prospered at the start of the twentieth century, the entertainment industry thrived, as well. Vaudeville reached its peak, and musical shows began to proliferate. Despite racial prejudice, talented black performers found their place on the stage. Although many were limited to the black vaudeville circuit, dozens of black performers learned their trade and thrived in vaudeville. For several years, black musicals also became popular and successful. Increasingly, they broke away from minstrel show themes and characters, becoming more sophisticated and daring in terms of subject, music, and dance. There was even an initial attempt to present black drama with the goal of stimulating social change.

Yet the period of creativity that had begun in the late 1890s largely came to a close after the production of *The Red Moon*. Among the chief reasons for this were the death of talented performers and writers such as George Walker and Bob Cole; Will Marion Cook's growing interest in other genres of music; and Bert Williams' movement from the black stage to white musical theater. But there was also another force at work, and that was increasing prejudice. By 1910, there began, in the words of James Weldon Johnson, a "term of exile of the Negro from downtown theatres of New York." By the early 1920s, African-American stage actors were usually not allowed to perform in white Manhattan theaters. No further black Broadway musicals would appear on the scene until after World War I, when the area of the city known as Harlem would experience a flowering of African-American culture.

With the death of George Walker and Bob Cole and a rise in racial prejudice, black musical comedies would disappear from the New York stage for a time. But within a few years, an explosion of African-American culture would bring talented new black playwrights, composers, and entertainers to the theaters of Manhattan.

In 1919, with the release of *The Homesteader*, Oscar Micheaux became the first African American to produce a feature-length film. Termed a "race film" because it was made for black audiences, *The Homesteader* was greeted as the "greatest of all Race Productions" and marked the beginning of Micheaux' long career in the cinema.

A national and international news agency, the Associated Negro Press (ANP) was established in 1919 by Claude Barnett. At a time when black newspapers had record circulations and great influence, the ANP sent out twice-weekly packets of information about people, events, and organizations of relevance to the lives of African Americans. It continued to operate until 1964.

# STARRING
# IN ORDER OF
# APPEARANCE

Anita Bush

Charles S. Gilpin

Regina Anderson Andrews

Garland Anderson

Paul Robeson

Eubie Blake

Noble Sissle

Flournoy Miller

Aubrey Lyles

Florence Mills

Josephine Baker

Adelaide Hall

Bessie Allison

Ethel Waters

Lena Horne

Bill "Bojangles" Robinson

Duke Ellington

Louis Armstrong

Sidney Bechet

Fletcher Henderon

# 3.

*The 1920s and the Harlem Renaissance*

Broadway reached its prime during the Roaring Twenties. Theaters and new shows proliferated, and the Great White Way was never more spectacular. Paul Morand, a visiting French novelist, wrote, "In Forty-Second Street, it is a glowing Summer afternoon all night. . . . Theaters, night clubs, movie palaces, restaurants are all lighted at every porthole."

Known as the Roaring Twenties, the 1920s was a time of economic prosperity and high spirits, and the world of entertainment thrived. Vaudeville, with its mass appeal, was still drawing an audience—although it now had plenty of competition from radio and motion pictures—and black performers remained an important part of the vaudeville phenomenon. At the same time, Broadway was growing stronger than ever. Between 1917 and 1928, the number of shows that opened each year more than doubled, rising from 126 to 264. Indeed, these were boom years for New York's theater district. It has been estimated that over 20 million people attended Broadway shows during the 1927-to-1928 season—about twice the number that attend now despite the fact that the city's population was far smaller then.

As Broadway burst with enterprise, exuberant black musicals, which had faltered in the previous decade, once again found a place on the Great White Way. But there was also a more serious side to the 1920s, which saw a new African-American movement gathering momentum uptown. Called the Harlem Renaissance, it was a blossoming of black culture, including literature, the visual arts, and the performance arts. People in the Renaissance movement placed their hope for a better future in the "New Negro," who would use intellect and art to destroy racial prejudice and "uplift" the race. It is easy to understand how this energetic era would inspire African Americans to embrace their heritage and start to forge a new role in the flourishing world of the theater.

Harlem became an influential cultural center when a new movement emerged there in the 1920s. Called the Harlem Renaissance, it was a blossoming of black literature, the visual arts, and the performing arts. Leaders of the movement believed that, through artistic expression, they could destroy racial prejudice and improve the lives of black Americans across the nation.

After the Ku Klux Klan was revitalized in 1915 in response to the film *The Birth of a Nation*, the group moved beyond the targeting of African Americans to direct its hatred toward Catholics and Jews, as well. In the 1920s, Klan membership swelled, and by engineering elections, the KKK was able to dominate state governments in Indiana and Oregon.

# HARLEM

Few people are aware that for nearly two hundred years, Harlem was a farming village inhabited by wealthy farm owners known as "patroons." Eventually, though, the soil became depleted by overcultivation, and by the mid-1800s, the farmers had fled and the once beautiful village had begun to crumble. Recovery came in the form of the City of New York, which in 1873, took the area over and made plans to extend the railway system to Harlem, opening it up to development. Soon, apartments and tenements were constructed, and the area became the destination of Jews, Italians, and other ethnic groups that were desperate to escape the overcrowded conditions of the Lower East Side. But in the ever-changing city, neighborhoods did not remain the same for long, and in 1904, as the earlier groups left the area, black residents arrived en masse. This resettlement was fed by the Great Migration of African Americans from the South to the North, as blacks streamed to major northern cities in search of better jobs, better education, and better living conditions. By 1920, central Harlem was essentially a black community. In fact, with over 150,000 people, it was the largest middle-class enclave of African Americans in the nation.

The movement of African Americans to northern cities was one of the chief factors that led to the Harlem Renaissance, since it concentrated highly motivated people in areas where they could encourage and support one another. Black intellectuals from other cities visited or settled in Harlem, sharing their ideas, but interestingly, no particular group of blacks monopolized the area. The Harlem of the 1920s was nothing if not diverse, and included the prosperous and the less well-to-do; the well-educated and the uneducated; native New Yorkers and immigrants from the southern states and even the West Indies. By uniting many different groups, Harlem became a fertile ground for cultural experimentation.

While Harlem provided a new home for African Americans, it was by no means an ideal home. Although most white Americans enjoyed soaring hopes and greater prosperity after the end of World War I, black Americans found themselves living in an increasingly racist society. During the 1920s, membership in the Ku Klux Klan surged, and the Klan had growing political influence in both the South and the Midwest. Even in the Northeast, job opportunities for blacks were limited and prejudice influenced every aspect of life. So the Harlem Renaissance also grew out of an awareness of the problems that black people were facing, not just in Harlem but throughout the United States. Leaders of the movement—including writers such as Langston Hughes and Zora Neale Hurston, and activists such as W.E.B. DuBois—believed that they could use art to challenge existing stereotypes, create pride in their unique African-American heritage, and ultimately achieve social and racial integration.

When the city's transportation network failed to meet the needs of the white immigrants who had moved to Harlem in the late 1800s, they abandoned the area, and African Americans began moving there en masse. By the time the planned roads and subways reached Harlem, many of the nation's most notable black artists, intellectuals, and entrepreneurs had settled there, setting the stage for the Harlem Renaissance.

Adopted in 1920, the Nineteenth Amendment guaranteed the right to vote to all American women. Although this meant that African-American women, too, were granted suffrage by the law, in the southern states, black women—like black men—were often prevented from exercising the right to vote through both legal and extra-legal measures.

In 1920, James Weldon Johnson—civil rights activist, educator, author, and songwriter—became the first black executive secretary of the National Association for the Advancement of Colored People. He remained manager of the group until 1930, when he resigned to accept the Spence Chair of Creative Literature at Fisk University in Nashville, Tennessee.

# BLACK THEATER GROUPS OF HARLEM

Even after the popularity of the minstrel show had faded, the stereotypes it created continued to influence the depiction of African Americans on the stage. This had been all too obvious in most of the vaudeville and theater productions mounted in the 1800s and early 1900s. With the dawn of the Harlem Renaissance, some black theater groups formed with the goal of creating drama that presented a more realistic, positive view of black people. Others were created simply to provide entertainment for a population that was not admitted into Broadway theaters. All of these companies, regardless of the plays they offered, provided a stage for many talented black entertainers.

One of the first successful African-American non-musical theater groups in the United States was created by Anita Bush. Born in 1883, Bush had worked as a dancer with the vaudeville team of Williams and Walker until a back injury brought an end to her dancing career. Determined to remain in the theater, the young woman turned to staging plays, and in 1915, she formed the Anita Bush Players, an all-black theater company. The Players performed in Harlem's Lincoln Theatre, which was the first black theater to cater to black clientele only. But after the group had presented a number of works, the owner of the theater demanded that Bush change the name of the troupe to the Lincoln Players. Bush declined and took her company to the nearby Lafayette Theatre, another Harlem venue. Soon afterwards,

In 1915, former dancer Anita Bush created one of the first professional African-American dramatic theater groups in the country. *The Girl at the Fort*, pictured above, was among the earliest productions of the Anita Bush Players.

Bush sold the group, which, ironically, then became known as the Lafayette Players. Actor Charles S. Gilpin took over management of the Players, which became the first black stock company. Until the group disbanded in 1932, it performed the classics, shows that were popular in white repertory theater, and shows that were being performed on Broadway. Although the Players did not stage works written by African-American writers about the black experience, they did make popular entertainment available to black people. They are also said to have trained over three hundred black performers.

◀ African-American artist Archibald Motley used his paintings to chronicle the black experience during the 1920s and '30s, and is considered one of the major contributors to the Harlem Renaissance. This painting captures the vibrant spirit of the times.

The Krigwa Players were able to perform in the basement of the Harlem library because of one of the group's founders, Regina Anderson Andrews. Andrews was the first African American to head a branch of the New York Public Library, and as an activist who fought against racism, she supported the writers and entertainers of the Harlem Renaissance by supplying a workspace in her library branch.

Another important theater company of the era was the Players' Guild. Run by the Circle for Negro War Relief, the Guild was formed in 1919. During the 1920s, it gave several performances at the Harlem YMCA, including one that featured a very young Paul Robeson. At the time, the theater company was commended for providing African Americans with an alternative to the "cheap melodramas and the cheaper musical comedy" offered by most of the theaters in Harlem. Because their productions were staged at the YMCA, the building became a new venue for black drama.

In an effort to produce plays written by and produced for African Americans, in 1925, W.E.B. DuBois, founder of the NAACP, teamed with playwright Regina Anderson Andrews to form the Krigwa Players Little Negro Theatre in Harlem. Krigwa—which was originally Crigwa, an acronym for Crisis Guild of Writers and Artists—performed in the basement of Harlem's 135th Street branch of the New York Public Library. There, it staged political theater, including some of Andrews' works, such as *Climbing Jacob's Ladder*, which focused on lynchings in the South, and *Underground*, which told the story of the underground railroad. At the group's foundation were DuBois' principles for New Negro theater. In his words, black plays must be "for us, by us, about us, and near us." Because of a financial dispute, the group disbanded in 1930 and later emerged as the Negro Experimental Theatre. After its dissolution, the space in the Harlem library was used by other black theater groups.

Before the twenties, the Alhambra Theatre, located in central Harlem, had been a vaudeville house that booked no black acts and seated African Americans in the balcony only. However, the theater eventually catered to black audience members, and in 1926, it hosted the Harlem premiere of *Lew Leslie's Blackbirds of 1926* before the revue was taken to Europe. (For more about the *Blackbirds* revues, see page 77.) Then, in 1927, it introduced the Alhambra Players. Composed of all black performers, the group was, by all accounts, essentially a repertory company that staged many kinds of plays, including works by white playwrights.

Named in honor of the nineteenth-century black actor Ira Aldridge, the Aldridge Players were formed by African-American playwright Frank Wilson. Situated in the Harlem library as guests of the Krigwa Players, this company was created specifically to perform three of Wilson's plays—*Sugar Cain, Flies,* and *Color Worship*—and was active only in 1926.

Not all of the theater companies inspired by the Harlem Renaissance met all the goals of Renaissance leaders like DuBois. They did, however, begin an important movement that would continue into the next decade, both within Harlem and beyond its borders.

The Negro National League (NNL)—the first successful organized black baseball league—was established in 1920 at a YMCA in Kansas City, Missouri. The League had teams only in the South and the Midwest, but three years later, in 1923, the Eastern Colored League (ECL) was formed as the second major black league circuit.

In May 1921, the all-black musical *Shuffle Along* premiered on Broadway. With songs by Eubie Blake and Noble Sissle, this wildly successful show is said to have launched the Harlem Renaissance. Among its contributions was the introduction of mixed-race seating. For perhaps the first time, black theatergoers were allowed to sit in the orchestra of a Broadway theater.

# Garland Anderson and *Appearances*

Born in Wichita, Kansas in 1886, Garland Anderson had little formal education and no training as a playwright. Yet his play *Appearances* is thought to be the first full-length drama by an African-American dramatist performed on a Broadway stage. The story behind Anderson's success is a fascinating one.

In 1924, Anderson was working as a bellhop and switchboard operator in San Francisco when he attended a performance of the morality drama *The Fool* by Channing Pollock. Inspired, Anderson decided to write a work that would share his own beliefs about the power of positive thinking. Within only three weeks, he had completed *Appearances*, a courtroom drama about a bellboy who is falsely accused of raping a white woman, but because of his moral convictions, is eventually acquitted and released. Anderson had met his first goal of writing a play, and now he set about getting it to the stage.

Garland Anderson was working as a bellhop and switchboard operator when he was inspired to write a courtroom drama titled *Appearances*. Then, through hard work, he raised the money needed to stage his play on Broadway in 1925.

At the suggestion of a friend, Anderson sent his play to performer Al Jolson, who provided him with enough money to travel to New York and find a producer. Once in Manhattan, the energetic playwright contacted local journalists, who were more than happy to interview Anderson and write about his quest for financial backing. The resulting wave of free publicity led to not only a public reading of his play at New York's Waldorf-Astoria Hotel, but also a meeting with President Calvin Coolidge in Washington, DC. Within a few months, through hard work, Anderson had raised the money he required to stage the play.

*Appearances* premiered at New York's Frolic Theatre on October 13, 1925, and ran for twenty-three performances. The play received only lukewarm reviews, but the critics applauded Anderson's persistence in getting his work onto a Broadway stage, especially considering its highly controversial subject matter and mixed-race cast. When the New York run ended, *Appearances* toured several cities in the United States and then London, where Anderson became the first black man accepted into the prestigious international writers' organization PEN.

Although Garland Anderson never had another play produced, he not only made his point about constructive thinking but also made theater history. In later years, he was to become a successful businessman and popular lecturer on the power of positive thinking and faith.

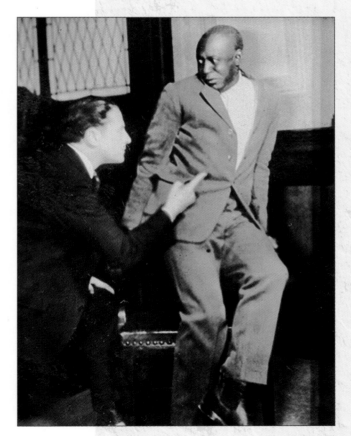

Considered the first full-length Broadway play written by an African American, 1925's *Appearances*—the story of a black bellboy falsely accused of raping a white woman—made it to the New York stage due to the sheer determination of first-time playwright Garland Anderson.

# THE PROVINCETOWN PLAYERS

At the same time that black theater groups were forming in Harlem, one white theater company produced several plays that centered on black characters and featured black performers. This was the Provincetown Players.

Originating in Provincetown, Massachusetts in 1915, the group was formed by writers and performers who spent their summer together in Cape Cod. The company was inspired by the period's Little Theater Movement, which sought to produce plays that were less influenced by commercialism and more experimental in nature. In 1916, the Provincetown Players were transplanted to New York, where they established a small performance space, which is often referred to as the Playwright's Theatre, at 139 MacDougal Street in Greenwich Village. In 1918, they would move to the Provincetown Playhouse at 133 MacDougal Street. It was in these two theaters that the group would stage a significant number of plays, several of which would eventually move uptown to Broadway.

When the Provincetown Players moved from Massachusetts to New York in 1915, their first home was 139 MacDougal Street in Greenwich Village. Then in 1918, they established the Provincetown Playhouse at 133 MacDougal (pictured above), and it was there that Eugene O'Neill's *The Emperor Jones* would premiere in 1920.

The Players' first hit was a production of Eugene O'Neill's *The Emperor Jones*, which tells the story of a black Pullman porter named Brutus Jones, who kills a man, goes to prison, and then escapes to a small Caribbean island, where he proclaims himself emperor. Obsessed with his own power, Jones alienates the people of the island, who turn against him. The story is related through flashbacks; when the play begins, Jones is trying to escape from his subjects through the forest.

*The Emperor Jones* opened at the Provincetown Playhouse on November 1, 1920. The role of Brutus Jones was played by black actor Charles S. Gilpin. Previously, black roles in integrated dramas had been taken by white actors in blackface, but O'Neill insisted on casting a black performer. (For more about Charles Gilpin, see the inset on page 67.)

The show was so successful and the demand for tickets so great that after only two weeks, *The Emperor Jones* had to be moved to a Broadway theater. This made Gilpin the first African-American actor to play a major role in a legitimate Broadway play. During its run, O'Neill's play was staged in

In this dramatic photo from Act I of *The Emperor Jones*, the self-proclaimed ▶ Emperor (Charles Gilpin) sits on a throne during the final days of his reign, talking to his "underling," the cockney trader Smithers (Jasper Deeter).

several venues, including the Selwyn Theatre and the Princess Theatre, for a total of 204 performances. It then toured the United States and, in 1925, it was staged in London, where Paul Robeson played the title role.

*The Emperor Jones* received rave reviews and launched O'Neill's career, but it did not present a positive African-American character to Broadway audiences. It also did not entirely please leading actor Charles Gilpin, who found some of the language so racist and degrading that he frequently changed O'Neill's words, enraging the playwright. Interestingly, W.E.B. DuBois—a leader of the Harlem Renaissance movement—defended O'Neill, stating, "The Negro today fears any attempt of the artist to paint Negroes. He is not satisfied unless everything is perfect and proper and beautiful and joyful. He is afraid to be painted as he is, lest his human foibles and shortcomings be seized by his enemies for the purposes of the ancient and hateful propaganda."

In a November 4, 1920 review of *The Emperor Jones*, critic Heywood Broun of *The New York Times* lavished praise on the drama's star, writing that Charles S. Gilpin "gives the most thrilling performance we have seen any place this season. . . . It is a performance of heroic stature."

Before *The Emperor Jones* was produced in 1920, most black characters in integrated dramas had been played by white actors in blackface, but playwright Eugene O'Neill insisted on casting veteran actor Charles S. Gilpin in the role of Brutus Jones.

# Charles Sidney Gilpin
# Critically Acclaimed Actor of the 1920s

One of the most highly regarded actors of the 1920s, Charles Sidney Gilpin was born on November 20, 1878 in Richmond, Virginia. By age twelve, Gilpin, a natural performer, was singing on stage, and at age eighteen, he began to travel with Bert Williams and George Walker's vaudeville show. After years of touring with various shows, the versatile performer became part of the Anita Bush Players and won a leading role in the company's production of *The Girl at the Fort*. When the group was sold and the name was changed to the Lafayette Players, Gilpin became its director, which placed him in charge of the first African-American stock company in New York City.

In 1919, Gilpin's growing reputation as a fine actor earned him the role of Reverend William Curtis in John Drinkwater's successful play *Abraham Lincoln*. Although it was a small part, the actor received critical praise, and his performance led to his being cast in the title role of Eugene O'Neill's 1920 production of *The Emperor Jones*. Again, Gilpin's performance was remarkable, and the Drama League of New York City invited him to a dinner at which he would receive an award for being among the ten people who had done the most for theater that year. A public controversy then arose. Because Gilpin was black, some felt that the honor should be withdrawn, while others believed that Gilpin should not attend the awards ceremony. The League, however, refused to withdraw the invitation, and Gilpin had no intention of declining it. When Gilpin accepted the award, he was given a standing ovation of unusual length.

Unfortunately, Gilpin's relationship with O'Neill was problematic throughout the run of *Emperor Jones*. Gilpin continually changed the wording of the script because of its racist nature, and the actor's drinking began to affect his performance. Before the 1925 revival of the play in London, O'Neill would replace Gilpin with Paul Robeson.

After the loss of his signature role, Gilpin never again performed on Broadway but worked only in occasional revivals of O'Neill's play as well as other relatively small productions. He died in 1930 at the young age of fifty-two. Playwright Moss Hart, who had seen Gilpin's performance in a 1926 revival, wrote, "He had an inner violence and a maniacal power that engulfed the audience. . . . Gilpin was the greatest actor of his race."

Charles Sidney Gilpin's electrifying performance in *The Emperor Jones* won him stellar reviews, and in 1920, Gilpin became the first African American to receive a Drama League of New York's award for making significant contributions to American theater.

In 1921, Bessie Coleman became the first African American to earn a pilot's license when she was awarded an international license by a French flying school—the only school that did not refuse to admit her because of her race and gender. When Coleman returned home, she was invited to attend *Shuffle Along*, where she received a standing ovation from both black and white audience members.

Founded in 1921 by Harry Pace, Black Swan Records was the first black-owned recording company to sell popular music to African-American audiences, and also the first company to record black classical musicians. Although it closed in 1923, Black Swan is credited with establishing an African-American presence in the music business.

# Paul Robeson
## Legendary Singer and Actor

One of the more overlooked of African-American actors, Paul Robeson enjoyed a stellar career in theater and film before his political beliefs all but removed him from popular history.

Born on April 9, 1898, Paul Robeson grew up in Princeton, New Jersey, and was awarded a scholarship to Rutgers University. During his college years, Robeson joined the debate team, sang with the glee club, and excelled at baseball, basketball, football, and track and field. After receiving an unprecedented twelve varsity letters, he graduated as class valedictorian. Robeson continued his education at Columbia Law School, and in the early 1920s, he worked at a New York City law firm while moonlighting as an actor with the Players' Guild of Harlem. When the firm's overt racism prompted Robeson to end his legal career, he decided to devote himself to acting full-time.

In 1921, the fledgling actor became a member of the chorus in Eubie Blake's dazzling musical *Shuffle Along*. Then in 1922, he was cast in the Broadway drama *Taboo*. Although the show ran for just three nights in New York, it then went on tour in London, and Robeson's stock as a performer rose quickly. Upon Robeson's return to the States, Provincetown Players' member Eugene O'Neill cast him in two of the group's productions—*All God's Chillun Got Wings* (1924) and a revival of *The Emperor Jones* (1925). The actor's reviews were

excellent, and throughout the 1920s and 1930s, Robeson continued to make his mark in the theater. His rendition of "'Ol' Man River" in the British revival of *Show Boat* (1928) is legendary, and his performance in the 1943 Broadway production of *Othello* contributed to the play's record-breaking run of nearly 300 performances.

Between 1930 and 1942, Paul Robeson was also in demand in films, and he appeared in a dozen motion pictures, including *The Emperor Jones* (1933), *Show Boat* (1936), *Song of Freedom* (1936), *King Solomon's Mines* (1937), and *Tales of Manhattan* (1942). A strong, highly expressive performer who took pride in his African-American heritage, Robeson would later draw great praise from the likes of James Earl Jones, Sidney Poitier, and Harry Belafonte.

During the 1930s, Robeson's political views and growing concerns about racial inequality in the United States began to overshadow his talents in the eyes of the American public, and, more important, in the eyes of the American government. Believing in a "new vision" that would elevate the value of the common man and promote equality of the races, the actor centered his dream of a brighter future on Stalinist Russia, which he felt was a model of a fair and just society. Although Stalin turned out to be a brutal dictator, for most of Robeson's life, the performer seemed blind to this reality. For this, he would pay a substantial price.

After the Second World War, when the United States and Russia shifted from being allies to being key participants in the Cold War, Robeson's political beliefs became the focus of government committees seeking to flush out Communists. During both the Tenney Committee hearings in 1946 and hearings before the House Committee on Un-American Activities in 1956, Robeson was repeatedly asked if he was a member of the Communist Party. He would not answer, and he refused to sign an affidavit affirming that he was not a Communist, stating, "Under no conditions would I think of signing any such affidavit, that it is a complete contradiction of the rights of American citizens." These actions resulted in his being blacklisted from domestic concerts, recording labels, and film studios. In 1950, Robeson was also deprived of his passport, and thus was cut off from the foreign performances that had long provided the bulk of his yearly income.

Despite the support of African-American activists, it would take Robeson eight years to get his passport back and even longer to overcome the blacklist. By then, failing health had resulted in his retirement. Paul Robeson died in 1976. Although his relationship with Russia and Communism remains controversial to this day, his extraordinary accomplishments in sports, academics, and theater are beyond reproach.

Although now often overlooked because of his political beliefs, Paul Robeson was a twentieth-century Renaissance man, excelling as a scholar, athlete, actor, and singer. His stage credits included 1924's *All God's Chillun Got Wings*, the 1925 revival of *The Emperor Jones*, the 1928 British production of *Show Boat*, and the long-running 1943 Broadway production of *Othello*.

In 1930, on the stage of London's Savoy Theatre, Paul Robeson became the first black actor to portray Othello since Ira Aldridge took the part in 1825. In 1943, when Robeson played the Moor of Venice on Broadway (pictured here), the production had a record-breaking run followed by a lengthy North American tour.

Eugene O'Neill's *All God's Chillun Got Wings* (1924) angered many Americans with its portrayal of a biracial marriage. Despite threats from the Ku Klux Klan, the play ran for five months.

In 1923, the Provincetown Players became the Experimental Theater, Inc., a name that better reflected the group's eye-opening productions. Within a few years, it would launch two additional plays that were significant to African-American theater.

Eugene O'Neill's *All God's Chillun Got Wings* premiered on May 15, 1924. It tells the story of a white woman (played by Mary Blair) who marries a black man (Paul Robeson), but, resenting him for his color, sets out to ruin his promising career as a lawyer. *All God's Chillun* drew front-page headlines when actress Mary Blair kissed the hand of African-American Paul Robeson on stage. The fervor over the mixed marriage and the kiss not

In 1922, Harvard-educated William Leo Hansberry—uncle of award-winning playwright Lorraine Hansberry—taught the first course in African history and civilization offered at an American school (Howard University). It would nevertheless be many years before academia acknowledged the achievements of ancient African civilization.

When twelve black men were convicted of killing five white men during a riot, the verdict was called into question because the trial had been dominated by an intimidating white mob. The 1923 Supreme Court case *Moore v. Dempsey* decided that the presence of the mob made it impossible for the men to receive a fair trial, and the accused men were freed.

only prompted the Ku Klux Klan to threaten O'Neill, but also had New York City's license commissioner attempt to shut down the play. Nonetheless, with police guarding the theater, the show continued to run at the Greenwich Village Theatre—across the street from the Provincetown Playhouse—for five months.

Paul Green's drama *In Abraham's Bosom,* which opened in 1926, relates the struggles of a southern farmer who is the son of a white slave owner and a black slave. The farmer, Abe (Charles Gilpin), tries to educate himself and to establish a school for fellow African Americans, but is repeatedly stifled by his white half-brother. This controversial play garnered excellent reviews but struggled to find an audience until it won the 1927 Pulitzer Prize for Drama.

Sadly, the stock market collapse of 1929 brought an end to the Experimental Theater. But within the group's relatively short period of existence, it made great strides in focusing attention on the black experience and getting black performers onto the stage of white Broadway theaters.

When a newspaper reported that *All God's Chillun Got Wings* included a scene in which a white actress kissed a black actor, the Ku Klux Klan sent threatening letters to playwright Eugene O'Neill. But the drama continued to run—with a strong police presence.

In 1926, the Provincetown Players again created controversy with Paul Green's drama *In Abraham's Bosom.* A year later, Green's story of a racially mixed young man garnered the Pulitzer Prize for Drama.

## THE MUSICALS OF THE 1920s

It was during the early 1920s that, after a ten-year absence, African-American musicals returned to Broadway. The show that led the way was *Shuffle Along*, but it was only the first of several musicals—either black-produced or white-produced with black cast members—that would capture the imagination of the public and contribute to the optimistic spirit of the Harlem Renaissance.

### *Shuffle Along*

One of the most successful and influential shows of the early 1920s was *Shuffle Along*. With music by Eubie Blake, lyrics by Noble Sissle, and book by Flournoy Miller and Aubrey Lyles, it premiered on May 23, 1921 at the Sixty-Third Street Music Hall—and almost immediately caused a sensation.

Noble Sissle and Eubie Blake's score mixed old compositions with new songs designed to fit *Shuffle Along*'s plot. The resulting "musical mélange" was spirited and jazzy—exactly what an early 1920s audience wanted.

The plot of *Shuffle Along* was thin, which was typical of the musicals of the time. Centered on an election for the mayor of Jimtown, it drew its comedy from the underlying political nonsense that always accompanies such elections. The characters were modeled after old minstrel-show stereotypes; they did not present the enlightened "New Negro." Yet this musical show is considered by many to be one of the events that launched the Harlem Renaissance, creating a buzz on Broadway that was felt further uptown in the theaters and clubs of Harlem.

*Shuffle Along* was a highly significant show for many reasons. First and foremost was the fabulous jazz music and spirited dances performed by a large and talented African-American cast, which included a young and beautiful Florence Mills; Josephine Baker, who, deemed too young to be in the show at fifteen, joined the cast a year later; Adelaide Hall, who would enjoy a career spanning more than sixty years; Bessie Allison, who went on to dance in the chorus line of Harlem's renowned Cotton Club; and Paul Robeson, who would achieve success both on the stage and in films. Perhaps most important, the musical had a mixed-race audience. Instead of being restricted to the balcony, black theatergoers could watch *Shuffle Along* from the orchestra. After so many years of segregated seating, this was a tremendous step forward.

Blake and Sissle had to overcome considerable roadblocks to get their show to the Broadway stage. Money was certainly an issue. During the previous decade, producers had been unwilling to take a chance on a "col-

*Shuffle Along's* cast, including this bevy of chorus girls, was entirely composed of African Americans. While it was not the first show to have an all-black cast, it was the first to allow black audience members to sit in the orchestra rather than relegating them to the uppermost balcony. In an era of segregated seating, this was a significant step forward.

In 1923, the Club Deluxe, originally owned by black heavyweight boxing champion Jack Johnson, had its name changed to the Cotton Club. Although it was a "whites only" establishment that would not serve blacks, this famous Harlem nightspot would launch the careers of several talented African Americans, most famously, Duke Ellington and Cab Calloway.

Published from 1923 to 1949, *Opportunity: A Journal of Negro Life* was created by the National Urban League to give voice to the black writers of the Harlem Renaissance. Edited by Charles S. Johnson, *Opportunity* featured works by Countee Cullen, Langston Hughes, and Zora Neale Hurston. Annual prizes were awarded to recognize the accomplishments of the group.

ored show." But Henry Cort, the son of well-to-do theatrical impresario John Cort, was willing to accept the risk, as were the owners of the empty Sixty-Third Street Music Hall. When local hotels refused to provide accommodations for black cast members, friends of the cast and crew took in out-of-town actors. Because of the show's small budget, it made use of secondhand costumes, old scenery, and makeshift props. Although Blake, Sissle, and Cort were nearly $20,000 in debt before the show even opened, they pinned their hopes and dreams on the talent and enthusiasm of the performers and the fabulous tunes and dance numbers. Their gamble paid off, as *Shuffle Along* was packing the house within two weeks of opening night and proceeded to run for more than 500 performances, setting the bar high for upcoming African-American musicals.

Entertainers in other Broadway shows were so curious about *Shuffle Along* that Blake and Sissle added special midnight performances on Wednesdays to accommodate them. Blake's music, which helped usher in the jazz era with its New Orleans flavor, also became the standard against which other musicals would be judged for years to come. One of the most popular songs, "I'm Just Wild about Harry," was a huge hit during the run of the show and would later re-emerge as the theme song for Harry Truman's 1948 presidential campaign.

The success of *Shuffle Along* demonstrated how eager white theatergoers were to see talented black performers on Broadway, and within the next three years alone, nine musicals written by and featuring African Americans were to keep Manhattan hopping. Two of these productions were *Strut Miss Lizzy* (1922) and

Lyricist Noble Sissle—shown here surrounded by *Shuffle Along* cast members—enjoyed a long, successful career as a singer, bandleader, jazz composer, and lyricist. Because of the popularity of this 1921 musical, Sissle is best known for his partnership with composer Eubie Blake.

*Runnin' Wild* (1923). Lizzy was a vaudeville production from the Minsky Brothers, while *Runnin' Wild* was a musical comedy that would run wild on Broadway for 228 performances. Although neither show generated great critical acclaim, *Runnin' Wild* is forever remembered for introducing the Charleston, which would initiate the national dance craze of the decade.

In 1924, the Negro League World Series—the first official competition between recognized black championship teams—was played between the Negro National League champions, the Kansas City Monarchs, and the Eastern Colored League champions, the Hilldale Giants. The Monarchs narrowly defeated Hilldale in a ten-game battle, five games to four, with one game tied.

At a time when Jim Crow laws were still being enforced, the Catholic organization known as the Knights of Columbus commissioned and published *The Gift of Black Folk: The Negroes in the Making of America*. Written by civil rights advocate W.E.B. DuBois, the book presented the contributions of African Americans from the colonial period through the First World War and the early 1920s.

# Eubie Blake
# Pioneering Ragtime and Jazz Composer

On February 7, 1983, nearly 1,500 guests ranging from noted musicians to political dignitaries attended two events—held at New York's Shubert Theater and nearby St. Peter's Lutheran Church—in honor of Eubie Blake's hundredth birthday. While the frail Blake remained at home in Brooklyn, New York City Mayor Ed Koch arrived with a bouquet of red, white, and blue flowers along with the bronze City of New York Seal of Recognition. Even President Ronald Reagan took time out from his busy schedule to send a telegram praising the legendary composer for making his "priceless gifts a part of our musical heritage." Five days later, Eubie Blake died, leaving behind a rich cultural legacy.

Born in Baltimore, James Hubert Blake learned to play the pump organ as a child, and originally performed in his local church. Very soon, though, Blake found that he preferred the freedom of playing ragtime music on pianos in the city's brothels and saloons. He was still in his teens when he wrote his first composition, "Sounds of Africa," which was later renamed the "Charleston Rag" and became a ragtime favorite. The piece was not committed to paper, though, until 1915, when Blake learned musical notation.

In 1916, Blake met Noble Sissle, a formally trained musician and composer, and the two immediately began writing songs together, with Blake composing the music and Sissle providing lyrics. At the same time, Blake and Sissle started their collaboration on a musical. Their plans were disrupted by Sissle's service in the First World War, but following the war, the team resumed work on their musical while performing on the vaudeville circuits as the tuxedo-clad Dixie Duo.

In 1921, Blake and Sissle's dreams of Broadway came true with the opening and outstanding success of *Shuffle Along*. (See page 72.) In 1924, the pair wrote and produced another musical, *The Chocolate Dandies*, which ran for only 96 performances.

After *Chocolate Dandies,* Blake and Sissle largely went their separate ways. But during the 1930s and 1940s, Blake would sometimes collaborate on songs with his original partner, although he most often worked with other lyricists—most famously, Andy Razaf. He also served as a conductor for many orchestras and bands, including those that entertained the troops during the Second World War. And in 1946, at an age when most people are contemplating retirement, Blake earned a degree from New York University.

For the next several decades, Blake performed in concerts worldwide with a host of musical talents. He also made television appearances and recorded albums, all while continuing to write songs. Blake received many awards for his contributions to both American music and African-American progress, but perhaps the greatest honor came in September 1978, when the Broadway musical *Eubie!* premiered at the Ambassador Theatre. Starring Maurice and Gregory Hines, the show featured two dozen of Blake's original compositions, including "Goodnight Angeline," the "Charleston Rag," "Shuffle Along," "In Honeysuckle Time," and "I'm Just Wild About Harry." *Eubie!* was an indisputable hit, with Blake fans filling the theater for some 439 performances. The cast recording was also a major success, demonstrating music lovers' ongoing enthusiasm for pioneering ragtimer and jazz composer Eubie Blake.

Known for his important contributions to jazz, Eubie Blake is pictured here wearing that symbol of the Jazz Age, a raccoon coat.

## *Lew Leslie's Blackbirds*

In 1928, an African-American Broadway revue actually topped the success of *Shuffle Along*. The show was *Lew Leslie's Blackbirds of 1928*.

Born Lewis Lessinsky, Leslie was a white producer who started as an impressionist in vaudeville before becoming an agent. Aware of the popularity and incredible potential of talents such as Florence Mills and Adelaide Hall, as well as the success of the Ziegfeld Follies, Leslie put together a strong cast of African-American performers for the 1926 *Blackbirds* revue. After a Harlem premiere at the Alhambra Theatre (see page 62), Leslie took the revue to Paris and London. The show's popularity overseas paved the way for the *Blackbirds* to nest comfortably at Broadway's Liberty Theatre for 518 performances. Billed as "A Distinctive and Unique Entertainment with an All-Star Cast of 100 Colored Artists," the show debuted on May 9, 1928 at the Liberty Theater. It featured the hit songs "Diga Diga Doo," "Doin' the New Low Down," "I Must Have That Man," and "I Can't Give You Anything But Love," all created by the white songwriting team of Jimmy McHugh and Dorothy Fields. McHugh and Fields later went on to pen numerous hit tunes for film and stage, including "On the Sunny Side of the Street," which was introduced in *Lew Leslie's International Revue.*

Not unlike Ziegfeld, Leslie would try to stage ongoing Broadway revues in 1930, 1934, 1936, and 1939. But even with highly gifted black performers like Bill "Bojangles" Robinson, Ethel Waters, and Lena Horne, none of these attempts quite captured the magic of the original, which made a mark at a time when revues featuring a little folly and a lot of great songs were a hot ticket.

For his 1928 *Blackbirds* revue, impresario Lew Leslie assembled top African-American performers such as Adelaide Hall, Bill Robinson, Tim Moore, and Aida Ward. While later *Blackbirds* revues would also feature great artists—including Ethel Waters and Lena Horne—none would meet with the success of Leslie's 1928 show.

*Lew Leslie's Blackbirds of 1928*, like all the *Blackbirds* shows, was intended for white audiences and included stereotypical sketches such as this poker skit. But even if it meant wearing blackface, most African-American actors were glad to perform in Leslie's grand-scale productions.

# Florence Mills and Adelaide Hall

The musical theater boom of the 1920s gave the country many great female performers. Two who not only wowed producers and audiences but also had a lasting influence on the profession were Florence Mills and Adelaide Hall.

Born on January 25, 1896, Florence Mills was a child prodigy, winning cakewalk contests by the age of five. As a teenager, she and older sisters Olivia and Maude formed a vaudeville act. Known first as the Mills Trio and then as the Mills Sisters, they played in Harlem theaters and the black vaudeville circuit.

Mills' big break came in 1921, when she was asked to replace Gertrude Helen Saunders as the lead in *Shuffle Along.* It was there that Mills introduced the Baltimore Buzz. More of a dance step than a distinct dance like the Charleston, the Buzz became widely popular, drawing more attention to the already successful musical. A year later, producer Lew Leslie launched the *Plantation Revue,* a black follies-style musical that featured Mills singing and dancing along with her backup dancers, the Six Gypsy Vamps. The show lasted for only thirty-three performances, but Mills was well on her way to becoming one of the most noteworthy entertainers of the period known as the Harlem Renaissance.

In 1926, Florence Mills became a featured player in Lew Leslie's *Blackbirds* revue, which was a great success in Europe on its way to Broadway. Sadly, Mills never made it to the celebrated

Florence Mills began her career in vaudeville. Then in 1921, she got her big break when she was asked to replace Gertrude Helen Saunders in *Shuffle Along.* In the years that followed, whether appearing in *Plantation Review* (1922) or the *Blackbirds of 1926,* Mills was a showstopper. This photo is from *Dover Street to Dixie,* the 1923 London musical that would become the 1924 Broadway show *Dixie to Broadway.*

*Blackbirds of 1928.* On October 25, 1927, Florence was hospitalized for a tuberculosis-related ailment. Aware that she was dying, she sang to her manager and nurses from her hospital bed to lift their spirits. Mills died on November 1 at the age of thirty-one. Her accomplishments were significant in a twenty-five-year career that ended way too soon.

# Leading Ladies of the Jazz Age

Born on October 20, 1901, Adelaide Louise Hall, like Florence Mills, got her break in 1921 in *Shuffle Along,* but unlike Mills, she started in the chorus. The native New Yorker would not have to wait long, though, before moving to a featured role on Broadway. In 1923, she was cast in the musical *Runnin' Wild,* and she later took the Charleston from Broadway to the stages of London, where she introduced the trendy new dance to the Brits.

Before returning to the Broadway stage, Hall would become one of the first females to record the scat style of singing in a song called "Creole Love Call" with Duke Ellington and his orchestra. The 1927 recording became a huge hit and has since been covered by numerous jazz greats on its way to becoming a jazz classic.

After her success with "Creole Love Call," Hall enjoyed celebrity status. Following the death of Florence Mills in 1927, the young actress won the lead in the *Blackbirds of 1928* opposite vaudeville star Bill "Bojangles" Robinson. First came a long Broadway run; after that, the show would "Take Paris by Storm," as the headlines read, and Hall would enjoy international fame.

For Adelaide Hall, the Harlem Renaissance and her Broadway tenure served as the starting point for a career that would span seven decades. Tremendously successful world tours and a long stint at the Cotton Club would lead to Hall's becoming one of the wealthiest performers in show business. In the 1930s, she moved to London, where she remained for most of her life, starring on stage, in films, and on television. She would, however, return to Broadway one more time, in 1957, to play opposite Lena Horne in the musical hit *Jamaica,* with music by Harold Arlen, lyrics by E.Y. Harburg, and book by Harburg and Fred Saidy.

After a long, successful career, Adelaide Hall died in 1993. She is remembered as one of the most important vocalists in the history of jazz, as well as an artist who was able to overcome the barriers that had previously kept African-American entertainers from reaching wide recognition.

Adelaide Hall's career began in 1921's *Shuffle Along* and continued for decades. One of the top black singers of her era, Hall was a popular recording artist and Broadway sensation who eventually would appear in films and on television, as well. Her last Broadway appearance would be in 1957, when she performed in the musical *Jamaica* by special request of the show's star, Lena Horne.

# Bill "Bojangles" Robinson
## Iconic Tap Dancer, Legendary Philanthropist

Born Luther Robinson on May 25, 1878 in Richmond, Virginia, the man who would eventually be known to all as Bill "Bojangles" Robinson began dancing for a living at the age of six. He was only fourteen when he started touring with Mayme Remington's troupe in the pickaninny chorus.

A year after joining Mayme Remington, Robinson made his way to New York City, where his unparalleled tap dancing ability immediately won him favor in prominent vaudeville circuits. Soon, he was teamed with vaudevillian George W. Cooper, since a rule restricted blacks from performing solo. The duo played the circuit for twelve years, without blackface, until 1915, when Robinson headlined at New York's prestigious Palace Theatre.

Robinson's talents and charm opened doors that were routinely closed to most entertainers, especially African Americans, and he was richly rewarded for his abilities. By the time he played the Palace, he was earning as much as $3,500 a week, which was greater than the annual salary of most Americans at the time. Wearing his own specially made tap shoes—which had no metal taps, but were constructed of wood—Robinson became the premier tap dancer of the era, and perhaps the best of all time. His signature Stair Dance, first introduced in 1918, was a work of great precision, carefully choreographed so that as he went up and down a staircase, each step emitted a different pitch to a different rhythm. The audience watched in awe.

After twenty-five years in vaudeville, Robinson made his Broadway premiere in *Lew Leslie's Blackbirds of 1928,* performing the hit song and dance "Doin' the New Low Down." He was featured in five more Broadway shows, including *Brown Buddies* (1930), *Blackbirds of 1933, The Hot Mikado* (1939), *All in Fun* (1940), and *Memphis Bound* (1945). While starring in *The Hot Mikado*, the now-famous performer celebrated his sixty-first birthday by dancing down Broadway from Columbus Circle to Forty-Forth Street.

Robinson was never at a loss for work, for he also enjoyed a busy film career that included more than a dozen big-screen roles. His first film was *Dixiana*, a 1930 film with a mostly white cast. Then in 1933, he appeared in *Harlem Is Heaven,* one of the first all-black movies ever made. Robinson also co-starred with Lena Horne and Cab Calloway in 1945's highly acclaimed *Stormy Weather.* Today's movie buffs may best remember him in the films he made with child star Shirley Temple, which included *The Little Colonel* (1935), *The Littlest Rebel* (1935), *Rebecca of Sunnybrook Farm* (1938), and *Just Around the Corner* (1938).

From the Stair Dance to his signature bow ties and his infectious smile, Robinson was a crowd-pleaser, confident in his unique abilities, which, oddly enough, included being able to run backwards as fast as most people could run forward. Robinson also gave back, taking part in numerous benefits and charitable activities, and donating a significant amount of his own earnings to a variety of causes. Throughout his life, he belonged to many clubs and organizations, and in 1937, he became a founding member and honorary president of the Negro Actors Guild (NAG), which was formed to create better opportunities for black performers. (See the inset on page 100 for more about NAG.) American jazz expert Marshall Stearns wrote, "To his own people, Robinson became a modern John Henry, who instead of driving steel, laid down iron taps." In 2002—over fifty years after his death—Bill Robinson was inducted into the Tap Dance Hall of Fame by the American Tap Dance Foundation.

The stories about entertainer Bill Robinson are legend. On his sixty-first birthday, he celebrated by dancing down Broadway from Columbus Circle to Forty-Fourth Street. At another time, he set a world's record for the 75-yard *backward* dash. This photo, taken on the streets of New York, shows the energy and enthusiasm that Robinson brought to everything he did, even when he wasn't on stage.

Bill Robinson is still remembered for his beautifully choreographed Stair Dance, shown here in a scene from the *Blackbirds of 1928*. It was said that the popular dancer produced a different pitch with each step he took. Audiences were mesmerized.

## *Show Boat*

Considered a groundbreaking musical, the Jerome Kern and Oscar Hammerstein II epic *Show Boat* opened on Broadway on December 27, 1927. Based on Edna Ferber's novel about life on the mighty Mississippi, and produced by Florenz Ziegfeld, *Show Boat* was a larger-than-life story that brought audiences multidimensional characters and several intriguing story lines.

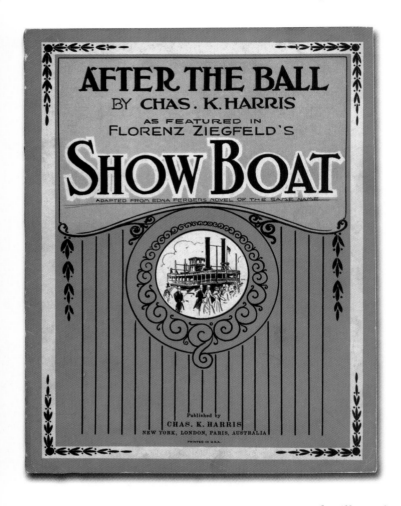

Groundbreaking in many ways, including its themes of racial inequality and interracial marriage, 1927's *Show Boat* is also known for its fabulous music. The highly popular "After the Ball," performed first in *A Trip to Chinatown* (1891) and later in *A Trip to Coontown* (1898), was part of the original Ziegfeld Theatre production of the play.

For Kern, Hammerstein, and Ziegfeld, *Show Boat* was a bold step, as it took a detour from the cheerful, frivolous follies and vaudeville-style revues that were then so popular. The play broke with convention in many ways, including controversial themes such as racial inequality, interracial marriage, and gambling addiction. There was a unique main character, Julie, a singer and actress of mixed race who's illegally married to a white man and tries to "pass" as white, but eventually is forced to leave the show boat because she is black. Before this, tragic characters with complex emotions had not been found in American musicals, but only in dramas and operas. And never before had story lines about black and white people been intertwined, nor had these characters shared equal importance in the show. Moreover, the show had a biracial cast, with white and black actors performing side by side.

Another distinctive aspect of the show was that the original songs were carefully integrated into the production, with the lyrics serving to move the stories forward. Kern and Hammerstein also provided diverse musical styles, which made a refreshing change from the single-style musicals that dominated the era. Backed by both a white chorus and a black chorus, the large cast brilliantly sang nearly two dozen songs, including romantic numbers like "Make Believe" and "Why Do I Love You?," vaudeville-style numbers like "I Might Fall Back on You," blues-tempo songs like "Can't Help Lovin' Dat Man," and, of course, spirituals such as "Ol' Man River," which was reprised several times. The song "After the Ball," originally from *A Trip to Chinatown* and later used in *A Trip to Coontown*, was also included in the original production.

Although Kern and Hammerstein—the latter of whom also wrote the show's book—incorporated many original elements in *Show Boat*, audiences were still greeted with the beautiful costumes, lavish sets, and superb cho-

Until 1943, the American Bar Association (ABA) did not accept black members. So in August 1925, the National Bar Association (NBA) was founded as a forum for African-American attorneys. The NBA addressed issues such as legal education, uniform state laws, and professional ethics, and, along with the NAACP, it tackled civil rights cases.

When Garland Anderson's play *Appearances* premiered at New York's Frolic Theatre in October 1925, it became the first full-length drama written by an African American and produced on a Broadway stage. Anderson also has the distinction of being the first man of color accepted into the prestigious international writers' organization PEN.

reography they had come to expect from Ziegfeld. The great impresario staged the production at the new Ziegfeld Theatre, which had opened earlier in the year with the musical *Rio Rita.* The show was an immediate hit with both critics and audiences, and it ran for 572 performances.

The popularity of *Show Boat* brought it back to Broadway just five years later, in 1932, and for subsequent, highly successful revivals in 1946, 1983, and 1994. The '94 version of the riverboat classic won a Tony Award for best revival of a musical and had the longest run in the history of the show, with 972 performances. In addition, stage versions have been mounted around the world to critical acclaim, and three film versions have been released— the first in 1936, the second in 1936, and the third in 1951. In some form or another, *Show Boat* continues to be one of the most produced musicals in theater history.

Although *Show Boat* may have provided audiences with some surprises, including both white and black choruses, it also offered the beautiful costumes and lavish sets that theatergoers had come to expect from impresario Florenz Ziegfeld.

In 1926, Carter Woodson, founder of the *Journal of Negro History,* launched Negro History Week to celebrate the contributions of black people to American life. Eventually evolving into Black History Month, this event has always taken place in February to mark the birthdays of Abraham Lincoln and Frederick Douglass.

Writer and activist Arturo Alfonso Schomburg was a passionate collector of books and artifacts on Africa, the Diaspora, and the African-American experience. In 1926, Andrew Carnegie purchased his collection, which became the basis for the Schomburg Center for Research in Black Culture, located in Harlem, New York.

# The Influence of Jazz on Mainstream Music

Born in the rural South and matured in the clubs of New Orleans, jazz combined African rhythms, the blues, and ragtime to produce a unique sound. In the 1920s, the loose beat of jazz exploded from its home into black enclaves in Chicago and New York. From there, it was only a matter of time before white Americans, too, began to hear and appreciate this exciting new form of music.

Mainstream America became aware of jazz mostly through the large-scale radio broadcasts introduced in the 1920s. Every week, thousands of Americans listened to Duke Ellington's performances in Harlem's famous Cotton Club. Also popular were the "potter palm" concerts—amateur and big-band jazz performances that were broadcast into people's living rooms. In this way, white Americans were able to hear the music of Louis Armstrong, Sidney Bechet, and Fletcher Henderson without ever leaving home.

Beginning in 1927, Duke Ellington and his musicians formed the Cotton Club's resident band, and frequent radio broadcasts brought the Duke's brand of jazz into American homes. Here, the Duke is seated at the piano, surrounded by members of his orchestra.

People who were lucky enough to live in or near New York could visit one of Harlem's many jazz clubs, the most famous of which was the Cotton Club. Owned by New York gangster Owney Madden, the trendy Cotton Club attracted the best that the black jazz world had to offer. But, like many Harlem clubs, although most of the staff and entertainers were African American, the Cotton Club catered to white patrons only. Black people could work there but were not admitted as guests.

Jazz also entered people's homes through Tin Pan Alley—the New York City songwriters and music publishers who dominated America's popular music through sheet music, radio, and phonograph recordings. Although always oriented to mainstream entertainment, starting in the 1920s, some true jazz as well as many jazz-style pop songs and blues numbers were produced by music publishers. As public enthusiasm grew, Tin Pan Alley favorites such as George Gershwin and Cole Porter wrote jazz pieces and jazz-based songs. These compositions helped increase jazz's popularity with white Americans, who eagerly attended musicals and concerts and bought recordings of jazz-influenced works like Gershwin's *Rhapsody in Blue* (1924). Young people, especially, embraced its sound and beat, just as they enthusiastically learned jazz dances like the Charleston and Black Bottom.

Unfortunately, racism remained a major aspect of American life during the Jazz Age. Tin Pan Alley might record black music or jazz-style songs, but for the most part, it did not accept black musicians as its own. Segregation was the status quo, so black and white musicians could not perform together. But the jazz craze offered people an unprecedented opportunity to interact with one another regardless of race, and even after the Jazz Age ended with the Great Depression, its new and vibrant music would live on in popular culture.

Located at the corner of Lenox Avenue and 142nd Street, ▶ Harlem's Cotton Club—the most famous of New York's nightclubs during the 1920s and early 1930s—offered performances by the leading jazz musicians of the day.

# THE LEGACY OF THE 1920s

For African Americans, the 1920s brought inspiration and a new optimism about the ability of black people to achieve success and win respect in American society. This was especially true in New York City, where the Harlem Renaissance fostered a new cultural identity and inspired a desire to improve society through education and art.

The twenties gave rise to powerful dramas written by African-American playwrights and staged by black theater groups, as well as dramas that were penned by white artists but focused attention on the black experience. This decade also marked the triumphant resurgence of black musicals on Broadway. From Eubie Blake to Bill Robinson, there were African-American stars the likes of which had never been known by American audiences. And there was the landmark musical *Show Boat*, which demonstrated, through both plot and the integration of white and black performers, that color boundaries could be dispensed with—if only for a few hours.

Ultimately, the joyful spirit of the Roaring Twenties ended in a whimper. The stock market crash of 1929 ushered in the Great Depression, which was followed by a war of unprecedented scale. During these trying times, the lights on Broadway would flicker but would not die.

◄ Archibald Motley's paintings reflect the urban experience of African Americans. Like many of his works, this one shows the diversity of black city life.

# STARRING
## IN ORDER OF
## APPEARANCE

| | |
|---|---|
| Langston Hughes | Evelyn Ellis |
| Hurst Amyx | Todd Duncan |
| Stuart Beebe | Eubie Blake |
| Rose McClendon | Nicholas Brothers |
| James Kirkwood | Ethel Waters |
| Mercedes Gilbert | Maurice Cooper |
| Jack Carter | Bill "Bojangles" |
| Edna Thomas | Robinson |
| Canada Lee | Freddie Robinson |
| Abram Hill | Rosetta LeNoire |
| Frederick O'Neil | Gwendolyn Reyde |
| Hilda Simms | Frances Brook |
| Alice Childress | Muriel Smith |
| Alvin Childress | Muriel Rahn |
| Sidney Poitier | Arna Bontemps |
| Harry Belafonte | Lena Horne |
| Ruby Dee | Countee Cullen |
| Ossie Davis | Pearl Bailey |
| Richard Wright | Harold Nicholas |
| Gordon Heath | Fayard Nicholas |
| Percy Verwayne | Rex Ingram |
| Frank Wilson | Ruby Hill |

# 4.

## Breadlines to Breakthroughs
## The 1930s
## and 1940s

When the Great Depression arrived in 1929, it immediately had an impact on the theater industry. Everyone from ushers to producers felt the devastating effects of the stock market crash, and many fled westward in search of jobs in the film industry. It has been estimated that Hollywood drew about 75 percent of its talent from the Great White Way.

The stock market crash of 1929 resounded from Wall Street to Broadway and beyond. Ticket lines at box office windows were considerably shorter than they had been just a few years earlier as the Great Depression took its toll on all aspects of American life. While the 1929-to-1930 theater season had seen 233 Broadway productions, the 1930-to-1931 season would see only 187. This trend would continue throughout the decade, with the number of shows falling to 98 by the depth of the Depression in 1939.

Fewer productions meant less revenue, so many of those working on Broadway—from directors, set designers, and performers to ticket takers and ushers—found themselves out of jobs. At the same time, a new gold rush of sorts was taking place out West, as the motion picture industry lured talented performers, writers, musicians, and producers to Hollywood. Even Ziegfeld packed up *Whoopee!* and headed west to take it to the big screen.

While Broadway was having its share of financial problems, vaudeville was completely vanishing. Of the nearly 1,500 theaters that had offered vaudeville to enthusiastic audiences in 1925, some 80 percent were movie theaters—or were at least sharing space with films—by 1930. Talkies were the new rage and were far cheaper to produce than live shows.

Despite the economic struggles caused by the crash of 1929, many bright lights continued to shine on Broadway. Producers like Lee and Jacob Shubert, who owned theaters across the United States, confidently continued to turn out creative, engaging shows. But the theater world could not hide from either the Great Depression or the world war that quickly followed. Instead, it offered audiences relief from reality in the shape of light-hearted musicals, and it used both dramas and musicals to explore important political and social issues of the time, including the struggles of blacks living in America.

Jessie Daniel Ames, a white Texas suffragist and civil rights activist, was determined to use women's organizations to solve racial problems. In 1930, Ames established the Association of Southern Women for the Prevention of Lynching. The ASWPL used both direct action and education to eliminate racially motivated killings—especially lynchings supposedly prompted by the need to protect white women.

In 1931, civil rights activist Walter White was named executive secretary of the NAACP. Highly dedicated, White remained in that position of leadership until 1955, becoming a powerful lobbyist for anti-segregation, anti-poll tax, and anti-lynching laws. Eventually, he would work with President Harry Truman on desegregating the armed forces.

# BLACK DRAMAS
# OF THE THIRTIES AND FORTIES

In the 1920s, activist W.E.B. DuBois had written about the need for black theater that was "for us, by us, about us, and near us." The 1930s would certainly offer productions that met DuBois' expectations in the form of Langston Hughes' *Mulatto* and various works staged by the African Negro Theater. But there would be other types of dramas, as well, as black actors took the stage both in classic dramas and in new works written by white playwrights and produced by white entrepreneurs. Not all of the productions would serve the black community in the way that had been visualized by leaders of the Harlem Renaissance, but all would make African-American performers an ever-growing presence in the theaters of New York.

## *Mulatto*

Written during the summer of 1930, *Mulatto: A Tragedy of the Deep South* was Langston Hughes' first full-length play. It opened at the Vanderbilt Theatre on October 24, 1935, starring Hurst Amyx, Stuart Beebe, and Rose McClendon.

*Mulatto* takes place during the Depression and details the conflict between a white plantation owner, Colonel Thomas Norwood (Beebe), and Robert Lewis (Amyx), one of the many children Norwood fathered with his black housekeeper and mistress, Cora Lewis (McClendon). While Norwood refuses to recognize Robert as his son, Robert persists in referring to himself as Norwood's son in public and declines to work in his father's cotton fields as a field hand. The play clearly focuses on white prejudice against black people, but it also explores the prejudice of black people against fellow African Americans. Robert, who is half-white, sees himself as being better than the darker-skinned workers who labor on the plantation. His beliefs and actions—which, at the time, were unacceptable to both whites and blacks—have tragic results for both him and his family.

*Mulatto* was a commercial success, running for 373 performances—longer than any black play that had come before it. (Not until 1959's *A Raisin in the Sun* would a new record be set.) After its Broadway run,

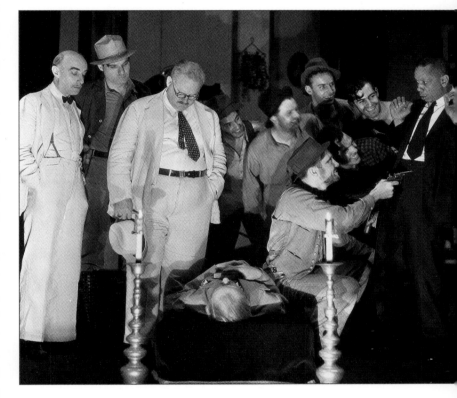

This scene from Langston Hughes' drama *Mulatto* illustrates the tension between whites and blacks in the Depression-era South, as drunken mourners threaten character Robert Lewis after his father's murder. Although critics did not give the play high marks, *Mulatto* had a long run and is now considered a fine example of African-American drama.

*Hocutt v. Wilson* was the first test case that involved segregation in higher education. In 1933, Thomas Hocutt, a student at the North Carolina College for Negroes, applied to the University of North Carolina pharmacy school and was denied admission based on race. Hocutt filed a lawsuit, and although he lost, his actions inspired later civil rights battles.

In 1934, after operating under different names—and always with a "whites only" policy—Harlem's Apollo Theater opened under its current name with a new focus on showcasing African-American talent. Its "Audition Night," which later became "Amateur Night," launched the careers of many talented black performers, from Ella Fitzgerald to Luther Vandross.

Although *Mulatto's* central focus is on the suffering of southern blacks at the hands of whites, like many writers of the Harlem Renaissance, playwright Langston Hughes was also concerned about the prejudices harbored by African Americans towards their own people.

Hughes' show toured for two years with a new cast. But despite the play's popularity with theatergoers, the critics panned it. Part of the problem may have been that producer Martin Jones added sensational elements like rape to the play to give it more audience appeal. This made the show so controversial that it was actually banned in Philadelphia. In addition, the African-American community disapproved of Hughes' use of stereotypical black dialect in the play. Now, however, *Mulatto* is considered to be one of the first great African-American plays ever produced.

*Mulatto* explores the heartbreak that can occur in a racist society when a white man and a black woman have a child that is accepted by neither race. Here, in a scene from *Mulatto's* touring company, the parents of tragic character Robert Lewis are played by James Kirkwood and Mercedes Gilbert.

After over two decades of involvement in the NAACP's fight for racial integration, W.E.B. DuBois reversed his stand on the issue in the 1930s, stating that separate but equal schools might provide a better education for black children. When, the NAACP asked him to retract his statement, he refused, and in 1934, DuBois resigned from the group.

The National Council of Negro Women (NCNW) was founded in 1935 by educator and activist Mary McLeod Bethune. It was created to improve the opportunities and quality of life for black women, their families, and their communities, both in the United States and in other countries. Today, it connects nearly 4 million women worldwide.

# Langston Hughes
# Poet, Playwright, and Activist

James Mercer Langston Hughes was born on February 1, 1902 in Joplin, Missouri. Shortly after his birth, his parents separated, and Hughes was raised by his maternal grandmother until her death. Now in his early teens, Hughes rejoined his mother, and the two moved to Cleveland, Ohio. It was during this time that Hughes discovered his love of books—especially poetry—and his talent for writing. The bright young man contributed to his high school's literary magazine and even submitted poems to poetry magazines. He was only eighteen years of age when, inspired by a train ride to Mexico, he wrote "The Negro Speaks of Rivers," which was to become one of his most famous works.

Hughes entered Columbia University in the fall of 1921, but stayed for only a year. Instead of attending college, he worked a series of odd jobs, travelled to Europe, and continued to develop his poetry. In 1925, with his work generating increasing attention, Hughes' poem "The Weary Blues" won first prize in a contest run by *Opportunity* magazine. He was also awarded a scholarship to Pennsylvania's Lincoln University, where he eventually completed his bachelor of arts degree.

In 1926, Hughes' first collection of poetry, also entitled *The Weary Blues*, was published by Knopf. DuBose Heyward—author of both the novel and play *Porgy*—praised the young author's work in the *New York Herald Tribune*:

> Langston Hughes, although only twenty-four years old, is already conspicuous in the group of Negro intellectuals who are dignifying Harlem with a genuine art life. . . . always intensely subjective, passionate, keenly sensitive to beauty and possessed of an unfaltering musical sense, Langston Hughes has given us a "first book" that marks the opening of a career well worth watching.

After graduating from Lincoln University, Hughes returned to Harlem, where he would spend most of his remaining years. There, his poetry, novels, and short stories would serve as an inspiration for African Americans during the Harlem Renaissance and for decades to come. Hughes' works emphasized the strengths, beauty, and courage of the African-American people and criticized divisions within the race. He was steadfast in his determination to reveal the true black experience, free of misinterpretation and racial stereotype. He wrote, "My seeking has been to explain and illuminate the Negro condition in America and obliquely that of all human kind."

While Hughes significantly influenced the Harlem Renaissance of the twenties, his work as a playwright came to fruition during the 1930s, when his drama *Mulatto* debuted on Broadway. (See page 91.) This story of a biracial family in crisis was his most successful Broadway play. Since much of Hughes' poetic works embraced the rhythms of African-American music, particularly blues and jazz, many of his subsequent plays were staged as musicals. These works included *Street Scene* (1947), *Tambourines to Glory* (1956), and *Simply Heavenly* (1957).

Long after his death in 1967, Langston Hughes continued to make his mark in the theater. His first play, *Mule Bone*, co-written with Zora Neale Hurston in 1930, would find its way to Broadway for a short run in 1991, more than sixty years after it had been completed. In 2007, Hughes' work would once again return to Broadway in a musical called *LoveMusik*, which ran for 60 performances at the Biltmore Theatre. And every year, his Christmas musical *Black Nativity* is staged in theaters, schools, and churches across America. (See page 151.) Hughes' words continue to touch new generations and remain as powerful today as they were when they were first written.

In the 1920s, Langston Hughes emerged as a major figure of the artistic and social movement known as the Harlem Renaissance. But *Mulatto*—Hughes' most successful play—did not reach the Broadway stage until 1935.

# Green Pastures
# A Broadway Fable

At a time when many Broadway shows were focusing on issues of the day, one play took a departure into biblical territory. Based on *Ol' Man Adam an' His Chillun*, a collection of short stories by Roark Bradford, Marc Connelly's *Green Pastures* reenacted tales from the Bible. The unique twist was that the action was set in Depression-era New Orleans, and all the characters—including God—were African-American and spoke in black dialect. Although not billed as a musical, the production also included black spirituals.

Connelly's play opened in New York's Mansfield Theatre on February 26, 1930. While it stirred some controversy on religious grounds and was actually banned in Great Britain, *Green Pastures* had an impressive run of 640 performances, and the playwright won the Pulitzer Prize for Drama. The production also went on five national tours. W.E.B. DuBois offered nothing but praise, calling it "an extraordinary appealing and beautiful play based on the folk religion of Negroes."

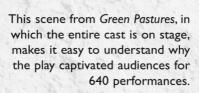

In Mark Connelly's *Green Pastures* (1930), heaven is a place of wondrous events, including eternal fish fries. While this interpretation of the Bible struck some as being irreverent, the play garnered Connelly a Pulitzer Prize for Drama.

This scene from *Green Pastures*, in which the entire cast is on stage, makes it easy to understand why the play captivated audiences for 640 performances.

# The Federal Theatre Project and "Voodoo *Macbeth*"

*Macbeth* was the play, Orson Welles was the twenty-year-old director, and John Houseman was the producer of a unique adaptation of a Shakespearean classic with an all-African-American cast. Debuting in 1936, *Macbeth* was funded by the Federal Theatre Project (FTP), a government program enacted in 1935 to create jobs for unemployed theater professionals during the Depression. Unsure as to whether the program would include the African-American population, civil rights activists had lobbied successfully for a Negro Theatre Project (NTP)—an offshoot of the FTP that would stage both contemporary works on black issues and classic dramas. Units of the NTP were set up in major cities across the United States, with the New York Negro Unit located at the Lafayette Theatre in Harlem.

*Macbeth*, one of the New York Negro Unit's first productions, came to life thanks largely to the imagination of Welles. Already established as a celebrity on radio, Welles felt that by moving the action to nineteenth-century Haiti, he would provide a more appropriate locale for the black cast.

Halli Flanagan, the national director of the Federal Theatre Project, named John Houseman head of Harlem's Negro Unit partly because he had shown sensitivity and skill when directing an opera with an all-black cast. Houseman believed that one part of the Negro Unit should perform plays by and for blacks, and the other should stage classical plays. To direct the unit's first classical drama, Houseman chose brash young Orson Welles.

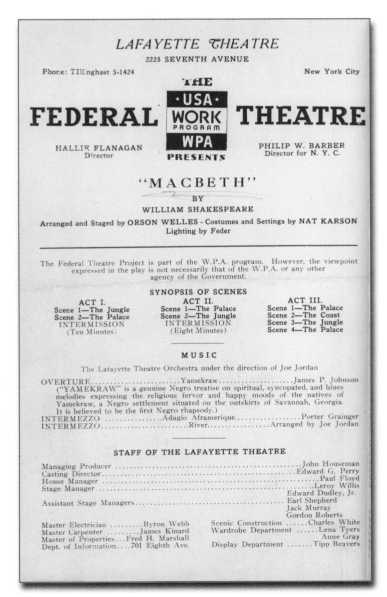

LAFAYETTE THEATRE
2225 SEVENTH AVENUE

Phone: TIllinghast 5-1424                                    New York City

# THE FEDERAL THEATRE

USA WORK PROGRAM WPA

HALLIE FLANAGAN
Director

PHILIP W. BARBER
Director for N. Y. C.

PRESENTS

## "MACBETH"

BY

WILLIAM SHAKESPEARE

Arranged and Staged by ORSON WELLES - Costumes and Settings by NAT KARSON
Lighting by Feder

The Federal Theatre Project is part of the W.P.A. program. However, the viewpoint expressed in the play is not necessarily that of the W.P.A. or any other agency of the Government.

### SYNOPSIS OF SCENES

| ACT I. | ACT II. | ACT III. |
| --- | --- | --- |
| Scene 1—The Jungle | Scene 1—The Palace | Scene 1—The Palace |
| Scene 2—The Palace | Scene 2—The Jungle | Scene 2—The Coast |
| INTERMISSION | INTERMISSION | Scene 3—The Jungle |
| (Ten Minutes) | (Eight Minutes) | Scene 4—The Palace |

### MUSIC

The Lafayette Theatre Orchestra under the direction of Joe Jordan

OVERTURE..................Yamekraw..................James P. Johnson
("YAMEKRAW" is a genuine Negro treatise on spiritual, syncopated, and blues melodies expressing the religious fervor and happy moods of the natives of Yamekraw, a Negro settlement situated on the outskirts of Savannah, Georgia. It is believed to be the first Negro rhapsody.)
INTERMEZZO ............Adagio Aframerique.................Porter Grainger
INTERMEZZO.......................River.................Arranged by Joe Jordan

### STAFF OF THE LAFAYETTE THEATRE

Managing Producer ........................................John Houseman
Casting Director..........................................Edward G. Perry
House Manager ...............................................Paul Floyd
Stage Manager ..............................................Leroy Willis
                                                         Edward Dudley, Jr.
Assistant Stage Managers..................................Earl Shepherd
                                                         Jack Murray
                                                         Gordon Roberts

| | | | |
| --- | --- | --- | --- |
| Master Electrician ........Byron Webb | Scenic Construction .....Charles White |
| Master Carpenter ......James Kinard | Wardrobe Department ......Lena Tyers |
| Master of Properties...Fred H. Marshall | | Anne Gray |
| Dept. of Information....701 Eighth Ave. | Display Department .......Tipp Beavers |

### CAST OF CHARACTERS

Duncan ....................(The King).................Service Bell
Malcolm ..................(Son to the King)..........Wardell Saunders
Macduff .....................................Maurice Ellis
Banquo .......................................Canada Lee
Macbeth ................NOBLES................Jack Carter
Ross ........................................Frank David
Lennox ..................................Thomas Anderson
Siward ....................................Archie Savage
First Murderer .............................George Nixon
Second Murderer ........................Kenneth Renwick
The Doctor .............................Lawrence Chenault
The Priest ...................................Al Watts
First Messenger .........................Philandre Thomas
Second Messenger .........................J. B. Johnson
The Porter ............................J. Lewis Johnson
Seyton ...................................Larrie Lauria
A Lord ..................................Charles Collins
First Captain ...........................Lisle Grenidge
Second Captain ..........................Gabriel Brown
First Chamberlain ........................Halle Howard
Second Chamberlain .....................Benny Tattnall
First Court Attendant.................Chauncey Worrell
Second Court Attendant...................George Thomas
First Page Boy..............................Viola Dean
Second Page Boy..........................Hilda French
Lady Macduff ...............................Marie Young
Lady Macbeth............NOBLE LADIES...........Edna Thomas
The Duchess ...............................Alma Dickson
The Nurse ...............................Virginia Girvin
Young Macduff .........................Bertram Holmes
Daughter to Macduff .......................Wanda Macy
Fleance ..................................Carl Crawford
Hecate ..................................Eric Burroughs
First Witch .........................Wilhelmina Williams
Second Witch ..........................Josephine Williams
Third Witch ...............................Zola King
Witch Doctor ................................Abdul

COURT LADIES—Helen Carter, Carolyn Crosby, Evelyn Davis, Ethel Drayton, Helen Browne, Bruce Howard, Aurelia Lawson, Margaret Howard, Lulu King, Evelyn Skipworth.
COURT GENTLEMEN—Herbert Glynn, Jose Miralda, Jimmy Wright, Otis Morse, Merritt Smith, Walter Brogsdale, Harry George Grant.
SOLDIERS—Benny Tattnall, Herman Patton, Emanuel Middleton, Ivan Lewis, Thomas Dixon, George Spelvin, Albert Patrick, Chauncey Worrell, Albert McCoy, William Clayton Jr., Allen Williams, Halle Howard, William Cumberbatch, Henry J. Williams, Amos Laing, Louis Gilbert, Theodore Howard, Leonardo Barros, Ollie Simmons, Ernest Brown, Merritt Smith, Harry George Grant, Herbert Glynn, Jimmy Wright, George Thomas, Richard Ming, Clifford Davis.
WITCH WOMEN—Juanita Baker, Beryle Banfield, Mildred Taylor, Sybil Moore, Nancy Hunt, Jacqueline Ghant Martin, Fannie Suber, Hilda French, Ethel Millner, Dorothy Jones.
WITCH MEN—Archie Savage, Charles Hill, Leonardo Barros, Howard Taylor, Amos Laing, Allen Williams, Ollie Simmons, Theodore Howard.
CRIPPLES—Clyde Gooden, Clarence Potter, Milton Lacey, Hudson Prince, Cecil McNair.
VOODOO WOMEN—Lena Halsey, Jean Cutler, Effie McDowell, Irene Ellington, Marguerite Perry, Essie Frierson, Ella Emanuel, Ethel Drayton, Evelyn Davis.
VOODOO MEN—Ernest Brown, Howard Taylor, Henry J. Williams, Louis Gilbert, William Clayton Jr., Halle Howard, Albert McCoy, Merritt Smith, Richard Ming.
DRUMMERS—McLean Hughes, James Cabon, James Martha, Moses Myers, Jay Daniel.

### CREDITS

Assistant Director .............................Thomas Anderson
Musical Arrangements under the direction of Virgil Thomson.
Voodoo Chants and Dances under the direction of Asadata Dafora Horton.
Dances under the direction of Clarence Yates.
Chorus under the direction of Leonard de Paur.
Costumes, Painting and Properties executed by the Federal Theatre Workshop.
Building by the Construction Staff of The Lafayette Theatre.
Masks executed by James Cochran.

The 1936 all-black production of *Macbeth* was so well publicized that on opening night, 10,000 people swarmed the area around the Lafayette Theatre, blocking traffic. *Macbeth* played to packed houses—mostly white—for nine weeks.

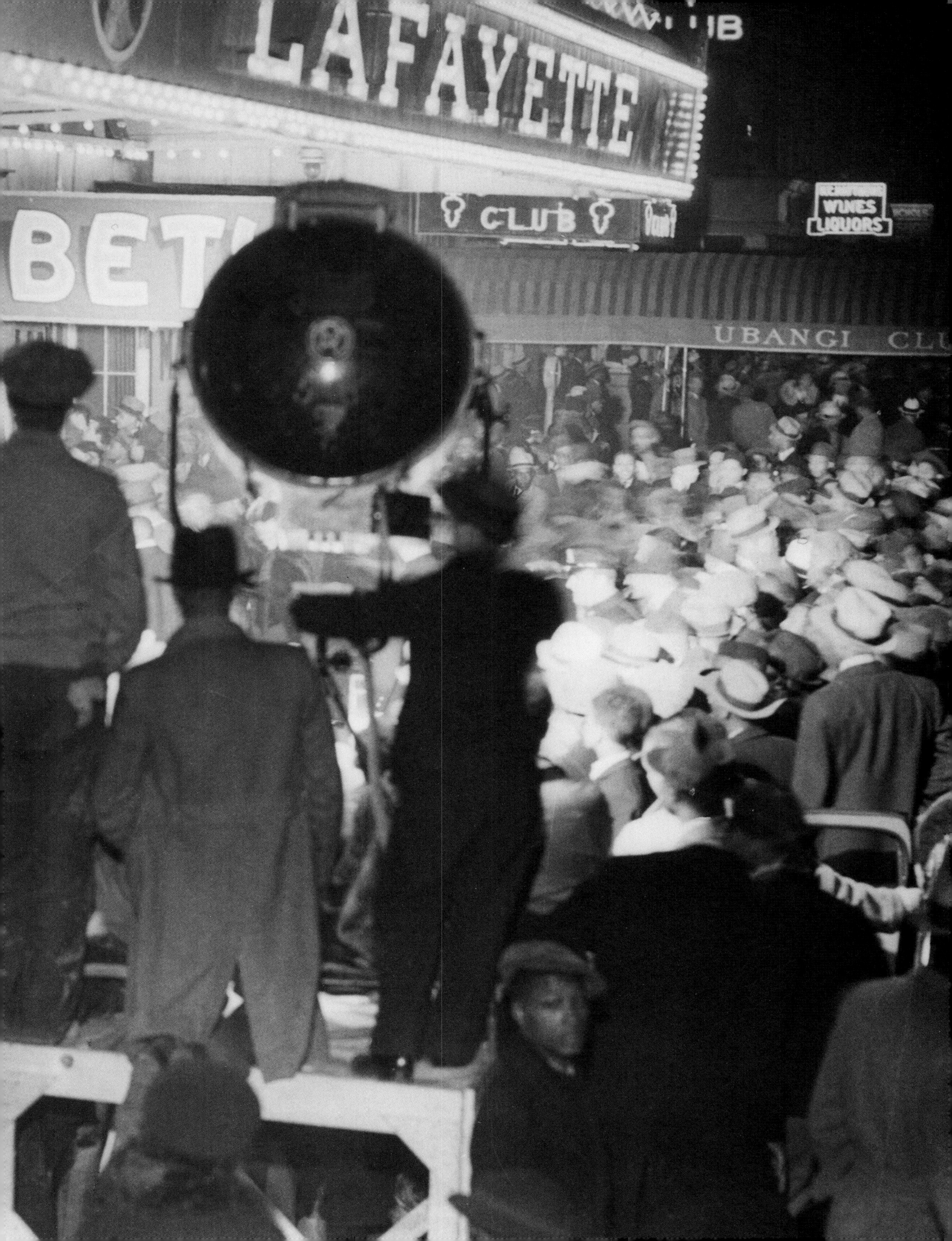

LAFAYETTE
CLUB
CLUB
WINES
LIQUORS
UBANGI CLU

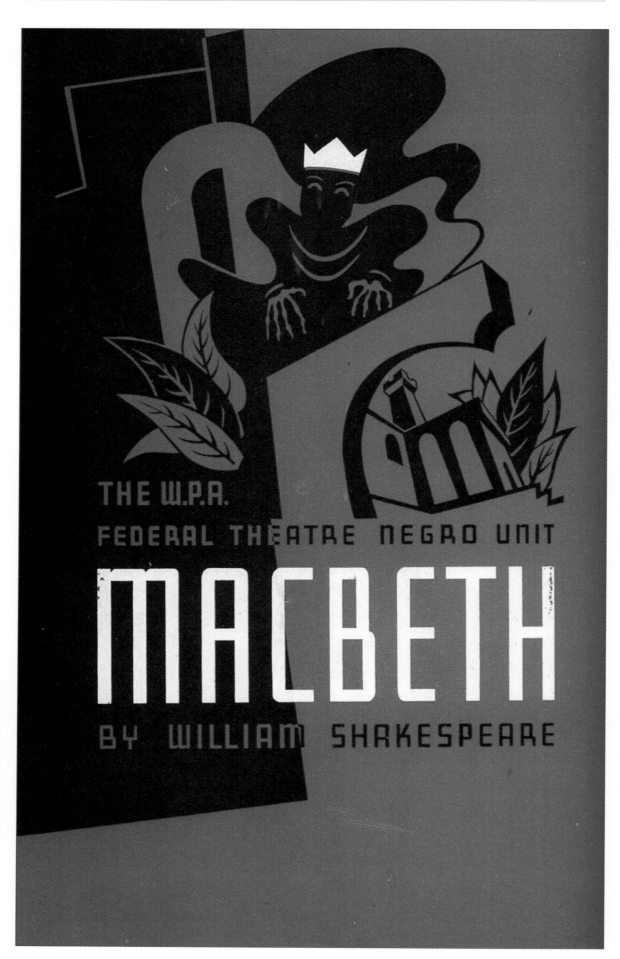

THE W.P.A.
FEDERAL THEATRE NEGRO UNIT
MACBETH
BY WILLIAM SHRKESPEARE

Between 1935 and 1939, twenty-three American cities hosted units of the federally funded Negro Theatre Project, an offshoot of the Federal Theatre Project. The most active unit was in New York City, where some thirty black productions were staged, the most famous being *Macbeth*.

The Scottish setting was replaced by a backdrop of palm trees and a jungle castle, and the medieval witchcraft became voodoo—which inspired people to refer to the production as "Voodoo *Macbeth*." Because Welles wanted to provide work for as many people as possible, the cast numbered over a hundred, and although the lead actors had Broadway experience, most of the players did not. Despite this drawback, Welles was confident that the play would draw large audiences and provide riveting entertainment. The reality must have exceeded even Welles' expectations.

The production was well publicized, and by 6:30 on opening night, April 14, 1936, 10,000 people crowded the area around the Lafayette Theatre, blocking traffic. The playhouse—all 1,223 seats—was sold out, and scalpers were doing a booming business. For those lucky enough to get inside the theater, the show was mesmerizing. The curtain rose on an extravagant set, a sea of colorful costumes, and the beat of voodoo drums, and the production held the audience's attention from the first scene to the last. When the curtain finally fell, thunderous applause filled the theater for fifteen minutes.

John Houseman and Orson Welles sought out experienced actors for *Macbeth*'s leading roles. Jack Carter, who had played Crown in 1927's *Porgy* and had also appeared in 1934's *Stevedore*, won the title role. Edna Thomas, who had also performed in *Porgy* and *Stevedore*, was Lady Macbeth. And Canada Lee, who had appeared in *Stevedore* and 1935's *Sailor, Beware!*, played Banquo.

By changing the setting of *Macbeth* from Scotland to Haiti, Orson Welles made it possible to offer a colorful jungle background and imaginative costumes.

In 1935, labor leader A. Philip Randolph established the National Negro Congress "to secure the right of the Negro people to be free from Jim Crowism, segregation, discrimination, and mob violence" and "to promote the spirit of unity and cooperation between Negro and white people." Although the Congress would disband in 1947, it served to unite over seven hundred African-American groups.

Established in 1935, the Federal Theatre Project (FTP) was a New Deal program designed to provide employment for performers, writers, directors, and other theater people during the Great Depression. An offshoot of the FTP, the Negro Theatre Project (NTP) specifically supported African-American theater in cities throughout the United States.

While the critics may have had mixed reactions to Welles' *Macbeth*, the African-American community responded more positively. Roi Ottley of the *Amsterdam News* wrote, "The Negro has become weary of carrying the White Man's blackface burden in the theatre. In *Macbeth* he has been given an opportunity to discard the bandanna and burnt-cork casting to play a universal character."

The critics were confused, to say the least. Some felt that the production was nothing more than a spectacle, while others were distressed by the unconventional adaptation of a classic work. But the displeasure of reviewers did not stop the buzz. In cities from New York to San Francisco, from Detroit to Dallas, the new *Macbeth* was an awakening, demonstrating how an innovative cultural adaptation could enlighten a new audience. The show also helped pave the way for integrated theater, as FTP policy stated that African Americans could buy seats and sit anywhere they chose. No one was excluded or relegated to the balcony.

Although FTP productions were designed to employ out-of-work theater people, and not necessarily to turn a profit, the shows were not expected to be quite as costly as *Macbeth*, which lost over $80,000. Tickets were less than half of the one to three dollars typically charged on Broadway, and in many cases, they were given away to encourage people to see the new productions.

*Macbeth* was one of 1,200 productions staged around the country for the enjoyment of more than 30 million Americans. Most significantly, the Federal Theatre Project created thousands of jobs at a time when they were sorely needed, and gave black performers—too often limited to singing and dancing for white audiences—an opportunity to take on the classics and other serious dramas.

The NTP provided assistance to African-American playwrights, directors, actors, and technicians from 1935 to 1939. Then, with the stroke of a pen, the program was abolished. The government shifted focus and began preparations for involvement in the war that was already underway in Europe.

# The Negro Actors Guild
# A New Voice, A New Presence

In the midst of the government's funding of African-American theater through the Negro Theatre Project, black entertainers who had established careers were also doing their part to help members of their industry. In 1936, after four years of planning, a group of dedicated black performers formed the Negro Actors Guild (NAG). The Guild's first president, composer and lyricist Noble Sissle, explained that the organization "would function along the lines of the Catholic, Jewish, and Episcopal Actors Guilds, that is, NAG would give the actors status." NAG would also work to generate greater acting opportunities for African Americans; help eliminate racial stereotypes from theater productions and films; and arrange transportation and hotel accommodations, provide health care, and finance funerals for its members. To fund the organization's new treasury, NAG was open to all races—not just African Americans. The treasury was further nourished by the many benefit concerts given by Bill "Bojangles" Robinson, a founding member who would eventually be named honorary president of the group.

By the early 1940s, the Negro Actors Guild had grown to include more than 700 professionals, including well-known entertainers like Louis Armstrong, Marian Anderson, Cab Calloway, Duke Ellington, Lena Horne, and Ethel Waters. Virtually every African-American actor and actress of the time belonged to the Guild. But beginning in the 1960s, increasing integration in the industry led many black performers to join the Actors' Equity Association rather than NAG. In 1982, having served the entertainment industry for nearly half a century, the Guild was disbanded.

# The American Negro Theater

As the American government geared up for a worldwide conflict and the NTP lost its funding, the American Negro Theater (ANT) picked up where the FTP had left off by providing a venue for black theater professionals. ANT was founded in June 1940 by black writer Abram Hill and black actor Frederick O'Neal. The goal of the new project was fourfold: to create and train a permanent black theater company, to produce plays that honestly presented contemporary black life, to provide inspiration and leadership for other black theater groups throughout the country, and to help develop racial pride within the black community. The name of the group was chosen partly for the acronym, ANT, which emphasized the need for cooperation, not competition, among black artists. The members were to share both the expenses and the profits of their work.

For several years, ANT flourished at a series of Harlem locations—first, at the Harlem Library Little Theatre; then, at the American Negro Theatre Playhouse created within the local Elks Club; and finally, in a loft on West 125 Street. Its first major production was *On Striver's Row*, Abram Hill's satire on black social climbing. Other shows included Phoebe and Henry Ephron's *Three Is a Family*, which eventually made its way to Broadway; Moss Hart and George Kaufman's classic *You Can't Take It With You*; Eugene O'Neill's *The Rope*; and Philip Yordan's *Anna Lucasta*. Over the course of a decade, the theater group staged nineteen plays, a dozen of which were original productions. An estimated 50,000 people attended ANT shows.

In 1942, ANT added a training program for young artists. Known as the Studio Theater, it launched the careers of a number of African-American actors, including Sidney Poitier, Harry Belafonte, Ruby Dee, and Ossie Davis. In addition, between 1945 and 1946, ANT hosted a series of weekly radio programs. Entitled *New World A-Comin'*, the programs presented dramatic readings from classic works like Shakespeare's *Romeo and Juliet* and operatic productions like Gilbert and Sullivan's *H.M.S. Pinafore*.

While *Anna Lucasta's* move from Harlem to Broadway might have contributed to the demise of the community-based American Negro Theater, the show had a long, successful run on the Great White Way. This photo of the Broadway production includes (left to right) Canada Lee, Hilda Simms, Alice Childress (who later turned to writing), and Alvin Childress.

The demise of the American Negro Theater began in the late 1940s, ironically, in part, because of the success of *Anna Lucasta*. After running for five weeks at ANT's Harlem theater in 1944, the play moved to the Mansfield Theatre on Broadway, where it ran for two years. This undermined the community-centered focus of the group, which had, from the start, rejected a "destination Broadway" attitude. The financial arrange-

---

By 1935, forty-five African Americans were members of the Federal Council of Negro Affairs, later referred to as the Black Cabinet. Appointed by Franklin D. Roosevelt, these informal public policy advisors provided the president with insights into the needs of African Americans and are often credited with laying the foundation of the civil rights movement.

In 1936, a group of dedicated black entertainers formed the Negro Actors Guild (NAG) as a welfare and benevolent organization for African-American performers. Under the leadership of Noble Sissle, the Guild's first president, the group worked to generate acting opportunities, eliminate stereotypic roles, provide health care, and otherwise help and protect its members.

"THE MOST IMPORTANT AMERICAN
COMEDY-DRAMA IN TWENTY YEARS"

ments, too, led to bitterness, as the Broadway production generated royalties of less than 2 percent for the struggling theater group. Adding insult to injury, the Broadway show used only a few of the original ANT actors. The members now aimed for Broadway success rather than social progress or the enhancement of African-American culture, and from that point on, they would produce only plays by known white playwrights. As a result, they lost the interest and support of the black community.

The American Negro Theater closed its doors in the early 1950s. Despite its relatively short existence, it played a significant role in fostering an awareness of both black theater and black issues. Just as important, it helped hone the skills of black playwrights, performers, and technicians who would achieve success in years to come.

A writer of novels, short stories, poetry, and nonfiction, Richard Wright focused largely on racial themes in his works. The 1941 play *Native Son*, based on Wright's 1940 best-selling novel of the same name, was adapted for the stage by Wright and white playwright Paul Green.

Adolf Hitler had hoped that the 1936 Summer Olympics in Berlin would prove his claim that the Aryan race was superior. But when African-American Jesse Owens won four gold medals in track and field, the German people hailed him as a hero. In 1984, a street in Berlin would be named in Owens' honor.

In 1937, young African Americans joined together to form the Southern Negro Youth Congress (SNYC). Members included individuals from black colleges, YMCA branches, and Girl Scout and Boy Scout chapters. Over the years, the SNYC helped rural blacks secure the right to vote, taught strategies for protest, and otherwise laid the groundwork for the civil rights movement.

# Other Significant Black Dramas of the Forties

One of the most controversial dramas of the 1940s was, not surprisingly, based on an equally controversial novel. Written by black author Richard Wright, the 1940 bestseller *Native Son* tells the story of a young, desperately poor African American named Bigger Thomas, who is driven to murder by racial injustice. The book was condemned by many critics for excusing crime and feeding white bigotry with its portrait of an unrepentant killer. No strangers to controversy, Orson Welles and John Houseman decided to mount a dramatic version of the story.

*Native Son* was adapted for the stage by Richard Wright and white playwright Paul Green. Premiering at the St. James Theatre on March 21, 1941, it starred Canada Lee in the lead role of Bigger Thomas. Both the play and Lee received enthusiastic reviews, with Lee being hailed as "the greatest Negro actor of his era and one of the finest actors in the country" by *The New York Times*. But the sympathetic portrayal of a man forced to kill a white woman caused the production to be condemned by a number of groups, including the National Legion of Decency. After running for three months (97 performances), under increasing pressure, *Native Son* closed and went on tour. In 1942, it would return to Broadway for 84 more performances. In later years, the powerful but divisive play would be staged several more times.

Already an experienced actor—he had performed in Orson Welles' all-black production of *Macbeth*, as well as other dramas—Canada Lee impressed critics with his searing portrayal of Bigger Thomas in *Native Son* (1941). *The New York Times* hailed Lee as "the greatest Negro actor of his era and one of the finest actors in the country."

Groups like the National Legion of Decency condemned *Native Son's* sympathetic portrayal of a black man who is driven to murder by racial injustice. Despite the fact that theatergoers and critics found the play riveting, this controversy caused the 1941 play to close and go on tour after a three-month run on Broadway.

Soon after the Negro Theatre Project (NTP) lost its government funding in 1939, the American Negro Theatre (ANT) picked up where the NTP had left off by providing a venue for black theater professionals. ANT's training program for young artists helped launch the careers of actors such as Sidney Poitier, Harry Belafonte, Ruby Dee, and Ossie Davis.

In 1939, the Daughters of the American Revolution denied black opera singer Marian Anderson the opportunity to perform at DAR-owned Constitution Hall because of her race. Hearing about the snub, Eleanor Roosevelt, herself a member of the DAR, resigned in protest and arranged for Anderson to sing on the steps of the Lincoln Memorial.

# The Apollo Theater

Located on 125th Street in Harlem, the Apollo Theater is one of the most important African-American theaters today. But it did not begin as a venue for black performers. Constructed in 1913, the Apollo was originally called Hurtig and Seamon's New Burlesque Theatre. At that time, the playhouse had a "whites only" policy. After it was purchased by Billy Minsky of Minsky's Burlesque in 1928, it continued to cater to white audiences and, except for the occasional black act, it hired mostly white entertainers.

Then in 1934, the theater underwent a much-needed renovation and retained new management. When it reopened, it was called the Apollo and was dedicated exclusively to showcasing African-American entertainment. The first major star to perform at the Apollo was Broadway's Adelaide Hall, who was featured in a production entitled *Chocolate Soldiers*. The critically acclaimed revue helped establish the new Apollo as Harlem's premier theater. That same year, with the introduction of "Wednesday Amateur Night" by producer Ralph Cooper, the theater began its tradition of launching careers. The competition was broadcast live by radio on a national network of twenty-one stations, so talented new performers soon became widely known. In November 1934, fifteen-year-old Ella Fitzgerald sang at Apollo's Amateur Night, and within a year, she was singing professionally with Chick Webb's band. Other black entertainers who debuted at this Harlem venue include Diana Ross and the Supremes, Aretha Franklin, Marvin Gaye, James Brown, and Luther Vandross.

In 1983, the Apollo received official status as a city landmark. Today, it continues to serve the community by presenting concerts and other cultural events, promoting black talent, and sponsoring outreach programs for the people of Harlem.

After its 1934 renovation, Harlem's Apollo Theater was dedicated to showcasing African-American entertainment. This marquee from the 1930s shows a wide variety of acts, from jazz great Count Basie to tap dancer Charles "Honi" Coles to comedian Jackie "Moms" Mabley.

*Deep Are the Roots* provides a snapshot of post-World War II race relations in America. Like so many black GIs, Brett Charles returns home expecting to be treated with the respect he received when he was fighting for his country. What he finds is a community that still regards him as a second-class citizen.

Another controversial play of the forties opened on September 26, 1945 at the Fulton Theatre. Written by Arnaud d'Usseau and James Gow, and directed by Elia Kazan, *Deep Are the Roots* tells the story of a black soldier who, after the Second World War, returns to the white southern household where he was raised by his servant mother. Having spent years out of the South and been decorated for bravery, the young man has new ideas about his place in life. His home town, however, has not greatly changed. Disturbed by his attitude, several members of the community wrongly accuse him of theft. Fortunately, one of the white girls with whom he grew up champions him and even suggests marrying him—a proposal that he refuses.

The topic of biracial marriage offended some conservative theatergoers. In fact, more than a few people were seen indignantly stomping out in the middle of the play. But because America was increasingly liberal at the time, for the most part, the production was lauded. A 1945 review in *Time* magazine, while critical of the play's melodramatic writing, called *Deep Are the Roots* "a bad play that is yet worth seeing." It ran for nearly 500 performances.

In the 1945 production of *Deep Are the Roots*, characters Brett Charles (played by Gordon Heath) and Genevra Langdon (Barbara Bel Geddes) offended some theatergoers by merely suggesting the possibility of biracial marriage. Nevertheless, the play ran for almost 500 performances.

# AND THE MUSIC PLAYED ON

Even as the theater world presented dramas of increasing social and political importance, it continued to offer new musical shows designed to raise the public's spirits during the Depression and the ensuing war years. Yet not all the musicals of the time were lighthearted. George Gershwin's *Porgy and Bess* dealt with serious issues and remained a subject of controversy for many years.

## *Porgy and Bess*

One of the most significant plays of the 1930s, *Porgy and Bess* was based on the 1925 novel *Porgy* by DuBose Heyward. Set in a fictitious black community in Charleston, South Carolina, the best-selling novel tells the story of passionate Bess, a woman whose life is blurred by alcohol and drugs; her violent lover, Crown; her drug dealer, Sportin' Life; and Porgy, a disabled black beggar who attempts to rescue Bess from the men who are destroying her. While white readers admired the vibrant characters and assumed that the author wrote from a wealth of knowledge about his subject, the black community felt that the book perpetuated damaging racial stereotypes. A review in a black newspaper questioned why, of all the people in the black community, Heyward had chosen to portray the poorest and the least sophisticated. Black poet Countee Cullen called *Porgy* "the best novel by a white man about Negroes." W.E.B DuBois, while praising the author's talents, noted that the story did nothing to enhance African-American culture or image.

Years before the musical *Porgy and Bess* was written, *Porgy*, a 1927 nonmusical dramatization of the DuBose Heyward novel of the same name, premiered on Broadway. Here we see (from left to right) Percy Verwayne as Sportin' Life, Frank Wilson as Porgy, and Evelyn Ellis as Bess.

Despite the criticism from African Americans, Heyward and his wife, Dorothy, were so inspired by the novel's success that they wrote a theatrical version, *Porgy*, which opened at New York's Guild Theatre in 1927 and ran for 367 performances. Both the book and the play that so quickly followed intrigued many people, including composer George Gershwin. He had, in fact, contacted Heyward in 1926 to propose collaboration on an "American folk opera," but his schedule prevented him from immediately working on the score. It would not be until 1935 that the show opened on Broadway.

The delay might have been beneficial, as during the early thirties, New York playwrights and performers were becoming increasingly interested in producing serious, socially conscious dramas. The Group Theater—founded in 1931 by Harold Clurman, Cheryl Crawford, and Lee

In 1940, Hattie McDaniel walked from a segregated table in the back of Los Angeles's Coconut Grove nightclub to accept the Academy Award for Best Supporting Actress in a film (*Gone With the Wind*). McDaniel was not only the first African American to win an Oscar, but also the first person of color to be admitted as a guest at the ceremony.

On October 25, 1940, after a long career in the army, Benjamin O. Davis, Jr. became the first African American to be promoted to the rank of brigadier general. Davis was also a professor of military science and tactics at Wilberforce University in Ohio, and a teacher of military science and tactics at the Tuskegee Institute in Alabama.

Although *Porgy and Bess* is now considered a great folk opera, when it premiered at the Alvin Theatre in 1935, the critics had mixed reactions, and the show closed after 124 performances before going on tour. It would return to Broadway four more times over the next fifty years, including a highly acclaimed 1953 production that ran for over 300 performances and featured Leontyne Price as Bess, William Warfield as Porgy, and Cab Calloway as Sportin' Life. With each new production, changes were made in both the dialogue and score, with black dialect being eliminated and more of the songs that had been trimmed by Gershwin being restored. Perhaps most influential in turning the tide of opinion was the 1976 revival by the Houston Grand Opera, which debuted in Houston before moving to Broadway's Uris Theatre. Based on Gershwin's *full* score, it became the only opera to win a Tony Award.

Strasberg—was dedicated to tackling significant political issues. In addition, black theater continued to attract white theatergoers, even if they did not fully grasp the struggles faced by the characters. In 1934, George Sklar and Paul Peters' play *Stevedore* focused on a black militant hero from the docks of New Orleans who defends himself after being wrongly accused of a crime. That same year, John Wexley's *They Shall Not Die* told the story of the Scottsboro Trial, in which nine black youths were accused of raping white women. Some years later, when Langston Hughes wrote about the 1930s, he stated, "Every season there was at least one hit play on Broadway acted by an all Negro cast." So by the time that *Porgy and Bess* opened, Broadway audiences were already familiar with shows that featured African-American performers dealing with black issues.

On October 10, 1935—exactly eight years to the day after the debut of *Porgy*—*Porgy and Bess* premiered at the Alvin Theatre, with music by George Gershwin, lyrics by DuBose Heyward and Ira Gershwin, and libretto by Heyward. Because of Gershwin's fame, there was great interest in the show and the debut was well attended. But while the audience was enthusiastic, reviewers had mixed reactions. Olin Downes of *The New York Times* stated that the show had "much to commend it from the musical standpoint," and *Stage Magazine* raved, "George Gershwin's brilliant and moving transcription into music of Heyward's Negro folk play is authentic and gripping from the first chord to the last." Many reviewers, though, disliked the combination of different musical styles. Virgil Thomson of the *New York Herald Tribune* called the mixture of jazz, blues, and opera "clumsily executed . . . crooked folklore and halfway-opera." Like a number of people in the black community, Thomson (who was white) also objected to a black story being told by

Composer George Gershwin personally chose Todd Duncan to play crippled beggar Porgy in the original 1935 production of *Porgy and Bess*. Duncan would also sing Porgy in the 1937 and 1942 revivals of the opera.

From 1940 to 1980, about 5 million African Americans left the South and moved to the cities of the North, Midwest, and West in search of greater opportunity and freedom from Jim Crow restrictions. Called the Second Great Migration, this movement provided many black Americans with greater political rights while transforming them into a highly urbanized population.

Led by future Supreme Court Justice Thurgood Marshall, the NAACP Legal Defense and Educational Fund was formed in 1940 to provide African Americans with information about the criminal justice system as well as legal assistance. Over the years, it has won a number of significant cases concerning discrimination in education, housing, voting, jury selection, and access to counsel.

white men: "Folklore subjects recounted by an outsider are only valid as long as the folk in question is unable to speak for itself, which is certainly not true of the American Negro in 1935." W.E.B. DuBois voiced his displeasure with the depiction of black people as gamblers, drug dealers, and people with loose morals, saying that these degrading stereotypes created an impediment to the African-American struggle for political and economic rights. Duke Ellington objected not only to the portrayal of black people but also to the music, which he claimed was not a true representation of African-American song.

*Porgy and Bess* closed after 124 performances and then went on tour of the United States until March 1936. It would return to Broadway four more times over the next fifty years, including a 1953 production that ran for over 300 performances and featured Leontyne Price as Bess, William Warfield as Porgy, and Cab Calloway as Sportin' Life. The musical also toured more than two dozen countries throughout Europe, the Middle East, and Latin America. With each new production, changes were made in both the dialogue and the score. The black dialect, which the African-American community found insulting, was eliminated, and many songs that Gershwin had cut to limit the length of the original show were added back. Eventually, *Porgy and Bess* would be regarded as a great folk opera, and songs like "Summertime" and "It Ain't Necessarily So" would become classics that were recorded and performed time and time again.

People who now view *Porgy and Bess* as a great American folk opera may be surprised to learn that the 1935 production was widely criticized, especially by the black community, which disliked the play's depiction of African Americans and felt that the music was not a true representation of black culture.

## Musical Revues of the Thirties

The vast majority of the musicals staged during this period were far lighter and less divisive than *Porgy and Bess*. One musical entertainment that had begun in the previous decade (see page 77) and continued in the 1930s was *Lew Leslie's Blackbirds*. Leslie's 1930, 1934, 1936, and 1939 shows were not as well received as his initial 1928 production, but they did continue to feature great African-American stars, including Ethel Waters (1930), Bill "Bojangles" Robinson (1934), the Nicholas Brothers (1936), and Lena Horne (1939). (To learn about Ethel Waters, turn to the inset on page 112.)

Eubie Blake also continued staging revues. In 1933, he brought his 1921 hit *Shuffle Along* back to Broadway for a short run. Then, in 1937, he introduced *Swing It* as one of the relatively few musicals produced through the Federal Theatre Project. Opening at the Adelphi Theatre in the middle of the summer, the production was a blend of minstrelsy, singing, dancing, spirituals, jazz, and swing. *Swing It* was considered "muted" compared with Blake's earlier work, and it ran for only nine weeks.

As the United States prepared for global war, the nation's black leaders protested that black workers were prevented from taking jobs in segregated defense factories. On June 25, 1941, President Franklin Delano Roosevelt signed Executive Order 8802 banning "discrimination because of race, creed, color, or national origin" in all federal agencies, unions, and companies engaged in war-related work.

At the start of World War II, draft boards usually passed over African Americans. Then the NAACP applied pressure to President Roosevelt to enlist blacks in accordance with their percentage in the population: 10.6 percent. Although this level was never reached, black numbers soon began to grow in the Army, Air Force, Coast Guard, Navy, and Marine Corps.

# Ethel Waters
## Versatile Performer of Stage, Screen & Television

Born on October 31, 1896, Ethel Waters grew up in an impoverished home in Philadelphia, Pennsylvania. But even as a child, Waters' singing and dancing skills not only made her life sweeter but also attracted notice. At seventeen, she performed on stage in Baltimore, and just a few years later, the tall, slim Waters debuted on the black vaudeville circuit as "Sweet Mama Stringbean," working, in her words, "from nine until unconscious." By the 1920s, her soft, subtle style of blues singing had earned her great popularity, and she was recording with the small Cardinal Records label. By 1925, she had a recording contract with better-known Columbia Records. And by '28, in addition to appearing in clubs, Waters had moved on to the so-called "white time" Keith Vaudeville Circuit—which was a rare feat at the time. Although Bert Williams had accomplished this years earlier, he had been forced to perform in blackface.

Ethel Waters' first work on Broadway included 1927's *Africana, Lew Leslie's Blackbirds of 1930,* and *Rhapsody in Black* (1931). Then in 1933, legendary composer and lyricist Irving Berlin heard her sing "Stormy Weather" at the Cotton Club, and immediately, he knew that he wanted Waters to appear in his upcoming musical revue, *As Thousands Cheer* (1933). There, Waters gave a powerful performance singing Berlin's "Suppertime," in which a woman struggles with the news that her husband has been lynched. Within a few months, Waters was elevated to co-starring status and became the first African American to receive billing equal to that of white performers. *As Thousands Cheer* ran for 400 performances.

Waters' success in Berlin's revue opened the door to many more Broadway roles, including leads in the 1940 drama *Mamba's Daughters* and the 1940 musical *Cabin in the Sky,* for which she received great praise. She would also enjoy sterling reviews in Vincente Minnelli's 1943 screen version of *Cabin.* Other movies in which Waters appeared include *Cairo* (1942), *Stage Door Canteen* (1943), *Pinky* (1950), *The Member of the Wedding* (1952), *Carib Gold* (1957), *The Heart Is a Rebel* (1958), and *The Sound and the Fury* (1959). The versatile performer also made a name for herself on television. In 1939, Waters starred in an early variety special entitled *The Ethel Waters Show,* which aired on NBC, and from 1950 to 1951, she starred in the ABC television series *The Beulah Show.* Over the years, she would make appearances in many other TV shows, including *General Electric Theater* (1955), *Route 66* (1961), *Vacation Playhouse* (1967), and *Owen Marshall, Counselor at Law* (1972).

While Ethel Waters enjoyed a career that spanned vaudeville, Broadway, film, TV, and more, she is best known for her vocal talents. Her version of the jazz classic "Stormy Weather," along with pop hits "Am I Blue?" and "Dinah," are in the Grammy Hall of Fame. During her long career, Waters performed with Will Marion Cook, Fletcher Henderson, Coleman Hawkins, Duke Ellington, Count Basie, and many other greats—all while recording hundreds of songs for Columbia Records. She remains a towering figure in the history of American music.

Ethel Waters began her career on the black vaudeville circuit, ▶ then moved on to "white time" vaudeville, and by 1930, was appearing in Lew Leslie's *Blackbirds* on Broadway. Later stage credits include *As Thousands Cheer* (1933), *Cabin in the Sky* (1940), and *The Member of the Wedding* (1950).

Although the cast of *The Swing Mikado* was praised, critics complained that the score—which had been revised only slightly—lacked sufficient "swingcopation." "It ought to swing from end to end," said *The New York Times*.

## The Battle of the Mikados

Late in the 1930s, the Federal Theatre Project had a hand in one of the true musical phenomena of the decade—a black version of Gilbert and Sullivan's operetta *The Mikado*. Called *The Swing Mikado,* the production was conceived, staged, and directed by Harry Minturn. After opening in Chicago in 1938, it moved to the New York Theatre in March 1939. To accommodate the all-black cast, the action was transplanted to a "Coral Island in the Pacific," and costumes were designed to harmonize with the new setting. Some dialogue was rewritten in an attempt to simulate black dialect, but most of the dialogue remained the same. Although a good many of the original songs were not changed, as you might expect from the name of the show, a handful were set to a syncopated rhythm and several popular dance numbers were added, including the cakewalk.

The 1939 opening of the FTP-funded *Swing Mikado* was a high-profile event that was attended by First Lady Eleanor Roosevelt; Colonel Francis Clark Harrington, director of the Works Progress Administration; Harry Hopkins, one of President Roosevelt's closest advisers; and New York City Mayor Fiorello LaGuardia. The reviews, however, were not entirely positive. While *New York Times* critic Brooks Atkinson pronounced Maurice Cooper "a Nanki-Poo of superior voice and articulate acting capability," he complained about the lack of swing. "They scarcely swing it enough," wrote Atkinson. "It ought to swing from end to end." John Mason Brown of the *New York Post* agreed that the show "takes no chances." Everyone seemed to want more "swingcopation."

Audiences and critics who yearned for a "swingier" *Mikado* did not have to wait very long. When *Swing Mikado* was still being planned, the Federal

Theatre Project had rejected producer Mike Todd's offer to manage the show. So Todd decided to produce his own adaptation. Featuring famous black performers like hoofer Bill "Bojangles" Robinson, who played the title role, Todd's *Hot Mikado* was jazzier than the FTP production, and also had a bigger budget that allowed for wild costuming and elaborate visual effects. Opening at the Broadhurst Theatre on March 23, 1939, the *Hot Mikado* was greeted with enthusiasm by both theatergoers and critics, with *Newsweek's* George Jean Nathan calling it the "best all-around musical show."

The Federal Theatre Project's *Mikado* ran into trouble in the summer of '39, when several members of Congress took steps to abolish the FTP and suggested that the shows it funded were damaging the theater industry. *Swing Mikado* was finally sold to commercial producers and moved to the Forty-Fourth Street Theatre, across the street from *Hot Mikado,* where head-to-head competition resulted in the demise of both productions. At the end of the "Battle of the Black Mikados," *Swing Mikado* had run for 86 performances and *Hot Mikado,* for 85. But because of its great popularity, *Hot Mikado* was soon moved to the New York World's Fair of 1939 to 1940. There, it proved to be a major attraction for two seasons.

The ample budget of *Hot Mikado* is evident in this photo of the full cast. The visually stunning show was so popular that after its Broadway run ended, it had a two-season run at New York's 1939–1940 World's Fair, where it proved to be a major attraction.

*Hot Mikado* provided audiences and critics with wilder costumes and better-known performers than the federally funded *Swing Mikado* could afford. This scene from 1939's "best all-around musical show" features (from left to right) Bill Robinson, Freddie Robinson, Rosetta LeNoire, Gwendolyn Reyde, and Frances Brook.

◀ To accommodate an all-black cast, 1939's *Swing Mikado* transplanted Gilbert and Sullivan's nineteenth-century comic opera from its original setting of Japan to a "Coral Island in the Pacific." This photo shows the lavish set.

## *Cabin in the Sky*

The cast of the 1940 musical fantasy *Cabin in the Sky* featured several experienced Broadway performers, including Ethel Waters, Todd Duncan, and J. Rosamond Johnson.

Billed as a musical fantasy, 1940's *Cabin in the Sky* had music by Vernon Duke; lyrics by John Latouche; book by Lynn Root, who had written the story "Little Joe" on which the play was based; and choreography by George Balanchine. Essentially a version of the Faust legend, the play tells the story of likeable but morally weak Little Joe, who is bound for hell after being killed over a gambling debt. But Joe's pious wife, Petunia, prays so hard that her husband is given six more months on earth to earn a place in heaven. Beings from heaven and hell then fight over Joe's soul, while Petunia and temptress Georgia Brown battle for his body.

When *Cabin in the Sky* opened in October 1940 at the Martin Beck Theatre, it received mostly good reviews. Brooks Atkinson of *The New York Times* called it "the best Negro musical this column can recall and the peer of any musical in recent years." The all-black cast was praised, and star Ethel Waters was lauded for playing Petunia "with force and frankness that are completely overwhelming." Waters' performance also turned the song "Taking a Chance on Love" into a hit. But, as Atkinson noted, while the show was highly enjoyable, it included stereotypical black characters and followed Broadway's "Negro formula" of hot dance numbers and "darktown comedy." Despite these shortcomings—or, perhaps, because of them—*Cabin in the Sky* ran for 156 performances on Broadway before moving to the West Coast for an extended run. A successful film version, released in 1943, featured original star Ethel Waters and cast sexy Lena Horne as her rival, Georgia Brown.

## *Carmen Jones*

With a libretto by Oscar Hammerstein II, 1943's *Carmen Jones* transplanted George Bizet's opera *Carmen* from Spain to the South, and gave it an all-black cast. But the story of love and betrayal remained the same.

On March 31, 1943, the newly formed writing team of composer Richard Rodgers and lyricist Oscar Hammerstein II debuted their musical *Oklahoma!* to rave reviews. Amazingly, less than nine months later, Hammerstein introduced yet another musical to Broadway. This time, he had translated George Bizet's 1875 opera *Carmen* from French into English. The music, for the most part, was left intact, but Hammerstein moved the action from a cigarette factory in Spain to a parachute factory in southern America. Most interestingly, *Carmen Jones* would have an all-black cast.

The contemporary Carmen, a worker at a factory, meets "fly boy" Joe, who's stationed nearby. Carmen steals Joe away from fiancée Cindy Lou, but always fickle, she soon begins wooing another man—prizefighter Husky Miller. Eventually, Joe, overcome with jealousy, kills the woman he loves.

The cast and chorus were "raw"—chosen for voice rather than reputation. Somehow, director Charles Friedman, under the supervision of designer Hassard Short, transformed the neophyte thespians into a cohesive

Formed in 1941, when the U.S. military was racially segregated, the Tuskegee Airmen were the first black military aviators in the United States Air Force. While many Americans thought that the Airmen couldn't do their job because of their race, after being given equal opportunity and training, the black flyers served with distinction in combat.

In April 1944, the United Negro College Fund (UNCF) was created to provide a steady stream of funding to the country's historically black colleges and universities, and thus support access to higher education for African Americans. Later, the UNCF would become known only by its acronym to reflect its support of Latino, Native American, and Asian American students.

Broadway cast within six weeks. With Muriel Smith and Muriel Rahn alternating in the title role of Ms. Jones, the exuberance of the young cast overshadowed any deficiencies and the show was a hit, running for over 500 performances. The excitement of the theatergoers was matched only by that of the critics. After the Broadway Theatre debut in December 1943, Harry Taylor's review in *The New Masses* not only praised the new production but also highlighted the need for greater representation of African Americans in the theater:

This is the most exhilarating and delightful thing that has happened to Broadway in a long time. With rich appreciation for their verve and creativeness, Oscar Hammerstein wrote the libretto about Negroes for Negro players: it is not possible to imagine the new *Carmen* done in white. It is not only a wonderful artistic triumph, it is a people's triumph; above all *the* people's triumph. I participated and was happy in the joy of the audience. But *Carmen Jones* gave us not only lavish evidence of the talent of the Negro people, it also reminded us that we have deliberately kept it from view and normal exhibition. I heard many ask each other variants of, "Why don't we have more plays with colored casts?" And the reply always was, "We must have more." Those of us who remember our great hope at the Negro *Macbeth* and the other productions of the Negro wing of the Federal Theatre will know that this generous directive to the theater cannot be carried through in much greater pace than our national progress toward equal opportunity for all. The cast of *Carmen Jones* like Paul Robeson in *Othello* makes eloquent argument for haste.

Although the cast of *Carmen Jones* was chosen for singing ability rather than experience—only one performer had ever acted on a Broadway stage—the show was a hit, with one reviewer pronouncing it "the most exhilarating and delightful thing that has happened to Broadway in a long time."

# A Noteworthy Pairing

On January 9, 1947, an "American opera" titled *Street Scene* premiered at the Adelphi Theatre on Broadway. With music by Kurt Weill, lyrics by Langston Hughes, and book by Elmer Rice, the play was, in Weill's words, "a simple story of everyday life in a big city." While *Street Scene* ran for just 148 performances—and never returned to Broadway—the pairing of Kurt Weill and Langston Hughes drew attention, for it was Broadway's first significant interracial musical collaboration. More of an opera than a musical, *Street Scene* would, in later years, be regularly produced on the opera stage.

After its long Broadway run, *Carmen Jones* took off on a tour of America. It then crossed the Atlantic to Great Britain. In 1954, it would be made into a movie starring Dorothy Dandridge, Harry Belafonte, and Diahann Carroll, and in 1992, a London revival would garner the prestigious Laurence Olivier Award.

## St. Louis Woman

When producer Edward Gross read Arna Bontemps' novel *God Sends Sunday*, he was determined to create a Broadway musical adaptation of the story to showcase the talents of Lena Horne. Harold Arlen and Johnny Mercer were signed on to write music and lyrics, and Countee Cullen was hired to write the book with Bontemp. Like the novel on which it was based, *St. Louis Woman* tells the story of a successful black jockey, Li'l Augie, who falls for Della, a St. Louis belle. Della, however, is the girlfriend of Biglow Brown, an abusive black bar owner. Meanwhile, the barmaid, Butterfly, has her eye on a less-successful jockey, Barney. Complications and misunderstandings ensue, resulting in the murder of the no-good bar owner, a curse, and other gloomy events.

*God Sends Sunday*—the novel on which *St. Louis Woman* was based—was written by Arna Bontemps and is considered by many to be the final work of the Harlem Renaissance. Although the book was praised, the play proved controversial.

The production of *St. Louis Woman* was plagued by problems. Countee Cullen died before rehearsals began, the choreographer had to be replaced, and the NAACP—concerned by characters that included a violent boyfriend, gamblers, and women of easy virtue—condemned the play for featuring "roles that detract from the dignity of our race." Lena Horne agreed with the NAACP and turned down the part of the

Pearl Bailey took the stage of 1946's *St. Louis Woman* amid much controversy. The NAACP had criticized the play for including "roles that detract from the dignity of our race," and Lena Horne had turned down the part of Butterfly for that very reason. While the play received poor reviews, Bailey's Butterfly did not, and the young actress's career took off.

This cheerful scene from the often-gloomy musical *St. Louis Woman* shows characters Li'l Augie (played by Harold Nicholas) and Della (Ruby Hill) holding hands, surrounded by the cast. Another bright spot of the play was the Harold Arlen-Johnny Mercer score.

barmaid, Butterfly. Worse yet, the plot was convoluted and seemed much too bleak for a musical.

Amid African-American protestors—and with Pearl Bailey taking the part designed for Lena Horne—*St. Louis Woman* opened at the Martin Beck Theatre in March 1946, starring Bailey, Rubie Hill, Harold Nicholas, Fayard Nicholas, and Rex Ingram. The reviews were lukewarm, and the show ran for only 113 performances, but there were bright spots. One was the Harold Arlen-Johnny Mercer score, which included "Any Place I Hang My Hat Is Home" and "Come Rain or Come Shine." The other was Pearl Bailey's Broadway debut, which launched the talented actress's career. (To read more about Pearl Bailey, see the inset on page 130.)

In November 1945, the first copy of *Ebony* magazine was published—and immediately sold out at 25,000 copies. A monthly coffee-table periodical, *Ebony* was modeled after *Life* and *Look* but was designed to focus on the achievements of African Americans as a means of providing "positive images of blacks in a world of negative images."

Always an accomplished athlete, Jackie Robinson began to play baseball professionally as a member of the Negro Leagues in 1944. Then on April 15, 1947, as a member of the Brooklyn Dodgers, Robinson played at Ebbets Field, becoming the first African-American player to compete in the major leagues. That same season, he was chosen as Rookie of the Year.

## LOOKING BACK

From *Mulatto* and "Voodoo *Macbeth*" to *Porgy and Bess* and the two *Mikados*, the black Broadway shows staged between 1930 and 1949 provided the public with a dazzling array of choices. Stories of race relations helped enlighten theatergoers and spurred them to learn more about the plight and progress of African Americans. "Swinging" musicals set audiences singing and dancing while highlighting great talents like Ethel Waters, Lena Horne, Pearl Bailey, Eubie Blake, and Bill Robinson.

Some of Broadway's portrayals of African-American life were drawn by black playwrights, but many were the work of white artists. Although not all the characters in black plays were accurate reflections of real black people and their lives, clearly, a revolution was occurring as the theater slowly moved away from vaudeville stereotypes towards fleshed-out human beings. Complex story lines and integrated casts stirred up controversy and, at the same time, filled seats. Just as important, more and more of those seats were being occupied by African Americans, who were finally gaining access to Broadway entertainment.

Meanwhile, outside the theater world, the 1940s saw Benjamin Oliver Davis become the first black man to reach the rank of Commanding General, Hattie McDaniel become the first African American to win an Oscar for Supporting Actress, and Jackie Robinson become the first black player in major league baseball. Society was changing—albeit, slowly—and every aspect of American life, including the theater world, was changing with it.

Between 1930 and 1949, despite an economic depression, the New York theater provided a wide range of shows, a number of which featured great black entertainers. While some were light musicals, several plays—including *Mulatto* (1935), *Native Son* (1941), and *Deep Are the Roots* (1945)—explored subjects central to the African-American experience.

In 1948, President Harry S. Truman issued an order to desegregate the military, and also established the President's Committee on Equal Treatment and Opportunity in the Armed Services. Because there was resistance to this order within the military, full integration did not take place until the Korean War, when heavy casualties forced segregated units to merge as a means of survival.

Black entrepreneur Jesse B. Blayton, Sr. made history in 1949, when he bought the Atlanta radio station WERD, becoming the first African American to own and operate a radio station in the United States. After Blayton and his son, Jesse Blayton, Jr., developed a "black appeal" format, WERD became a great success with African-American listeners.

# STARRING
## IN ORDER OF APPEARANCE

| | |
|---|---|
| Todd Duncan | Mantan Moreland |
| Diahann Carroll | Earle Hyman |
| Pearl Bailey | Bert Chamberlain |
| Juanita Hall | Alice Childress |
| Alvin Ailey | William Blackwell |
| Arthur Mitchell | Branch |
| Geoffrey Holder | Loften Mitchell |
| Sammy Davis, Jr. | Robert Graham |
| Sammy Davis, Sr. | Brown |
| Olga James | Diana Sands |
| Lena Horne | James Earl Jones |
| Josephine Premice | Lorraine Hansberry |
| Ossie Davis | Sidney Poitier |
| Adelaide Hall | Claudia McNeil |
| Harry Belafonte | Ruby Dee |
| Ethel Waters | Louis Gossett, Jr. |
| Rex Ingram | Lloyd Richards |

# 5.

## Postwar
## Broadway
## The 1950s

Although black composers and lyricists seemed to disappear from Broadway during the 1950s, the decade brought a number of musicals that featured talented African-American performers, including one show that explored racism in South Africa. Serious dramas written by black playwrights were, for the most part, found only off-Broadway—until the end of the decade, when a groundbreaking drama found its home on the Great White Way.

Following the Second World War, America experienced a booming economy as GIs returned home to launch businesses, marry their sweethearts, purchase houses, and give birth to the Baby Boom generation. Not unlike the Roaring Twenties, which also followed a world war, the fifties were a time of optimism and enthusiasm, and society's buoyant spirit was reflected in the music, movies, and theater of the era. A popular new entertainment medium, television, had taken the country by storm, but despite the fact that Uncle Miltie and a host of other entertainers—including Ethel Waters in *The Beulah Show*—could now be viewed in the comfort of people's living rooms, Broadway enjoyed a broader-based audience than ever before. Ramped-up automobile production, new highways, and increased air travel made it easier for out-of-towners to vacation in New York City and take in the shows. It has been estimated that one third of 1950s Broadway audiences were not from New York City but from other states in the union or even abroad.

To the delight of theatergoers, the Golden Age of Musicals, which had begun in the forties, showed no sign of losing its glow. Writing teams like Richard Rodgers and Oscar Hammerstein II and choreographers like Jerome Robbins produced some of the most memorable, highly acclaimed musicals in Broadway history. These were bold productions with lavish costumes, story lines that crossed generations, and music that had

In 1950, Gwendolyn Brooks became the first African American to be awarded the Pulitzer Prize for Poetry when she won the honor for her 1949 collection *Annie Allen*. Brooks was also poet laureate of the State of Illinois, as well as the first black woman to serve as poetry consultant to the Library of Congress.

Singer and actress Juanita Hall was personally chosen by Richard Rodgers and Oscar Hammerstein II to play Bloody Mary in the 1949 Broadway production of *South Pacific*. In 1950, Hall's portrayal won her the Tony Award for Best Featured Actress in a Musical, making her the first African American to win a Tony.

America singing. Seven of these shows—*Guys and Dolls, The King and I, The Pajama Game, Damn Yankees, My Fair Lady, The Music Man*, and *The Sound of Music*—topped the 1,000-performance mark.

This was also a decade in which African-American composers and lyricists all but vanished from the Great White Way. While a number of shows featured talented black performers, the musicals themselves were almost always the work of established white songwriting teams. On the other hand, the 1950s would produce the critically acclaimed *A Raisin in the Sun* by African-American Lorraine Hansberry, as well as several other black-authored dramas, some of which made it to Broadway and some, to off-Broadway. Moreover, New York theaters would feature a number of significant African-American performers, including Alvin Ailey, Pearl Bailey, Diahann Carroll, Lena Horne, Ruby Dee, Sammy Davis, Jr., Harry Belafonte, Sidney Poitier, Louis Gossett, Jr., and James Earl Jones—dancers, singers, and actors who would remain major figures in the entertainment industry for decades to come.

## THE MUSICAL FIFTIES

Black composers and lyricists were conspicuously absent from Broadway during the fifties. Fortunately, this did not stop the rise of great African-American actors, singers, and dancers, who appeared in musicals ranging from serious social commentaries to light romantic comedies.

### Lost in the Stars

The first significant African-American musical of the fifties was *Lost in the Stars*, which technically opened in the final weeks of 1949 at the Music Box Theatre. Based on Alan Paton's 1948 novel *Cry, the Beloved Country*, the musical drama had book and lyrics by Maxwell Anderson and music by Kurt Weill. Set in Johannesburg, South Africa, *Lost in the Stars* tells the story of a black country parson who learns that his son has committed a robbery to escape a lifetime of work in the mine, and that during the crime, he accidentally killed a white man. In addition to focusing on the repentant young man, the play explores the friendship that develops between the

In 1950, Dr. Ralph Bunche became the first African American in the world to receive the Nobel Peace Prize for his work in bringing about an armistice between Arabs and Israelis. Bunche continued his diplomatic efforts for the rest of his life, always guided by a strong belief in the power of negotiation and diplomacy.

The 1950-1951 basketball season marked the appearance of the first black players in the history of the National Basketball Association. The first African American to be drafted was Chuck Cooper, when he was chosen by the Boston Celtics. Nathaniel Clifton was the first to sign a contact, and Earl Lloyd was the first to play in a regular-season game.

Based on Alan Paton's 1948 best-selling novel *Cry, the Beloved Country*, the musical *Lost in the Stars* tells the story of a black clergyman whose family is tragically affected by racial discrimination in South Africa. Todd Duncan, the original Porgy in 1935's *Porgy and Bess*, won critical acclaim for his portrayal of country parson Stephen Kumalo

parson and the victim's father, who are drawn together by the tragedy. Actor Todd Duncan, who had begun his Broadway career as Porgy in the original 1935 version of *Porgy and Bess*, took the starring role of the parson.

The reviews for *Lost in the Stars* were respectful if not entirely positive. Brooks Atkinson of *The New York Times* called the play "patchy," but also wrote that the climax was "grand and enlightening" and the music, "eloquent." He had nothing but praise for the performances of Todd Duncan and the rest of the cast, including the black choir. The original production ran for 273 performances. In the late 1950s, *Lost in the Stars* would be staged again, this time at the New York City Opera, and in 1972, it would return to Broadway for a short run at the Imperial Theatre.

On December 3, 1951, a decade after President Franklin Roosevelt outlawed discrimination in federal agencies and defense industries, President Harry S. Truman issued Executive Order 10308. By creating the Committee on Government Contract Compliance, Truman's order helped insure the compliance of federal contractors with FDR's non-discrimination provisions.

One of the greatest Supreme Court cases of the twentieth century, 1954's *Brown v. Board of Education* overturned the 1896 decision *Plessy v. Ferguson* by declaring it unconstitutional for states to establish separate public schools for black and white students. A major victory for the civil rights movement, this case paved the way for the integration of public schools.

# Diahann Carroll
# Sophisticated Lady of the Stage

Diahann Carroll's cool, elegant, sophisticated image has long set her apart from other performers and helped her enjoy decades of success in the entertainment industry. Born on July 17, 1935, Carroll grew up in New York City, where she attended a high school that specialized in the performing arts. In January 1954, when Carroll was only eighteen years of age, her career took off when she won the $1,000 grand prize on the television series *Chance of a Lifetime* with her rendition of Kern and Hammerstein's "Why Was I Born?" This led to bookings at the prestigious Latin Quarter and the Café Society nightclub, as well as a role in the film version of *Carmen Jones* (1954). That same year, the talented young actress made her Broadway debut alongside Pearl Bailey and Juanita Hall in *House of Flowers*. (For more about *House of Flowers*, see page 128.)

In 1962, Diahann Carroll won her chance to star in a major Broadway musical. After seeing her perform on *The Jack Parr Show*, Richard Rodgers asked if she would accept the female lead in his upcoming musical *No Strings*, which he was writing on his own following the death of partner Oscar Hammerstein II. It didn't take long for the talented young actress to say "yes." Progressive casting had Carroll starring opposite white actor Richard Kiley, and her performance made her the first African American to receive a Tony Award for Best Performance by a Leading Actress in a Musical.

Carroll would return to Broadway more than twenty years later in *Agnes of God* (1983). In between, she would break new ground as an African-American single mom in the television series *Julia*, which debuted in 1968. Her role—which was unusual for the time, as she played a professional rather than a domestic—won her the Golden Globe Award for Best Actress in a Television Series.

Diahann Carroll has enjoyed a long and busy career as a multifaceted performer. She has headlined in Las Vegas, acted on both the silver screen and the small screen, and recorded a number of albums, including the music of Harold Arlen and a tribute to Ethel Waters. And, of course, she has graced the Broadway stage in both dramatic plays and high-profile musicals.

Tall, slim, and elegant, with talent to spare, Diahann Carroll was a night-club performer before she made her Broadway debut in 1954's *House of Flowers*. Among Carroll's many stage credits are *No Strings* (1962), *Same Time, Next Year* (1977), and *Bubbling Brown Sugar* (2004).

# *Porgy and Bess,* Revived

When *Porgy and Bess* debuted on Broadway in 1935, the critics fired off mixed reviews, and the show ran for only 124 performances. (See page 107 for details.) But the story was very different when the folk opera returned to Broadway in 1953. Starring William Warfield as Porgy, Leontyne Price as Bess, and, in his Broadway debut, jazz musician Cab Calloway as Sportin' Life, the revival inspired *New York Times* critic Brooks Atkinson to write, "This is what a theatre classic ought to be—alive in every fiber, full of passion." Running for a total of 305 performances at the Ziegfeld Theatre, *Porgy and Bess* had become an overwhelming success nearly two decades after its premiere.

## *House of Flowers*

Among *House of Flower's* talented cast was an extraordinary group of male dancers, including Alvin Ailey, Arthur Mitchell, Geoffrey Holder, Louis Johnson, and Walter Nicks. Holder was co-choreographer on many of the dance numbers.

In 1954, Truman Capote's unconventional musical *House of Flowers*—based on one of Capote's short stories—opened at the Alvin Theatre. Harold Arlen composed the music, Capote wrote the book, and Capote and Arlen teamed up on the lyrics. The offbeat love story focuses on two competing bordellos on a Caribbean Island and the prostitute who spurns the advances of a rich man in favor of a poor local boy. One of the madams tries to thwart true love, but, of course, it wins in the end. The cast included Pearl Bailey and Juanita Hall as the two madams and Diahann Carroll as the love-sick prostitute, as well as Alvin Ailey, Carmen de Lavallade, Ray Walston, and Geoffrey Holder, who choreographed some of the dances. Both Carroll and Ailey made their stage debuts in the play.

The reviews for *House of Flowers* were mixed. Critics thought the plot was weak, but Bailey and Carroll both won raves, as did Harold Arlen's score, the costumes, and the dancing. Although the show ran for only 165 performances, one of the songs—"A Sleepin' Bee"—became a classic and was later recorded by Mel Tormé, Barbra Streisand, Tony Bennett, and many other artists.

With music by Harold Arlen, Truman Capote's *House of Flowers* (1954) ▶ featured a trade war between two competing brothel owners—Madame Tango, played by Juanita Hall, and Madam Fleur, played by Pearl Bailey. Also in the show was Diahann Carroll, who made her stage debut.

In 1954, Frankie Freeman became the first black woman to win a major civil rights case when she was lead attorney for *Davis et al. v. The St. Louis Housing Authority*, which ended racial discrimination in the city's public housing. Ten years later, Freeman would become the first black woman to serve on the U.S. Commission on Civil Rights.

On December 1, 1955, Rosa Parks refused to relinquish her seat on a Montgomery, Alabama bus to make way for a white passenger after the bus's "colored" section had been filled. When Parks was arrested, the black community protested by boycotting the bus for 381 days. Ultimately, the law requiring segregation on public buses was repealed.

SAINT SUBBER presents

# TRUMAN CAPOTE and HAROLD ARLEN'S new musical

## House of Flowers

starring PEARL BAILEY

direction
**PETER BROOK**

sets and costumes
**OLIVER MESSEL**

choreography
**GEORGE BALANCHINE**

with
| DIAHANN | JUANITA | JOSEPHINE | DINO | RAWN | JACQUES | GEOFFREY |
| CARROLL | HALL | PREMICE | DiLUCA | SPEARMAN | AUBUCHON | HOLDER |

and **FREDERICK O'NEAL**

musical director JERRY ARLEN     lighting JEAN ROSENTHAL     orchestrations TED ROYAL

# ALVIN THEATRE
52nd ST. W. of B'WAY                    MATS. WED. & SAT.

# Pearl Bailey
# Musical Star and Humorist

Pearl Bailey began her career in vaudeville and became a popular nightclub entertainer before landing her first Broadway role in *St. Louis Woman* (1946). Bailey's later stage credits include *House of Flowers* (1954) and, of course, 1967's famous all-black production of *Hello, Dolly!*

Known for a unique slurred delivery and comic touch, Pearl Bailey was a hit on Broadway, on the silver screen, and on TV, as well as in the record stores. She was, in fact, one of America's most beloved all-around entertainers.

Born on March 29, 1918 in Virginia, Pearl Mae Bailey was first drawn to music in the evangelistic church in which her father was a minister. By the time she was in her early teens, she was performing in vaudeville, and later, she danced and sang with the jazz bands of Noble Sissle, Cootie Williams, and Edgar Hayes. Bailey's relaxed stage presence and lightning-quick banter soon made her a hit with nightclub audiences as well as with the troops she entertained through the USO during World War Two.

It was shortly after the war that Bailey would land her first role on Broadway in the much-maligned musical *St. Louis Woman* (1946). While the NAACP criticized the musical for characters "that detract from the dignity of our race," Bailey drew nothing but praise for her performance. For the next several years, however, Bailey would focus greater attention on her film career, appearing in *Variety Girl* (1947), *Isn't it Romantic?* (1948), and *Carmen Jones* (1954). In 1954, she returned to the stage to star in the musical *House of Flowers*. (See page 128.)

In the sixties, Bailey mastered a new medium—television—where her wit, wisdom, and buoyant personality made her a favorite on talk and variety shows. She appeared on *The Ed Sullivan Show* twenty-three times, performing songs solo or with other entertainers, both black and white. When Ed Sullivan hugged the popular African-American performer, it's said that phones rang in TV stations all over the South.

In November 1967, Pearl Bailey's already successful career took another step forward when she accepted the role of Dolly Gallagher Levi in an all-black production of *Hello, Dolly!* Playing opposite Cab Calloway, who came out of retirement to assume the role of Horace Vandergelder, Bailey was praised by critics and audiences and recorded one of the show's three cast albums. In 1975, she returned to the stage for a revival of the musical.

In a career spanning six decades, Bailey recorded over thirty albums, including some featuring her Broadway favorites, such as *The Songs of Harold Arlen*. She also had her own television show, *The Pearl Bailey Show*, in 1971, and in 1986, she joined the cast of the long-running soap opera *As the World Turns*.

Pearl Bailey was not just a performer but also a humanitarian. She was a frequent supporter of the USO and was appointed special ambassador to the United Nations in 1975. In 1988—two years before her death—she had the honor of receiving the Presidential Medal of Freedom in recognition of exceptional meritorious service to her country.

## *Mr. Wonderful*

The year 1956 saw the debut of *Mr. Wonderful*, with original music and lyrics by Jerry Bock, Larry Holofcener, and George David Weiss, and book by Joseph Stein and Will Glickman. This tale of a struggling young entertainer named Charlie Welch was fashioned to showcase the talents of Sammy Davis, Jr. This it did quite well, letting the rising young star bring much of his Vegas act to Broadway. The play also featured Chita Rivera; Jack Carter; Olga James; Davis' father, Sammy Davis, Sr.; and Will Mastin, the performer with whom Davis and his father had worked for many years.

Debuting at the Broadway Theatre, *Mr. Wonderful* ran for 383 performances despite somewhat tepid reviews that criticized the thinness of the plot. But no one could deny the exceptional singing, dancing, and impersonations of the show's rising star.

After years of performing on stage—first, as a member of vaudeville's Will Mastin Trio; later, as a headliner in nightclubs—Sammy Davis, Jr. made his Broadway debut in 1956's *Mr. Wonderful*. He would return to Broadway in *Golden Boy* (1964), *Sammy* (1974), and *Stop the World—I Want to Get Off* (1978).

In addition to rising young star Sammy Davis, Jr., the cast of *Mr. Wonderful* included Olga James (pictured here), Chita Rivera, Jack Carter, and Davis' dad, Sammy Davis, Sr.

In the wake of Rosa Parks' arrest, Martin Luther King, Jr.—pastor of the Dexter Avenue Baptist Church in Montgomery, Alabama—was elected president of the newly established Montgomery Improvement Association in 1955. As leader of this grassroots movement to end segregation on Montgomery's buses, King would rise to national prominence.

Black opera singer Marian Anderson made inspiring headlines throughout the fifties. In 1955, she became the first black person to perform with New York's Metropolitan Opera. In 1957, she sang at the inauguration of President Dwight D. Eisenhower. And in 1958, she became a delegate to the United Nations. She would also sing at John F. Kennedy's 1961 inauguration.

## *Jamaica*

In 1957, Broadway theatergoers took a musical journey to Jamaica thanks to a score by Harold Arlen, lyrics by E.Y. Harburg—who, at the time, was blacklisted in Hollywood—and book by Harburg and Fred Saidy. *Jamaica* was originally written with Harry Belafonte in mind, but when Belafonte withdrew because of illness, the production was altered to star the lovely Lena Horne. Also featured were Ricardo Montalban, Alvin Ailey, Ossie Davis, Josephine Premice, and Adelaide Hall in her final Broadway role.

*Jamaica* tells the story of villagers who are trying to preserve their quiet life in the face of growing commercialism, and of the beautiful village woman, Savannah (Lena Horne), who dreams of escaping her small island home and moving to New York City. When the show opened at the Imperial Theatre, *Time* magazine wrote that the script was overly simplistic and the calypso-inspired score was less than memorable, but that Horne was "accomplished in a way all her own" and demonstrated "elegant sexuality." *Time* also praised the gorgeous costumes and the airy sets. *Jamaica* must have hit just the right note with audiences, as the popular musical ran for 558 performances. It also received seven Tony Award nominations, including Best Musical, Best Leading Actor (Ricardo Montalban), Best Leading Actress (Lena Horne), Best Featured Actor (Ossie Davis), Best Featured Actress (Josephine Premice), Best Costume Design (Miles White), and Best Scenic Design (Oliver Smith).

Although *Jamaica* didn't receive rave reviews, the show and several members of its cast were nominated for Tony Awards, including (left-hand photo, left to right) Lena Horne, Josephine Premice, and Ossie Davis. Premice received particular notice when *New York Times* dance critic Jennifer Dunning described her as "a razzle-dazzle lead performer who was hot flame to Horne's cool fire."

◀ *Jamaica* (1957) was originally written to showcase the talents of singer Harry Belafonte, but when Belafonte withdrew, the musical was altered for Lena Horne, who dazzled audiences with her "elegant sexuality."

# Lena Horne
# A Woman of Talent and High Ideals

During her career, Lena Horne avoided the stereotypical roles that were too often created for African-American performers. While this meant refusing at least one offer of Broadway fame, Horne stood her ground and eventually won accolades for her work in 1957's *Jamaica* and 1981's *Lena Horne: The Lady and Her Music.*

Born Lena Mary Calhoun Horne on June 30, 1917 in Brooklyn, New York, Lena Horne learned about show business at a very early age. Her mother, Edna Louise Scottron, was an actress with a black theater troupe, so throughout her childhood, Horne alternated between accompanying her mother on the road and living with family members in Georgia, New York, and Pennsylvania. When she was only sixteen years of age, the talented Horne left school and began performing in the chorus line of Harlem's famed Cotton Club. She had the good fortune to be taken under the wing of performers Cab Calloway, Duke Ellington, and Adelaide Hall, and before long, Horne was a successful singer, touring with Noble Sissle's Orchestra and bandleader Charlie Barnet.

If she had remained a nightclub performer, Lena Horne would still have ensured a name for herself in the entertainment industry, but her versatility and stunning looks led her to other venues, as well. She made her Broadway debut as "a Quadronne Girl" in 1934's short-running play *Dance with Your Gods.* She was also featured in *Lew Leslie's Blackbirds of 1939*—again, for only a short run, although she managed to catch the eye of *New York Times* reviewer Brooks Atkinson, who described her as "a radiantly beautiful sepia girl." Although the musical *St. Louis Woman* (1946) was originally conceived as a vehicle for Lena Horne, she refused the offered role, explaining that playing "a flashy lady of easy virtue" would be demeaning to her race. She did, however, accept a starring role in the 1957 hit musical *Jamaica*, for which she received a Tony nomination for Best Leading Actress. (See page 133.)

Meanwhile, Hollywood, too, had taken note of Horne's abilities. Because of her race and her refusal to play stereotypical black characters, her film roles were limited, and in some cases, her scenes were shot so that they could be easily deleted when the movies were shown in the segregated South. Nevertheless, Horne delivered noteworthy performances in the all-black musicals *Stormy Weather* (1943) and *Cabin in the Sky* (1943) and appeared in a number of other films as well, although usually in minor parts.

When her film career stagnated in the fifties, Horne once again focused on nightclub work, establishing herself as a premier performer and headlining at clubs throughout the United States, Canada, and Europe. She also began making appearances on television variety shows such as *The Ed Sullivan Show* and *The Kraft Music Show.*

Horne returned to the Broadway stage in 1981 in a musical revue entitled *Lena Horne: The Lady and Her Music.* The show—which included a variety of popular songs, jazz standards, and numbers that she had performed on the silver screen—met with overwhelming success, with *Newsweek* calling Horne "the most awesome performer to have hit Broadway in years." *The Lady and Her Music* ran for 333 performances at the Nederlander Theatre before going on tour in the United States and Canada. The musical won a special Tony Award, and the cast album, produced by Quincy Jones, won a Grammy Award.

In May 2010, Lena Horne died at the age of ninety-two. Friend and collaborator Quincy Jones said, "Lena Horne was a pioneering groundbreaker, making inroads into a world that had never before been explored by African-American women, and she did it on her own terms."

## *John Murray Anderson's Almanac*

Although Harry Belafonte wasn't able to take the stage in *Jamaica*, earlier in the decade, he not only appeared in but also garnered critical acclaim for his part in the 1953 musical revue *John Murray Anderson's Almanac*. Conceived and staged by Anderson, with most of the music created by the songwriting team of Richard Adler and Jerry Ross, the show also starred Hermione Gingold, Polly Bergen, Orson Bean, Tina Louise, Monique van Vooren, and Billy De Wolfe. After opening at the Imperial Theatre in December 1953, the *Almanac* ran for 229 performances—until June 1954. For his "Mark Twain" routine, which is said to have stopped the show, Harry Belafonte won a Tony Award for Best Featured Actor in a Musical, and he and Orson Bean both received Theatre World Awards for their outstanding performances. *New York Times* reviewer Brooks Atkinson called the show "bright and brilliant" and stated that Belafonte's "expository style as a singer and actor makes it [the Mark Twain piece] the *Almanac's* high point in theatrical artistry."

A musical revue, *John Murray Anderson's Almanac* (1953) featured Harry Belafonte as well as Hermione Gingold, Polly Bergen, Orson Bean, Tina Louise, Monique van Vooren, and Billy DeWolfe. Belafonte's "Mark Twain" routine garnered him a Tony Award for Best Featured Actor in a Musical.

## THE DRAMAS OF THE FIFTIES

After the end of the Second World War, most Americans were enjoying greater opportunity than ever before. The Depression was over, and returning GIs were provided with money towards training and education as well as guaranteed home and business loans. But many black Americans did not have the same bright prospects—especially those living in the South, where segregation was the rule in residential communities and schools. For this reason, throughout the fifties and continuing into the sixties, the African-American community focused on making strides against racial inequality and segregation. Following a three-year battle, with the support of the local NAACP, *Brown v. Board of Education* made its way to the Supreme Court, and in May 17, 1954, there was a unanimous decision that the Topeka Board of Education's policy of segregation violated the Equal Protection Clause of the United States Constitution. The next year, Rosa Parks refused to surrender her seat to a white passenger on a bus in Montgomery, Alabama, sparking a year-long Montgomery Bus Boycott. In the end, the Supreme Court ruled that segregated buses were unconstitutional. This victory inspired Martin Luther King, Jr. to start the Southern Christian Leadership Conference (SCLC), which he organized to fight for further civil rights.

On February 25, 1956, Senator Harry F. Byrd, Sr. of Virginia declared Massive Resistance, a group of laws intended to prevent the integration of schools. The linchpin of Byrd's strategy was a law that closed any public schools that took steps to integrate. Although this was declared unconstitutional, Virginia schools remained segregated for many years.

The Southern Manifesto, drafted by Strom Thurmond and signed in 1956, condemned the 1954 Supreme Court decision *Brown v. Board of Education*. To block school integration, politicians from Alabama, Arkansas, Florida, Georgia, Louisiana, Mississippi, North Carolina, South Carolina, Tennessee, Texas, and Virginia signed the resolution, calling the *Brown* decision a "clear abuse of judicial power."

# Juanita Hall
# A Musical Star Who Made Broadway History

Juanita Hall made her Broadway debut in 1930's *Green Pastures*. While also featured in *St. Louis Woman* (1946) and *House of Flowers* (1954), Hall is best known for her portrayal of Bloody Mary in 1949's *South Pacific* and Madam Liang in 1958's *Flower Drum Song*.

Juanita Hall is perhaps best remembered by today's audiences as Bloody Mary in the film version of *South Pacific.* But Hall began her musical career in singing and choir directing, and as many theater buffs know, she also made Broadway history.

Juanita Long was born in New Jersey on November 6, 1901. Her father, Abram Long, was African American, and her mother, Mary Richardson, was Irish American. She became Juanita Long Hall after marrying Clement Hall.

Hall attended the Julliard School of music in New York, and spent her early career directing the Works Progress Administration Chorus, the Westchester Chorale and Dramatics Association, and the Juanita Hall Choir, which performed in the 1948 film *Miracle in Harlem.* At the same time, Hall's Broadway career began to blossom as she took roles in *Deep Are the Roots* (1945 ) and *St. Louis Woman* (1946). But her big break came in 1949, when, as a leading actress of her day, Hall was personally chosen by Richard Rodgers and Oscar Hammerstein II to portray Bloody Mary in the Broadway musical *South Pacific.* Hall would go on to play Bloody Mary for more than 1,900 performances, and in 1950, her portrayal garnered her the 1950 Tony Award for Best Featured Actress in a Musical, making her the first African American to win a Tony.

With her career going strong, in 1954, Hall accepted the role of a brothel keeper in *House of Flowers*, working with Pearl Bailey and Diahann Carroll. Then in 1958, she rejoined Rodgers and Hammerstein to take the role of Madam Liang in the 1958 hit *Flower Drum Song.* Hall was also chosen to reprise both her *South Pacific* and *Flower Drum Song* roles in major film adaptations of the popular musicals.

Although *Flower Drum Song* was to be Juanita Hall's last Broadway production, she did not retire from show business. Throughout the fifties and early sixties, she appeared on television programs such as *The Perry Como Show* and *The Ed Sullivan Show.* In 1957, she recorded *Juanita Hall Sings the Blues* backed by an impressive group of jazz musicians, including Coleman Hawkins on tenor sax, Buster Bailey on clarinet, and Jimmy Crawford on drums. While this may have surprised many people, Hall had begun her career in singing, and she never lost her interest in vocal music. After her death in 1968, composer and jazz pianist Leonard Feather praised the talented performer as "an expert student and practitioner in the art of singing the blues." But lovers of Broadway will always remember Juanita Hall for her contributions to the musical-comedy stage.

On November 13, 1956, the U.S. Supreme Court upheld a district court's ruling (*Browder v. Gayle*) that the ordinances requiring segregated buses in Montgomery, Alabama were unconstitutional. Along with the 1954 case *Brown v. Board of Education*, this decision was one of the precedents used to end segregation in the United States.

In 1956, popular singer Nat King Cole made history when he became the first African American to host a prime time variety show on national television. Named *The Nat King Cole Show*, it was cancelled after fourteen months because of struggling ratings and a lack of national sponsors willing to support a program hosted by a black performer.

While important victories were being won by black activists, the concerns of black Americans did not immediately translate into Broadway productions that explored serious black issues. Theater owners and producers were not sure how audiences would react to black shows, so they stuck with proven commodities—lavish musicals, most of them with white casts. Other than star vehicles written for major box office draws like Lena Horne and Sammy Davis, Jr., there was a dearth of major roles for black performers, and those roles that were available were not always attractive to African-American performers who were dedicated to social reform.

Exemplifying the situation was the Critics' Circle Award-winning play *The Member of the Wedding* (1950), based on the novel by Carson McCullers. The story focuses on a lonesome, alienated twelve-year-old girl, Frankie, and her relationship with her African-American maid/mammy, Berenice. Played by Ethel Waters in the original production, Berenice serves as a surrogate mother to both Frankie and her six-year-old cousin, John Henry. Although Waters drew critical acclaim and the show ran for over 500 performances, the stereotypical role of a servant was not one that would advance the progress of African Americans in the theater.

Fortunately, off-Broadway theater, less concerned with staging blockbusters, was willing to take on some of the issues that big-budget producers were ignoring. And at the end of the decade, the Great White Way would present *A Raisin in the Sun*—a black play that was not only of social significance, but also of high quality.

Between 1910 and 1920, off-Broadway theaters like the Provincetown Playhouse began cropping up to promote experimental works. By the 1950s, these smaller theaters had become more numerous, and they served as attractive venues for black playwrights whose dramas weren't considered commercial enough for pricey Broadway theaters.

Ethel Waters won critical praise for her portrayal of maid and surrogate mother Berenice Sadie Brown in 1950's *The Member of the Wedding*. Here she is shown with costars Julie Harris (left) and Brandon De Wilde (right).

During the battle for black rights in the 1950s and 1960s, the Alabama Christian Movement for Human Rights (ACMHR) was the most important civil rights organization in Birmingham, Alabama. Formed in 1956 by pastor Fred Shuttlesworth, the ACMHR organized bus boycotts, sit-ins, and other forms of protest.

Alice Childress worked at the American Negro Theatre (ANT) as an actress, director, and drama coach before she began writing plays. In 1956, *Trouble in Mind*, the playwright's first full-length drama, won an Obie Award for the best original off-Broadway show, making Childress the first African-American woman to win an Obie.

# Waiting for Godot

Samuel Beckett's "Theater of the Absurd" play *Waiting for Godot* premiered in Paris in 1953, and was first seen by American audiences at Florida's Coconut Grove Playhouse in 1956. Then in 1957, an all-black production of the tragicomedy was produced in Boston before being transferred to Broadway. During a decade when few nonmusicals with black casts would appear on the Great White Way, *Godot* opened at the Ethel Barrymore Theatre on January 21, 1957. The production featured Rex Ingram, Mantan Moreland, Earle Hyman, Bert Chamberlain, and—in his second Broadway appearance—Geoffrey Holder. Six performances were given before the run ended on January 26.

## Off-Broadway

Alice Childress began her career as an actress in the 1940s, but her dissatisfaction with the stereotypic roles offered to African Americans inspired her to write plays instead of acting in them. Her 1955 play-within-a-play *Trouble in Mind* was designed to explore racism in the theater by giving audiences a peek at the inner workings of a production that has a black cast but was written and produced by whites.

During the fifties, New York's off-Broadway theaters teemed with plays written by talented African-American writers. Although both the audience and the runs were often small, this didn't stop the playwrights from receiving attention, nor did it stop the productions from making important statements regarding society's treatment of blacks and even about black theater itself.

Alice Childress began her career as an actress, but soon grew tired of being cast in stereotypical black roles, so she turned her hand to writing plays. Her drama *Trouble in Mind* opened in November 1955 at the Greenwich Mews Theatre. A play-within-a-play, it centers on the troubled production of a fictional anti-lynching show called *Chaos in Belleville*, which has been written and produced by whites, but includes a mostly black cast. Well-meaning but patronizing, *Chaos* leads to feuds between various members of the cast, as well as the cast and the director, as the black actors rebel against a script that doesn't accurately represent them or their culture.

*Trouble* allowed Childress to address the disparity between plays that were written by white playwrights about blacks and met with great success, and works that were written by black playwrights yet received far less attention. But the production of *Trouble*, too, had its troubles, including script problems and difficulty with the director. Although it ran for only 91 performances, the play was praised by both audiences and critics and won the 1956 Obie Award for the best original off-Broadway show, making Childress the first African-American woman to win an Obie.

When President Dwight D. Eisenhower signed into law the Civil Rights Act of 1957, it marked the first time since Reconstruction that the Federal Government had taken steps to prevent discriminatory practices. Although the final legislation was watered down and not effective, it began a series of government actions designed to protect voters' rights.

In 1957, school officials in Little Rock, Arkansas took steps to integrate all-white Central High School by accepting nine black students. When Governor Orval Faubus used the Arkansas National Guard to prevent the children from entering Central High, President Dwight D. Eisenhower dispatched army troops to ensure that the "Little Rock Nine" gained admittance.

Other significant off-Broadway plays of the era included two dramas by young African-American playwright William Blackwell Branch. The first, *A Medal for Willie*, was produced in 1951 by the Committee for the Negro in Arts, at Harlem's Club Baron. The play explores a southern town that is willing to honor an African-American soldier after he is killed in the Second World War, but had no regard for him or his family during the soldier's lifetime. As the play takes the audience through the day in which the town pays tribute to Corporal Willie Brown, we learn who Willie was and how the community caused him pain—and, ultimately, caused his death.

The opening-night audience responded enthusiastically to *A Medal for Willie*. Ironically, Branch could not enjoy his success, for the next morning, he was inducted into the Army.

*In Splendid Error* was written by William Branch while he served in the military in the early 1950s. Set a century earlier, it recounts the discussions between former slave and social reformer Frederick Douglass and white abolitionist John Brown. The play opened at the Greenwich Mews Theatre in October 1954 and ran for four months despite mixed reviews.

Among the most topical off-Broadway plays of the time was Loften Mitchell's *A Land Beyond the River*. The 1957 drama tells the real-life story of Reverend Joseph A. DeLaine, whose battle for desegregation of a southern school evolved into the landmark court case *Brown v. Board of Education*. Robert Graham Brown played the leading role, and Diana Sands—who would later go on to roles in nine Broadway shows, including *A Raisin in the Sun*—was featured in the cast. After a long run at the Greenwich Mews Theatre, *A Land Beyond the River* was published as a book.

After studying screenwriting at the Yale School of Drama and briefly performing as an actor, William Blackwell Branch became convinced that only African Americans could write theater about and for people of color. Eventually, he would write several plays, including *A Medal for Willie* (1951) and *In Splendid Error* (1954).

## Sunrise at Campobello

Dore Schary's drama *Sunrise at Campobello* debuted at the Cort Theatre in January 1958, and ran for over 550 performances. Its riveting story focused on Franklin Delano Roosevelt's struggle with polio at his family's summer home on Campobello Island in New Brunswick, Canada. Along with Ralph Bellamy's Tony Award-winning performance as FDR, the play is noteworthy because it marked the debut of a young actor from Arkabutla, Mississippi named James Earl Jones. While this was just the starting point for Jones' phenomenal career, it did provide him with the opportunity to meet two important audience members—Eleanor Roosevelt and Harry Truman.

Inspired by the Montgomery bus boycott, in 1957, Martin Luther King, Jr. invited southern black ministers to join together and coordinate the action of local protest groups. The result was the Southern Christian Leadership Conference (SCLC), which would help lay the groundwork for the Civil Rights Act of 1964 and the Voting Rights Act of 1965.

Referred to as the "Jackie Robinson of ice hockey," Canadian-born Willie O'Ree broke the black color barrier in the sport in 1958, when he replaced an injured player on the Boston Bruins. O'Ree's NHL debut received little publicity, and there would be no other black players in the NHL until Mike Marson was drafted by the Washington Capitals in 1974.

PHILIP ROSE and DAVID J. COGAN present

# SIDNEY POITIER

# a raisin in the sun

A new play by LORRAINE HANSBERRY

with

## CLAUDIA McNEIL    RUBY DEE
## LOUIS GOSSETT    DIANA SANDS

JOHN FIEDLER    IVAN DIXON

Directed by LLOYD RICHARDS
Designed and Lighted by RALPH ALSWANG
Costumes by VIRGINIA VOLLAND

# BARRYMORE THEATRE

47th STREET WEST OF BROADWAY    MATS. WED. & SAT.

Printed by Artcraft Litho. & Ptg. Co., Inc., N.Y.C.    491

## *A Raisin in the Sun*

When Lorraine Hansberry's *A Raisin in the Sun* opened on March 11, 1959 at the Ethel Barrymore Theatre, it became the first play written by an African-American woman to make it to Broadway, as well as the first play directed by a black man. For African Americans, this meant that the decade of theater would end on a triumphant note, with a stellar cast in a critically acclaimed drama that would become a modern classic. The play also served as a much-needed reminder of how power- ful theater could be when exploring issues that divide a nation, such as racial discrimination.

Set after the Second World War but before 1959—a piv- otal time when African Americans were just beginning to address the problem of racial inequality—*A Raisin in the Sun* tells the story of the Youngers, a black working-class family living in close quarters in a Chicago tenement. When the family gets a large check from a life insurance policy, they have a chance at a new beginning, but different family members have different plans for the money. Lena, the matriarch, wants to move to a larger house in a white neigh- borhood despite the segregationist attitude of the area. Beneatha, Lena's bright and ambitious daughter, yearns for tuition to go to medical school. A woman ahead of her time, Beneatha also embraces her African-American heritage. Walter, Lena's married son, wants to use the money as a down payment on a liquor store. His wife, Ruth, has no spe- cific plans for the money; she just wants to see her family happy, and she works both in her own home and in other people's homes to give her husband and their son, Travis, what they need.

First-time producer Philip Rose had trouble finding fund- ing for the show. An old friend of Hansberry and a former record company executive, he believed in the play, but because of the black cast and the subject matter, *A Raisin in the Sun* was considered a risky venture at a time when audiences were pre- dominantly white. It took Rose a year to raise the money for the initial tour. Fortunately, the play toured to positive notices, which were due in no small part to the cast. Claudia McNeil, who played matriarch Lena Younger, was new to Broadway audiences but was not a novice per- former. She had sung in both vaudeville and nightclubs, and had acted in Langston Hughes' play *Simply Heavenly* (1957). Diana Sands (Beneatha Younger), had already appeared in several plays, including classics like

When *A Raisin in the Sun* opened in 1959, Sidney Poitier had already appeared in the plays *Lysistrata* (1946) and *Anna Lucasta* (1947), and his performance in the 1950 film *No Way Out* had garnered him both notice and further movie offers. With audiences eager to see more of the actor, Poitier could now choose among leading roles on the stage and screen.

◀ First-time producer Philip Rose had trouble getting financial backing for *A Raisin in the Sun*, because nobody thought that a black drama could succeed. Yet this glimpse into the life of African Americans packed theaters for well over 500 performances, attracting both white and black theatergoers.

George Bernard Shaw's *Major Barbara*. Sidney Poitier (Walter Younger), had received training at the American Negro Theatre, and had appeared in productions of *Anna Lucasta* and *Lysistrata*, as well as in films such as 1950's *No Way Out*. Like Poitier, Ruby Dee (Ruth Younger) had begun her training at the American Negro Theatre and had performed in *Anna Lucasta*, as well as other Broadway shows. Louis Gossett, Jr. (George Murchison, one of Beneatha's suitors), had landed his first role at the age of sixteen, when he was given the lead in the Broadway play *Take a Giant Step*. The cast members were not equally experienced, but they were all immensely talented.

When it finally opened at the Ethel Barrymore Theatre, *A Raisin in the Sun* was a success. The audience was wildly enthusiastic, and the critics were full of praise. Hailed as a watershed in American drama—*The New York Times* stated that it "changed American history forever"—it won the New York Drama Critic's Award as Best Play of the Year and garnered four Tony Award nominations, including Best Play, Best Actor in a Play (Sidney Poitier), Best Actress in a Play (Claudia McNeil), and Best Direction of a Play (Lloyd Richards). The show ran for 530 performances, first at the Barrymore and then at the Belasco Theatre, both of which had seating capacities of more than 1,000 people. Besides giving white audiences a glimpse into the true lives of black Americans, *A Raisin in the Sun* was noteworthy for drawing a new audience to Broadway, for black people finally had a play that accurately represented their lives, their hopes, and their dreams.

Lorraine Hansberry's masterpiece was so popular that within two years, a film version was released featuring most of the original Broadway cast. This led to Golden Globe Award nominations for both Sidney Poitier and Claudia McNeil. The play has been translated into thirty languages and has been continually staged in school auditoriums, community centers, church basements, and professional theaters. In 1973, it was transformed into the Tony Award-winning musical *Raisin*, and in both 2004 and 2014, it was again produced as a Broadway drama.

The success of *A Raisin in the Sun* was due not only to the talents of playwright Lorraine Hansberry, but also to its marvelous cast, which included (top photo, left to right) Sidney Poitier, Claudia McNeil, Ruby Dee, Glynn Turman, and Diana Sands. Louis Gossett, Jr. was also in the original production.

# Lorraine Hansberry
# Groundbreaking Playwright & Activist

Born on May 19, 1930, Lorraine Hansberry grew up in Chicago during the Great Depression, but was fortunate to have a family that was financially successful, educated, and politically aware. Her father was a real-estate broker; her mother, a school teacher and, later, a ward committeewoman; and her uncle, a professor at Howard University. Family friends included W.E.B. DuBois, Paul Robeson, and Langston Hughes.

After graduating from high school, Hansberry enrolled in the University of Wisconsin, but left after two years to become a writer. In 1950, she moved to New York City and got a job working for *Freedom*, the newspaper that Robeson helped found. This put her in the middle of Harlem's cultural and political life, and Hansberry not only wrote articles but also read widely on black history, politics, philosophy, and the arts.

When Hansberry was in her mid-twenties, she began working on *A Raisin in the Sun,* a play that was influenced greatly by her personal experiences. Like the families that had rented her father's properties in Chicago, the Youngers are struggling members of the working class. Like her own family, they will face discrimination when they move to a white neighborhood in an effort to better their lives. The play also reflects Hansberry's interest in issues such as women's liberation and black pride.

After the success of *A Raisin in the Sun,* the young playwright was in demand as a public speaker, and she lectured on civil rights as well as other significant political issues of the time. She also worked on several plays. *The Sign in Sidney Brustein's Window* premiered on Broadway in 1964, but it had only a short run, during which Hansberry battled pancreatic cancer. She died in January 1965, leaving a number of finished and unfinished works. These works have continued to live on through her husband, Robert Nemiroff, and through political activists who committed themselves to making Lorraine Hansberry's progressive political and social views known to future generations.

**Lorraine Hansberry was in her mid-twenties when she began writing *A Raisin in the Sun*. She based the story on her family's experience of racial discrimination after moving to an all-white Chicago neighborhood. This harrowing episode—as well as contact with activists Paul Robeson, Langston Hughes, and W.E.B DuBois—helped transform Hansberry into a dedicated civil rights advocate.**

Founded in 1958, the Alvin Ailey American Dance Theater, a repertory company of African-American dancers, soon was recognized as the preeminent black dance group in the country. At first, all performers were African Americans, many of whom had faced discrimination elsewhere in the industry. In 1963, the troupe would become racially integrated.

In 1958, at the very first Grammy Awards, Ella Fitzgerald became the first African-American woman to win a Grammy when she took home the awards for Best Female Vocal Performance and Best Individual Jazz Performance. That same year, Count Basie became the first black man to win a Grammy when he garnered the award for Best Group Jazz Performance.

# What Happened to the Cast of *A Raisin in the Sun?*

Part of what made *A Raisin in the Sun* such an overwhelming success was the original 1959 cast. In turn, the highly acclaimed play focused the public's attention on the performers, many of whom went on to have long and impressive careers.

After the Broadway run of *A Raisin in the Sun,* Claudia McNeil (Lena Younger)—like most of the original cast—reprised her role in the 1961 film adaptation. *The New York Times* said that McNeil had a "commanding presence" and was "solid, voluminous, and serene as a mother trying to control her son (played by Sidney Poiter) and wanting to buy her family a respectable home." In later years, McNeil appeared in a number of films, such as *The Last Angry Man* (1959) and *Black Girl* (1972); starred in plays such as James Baldwin's *The Amen Corner* (1965); and performed in TV miniseries such as *Roots: The Next Generations* (1979). Yet she was always best remembered as the matriarch in Lorraine Hansberry's enduring drama.

*A Raisin in the Sun* was Sidney Poitier's (Walter Younger) most significant Broadway role, but by the time the play hit New York, the actor's film career had already been launched. Poitier would become one of the most prominent screen actors of the twentieth century, starring in more than forty films, including *Blackboard Jungle* (1955), *Porgy and Bess* (1959), *The Defiant Ones* (1959), *Lilies of the Field* (1963), *A Patch of Blue* (1965), *To Sir With Love* (1967), *In the Heat of the Night* (1967), and *Guess Who's Coming to Dinner* (1967). His role in *Lilies of the Field* won him an Oscar, making him the first black actor to receive the Academy Award for Best Actor in a Leading Role.

In 1961, the same year that Ruby Dee (Ruth Younger) appeared in the film version of *A Raisin in the Sun*, she joined husband Ossie Davis in the play *Purlie Victorious,* which Davis had written. In 1963, the pair reprised their roles for the silver screen. Throughout the sixties, seventies, and eighties, Dee played numerous parts on stage, in films, and on television. In 1979, she received an Emmy nomination for her role in *Roots: The Next Generations,* and in 1991, she won an Emmy for her work on the television movie *Decoration Day.* Her career spanned more than fifty years.

The role of Beneatha Younger marked Diana Sands' Broadway debut. Sands would appear in seven more Broadway plays throughout the 1960s, including the two-person hit comedy *The Owl and the Pussycat* (1964), in which she costarred with Alan Alda. For her role as Doris W., the part-time prostitute, she received a Tony Award nomination for Best Actress in a Leading Role. One of the fastest-rising stars of the 1960s, Sands also appeared in film and television productions throughout the decade, earning two Emmy Award nominations. Sadly, the talented actress passed away in 1973 at the young age of thirty-nine.

After his watershed role in *A Raisin in the Sun*, Louis Gossett, Jr. would move on to a half-dozen Broadway roles, including the highly successful musical version of Clifford Odets' *Golden Boy* (1964) with Sammy Davis, Jr. After his screen debut in the 1961 film adaptation of *A Raisin in the Sun*, he would appear in over 150 film and television roles. He is perhaps best known for his Emmy-winning role in the 1977 miniseries *Roots*, and for his Academy Award-winning role as the demanding drill sergeant in 1982's *An Officer and a Gentleman.*

# LOOKING BACK AT THE FIFTIES

During most of the fifties, Broadway seemed unwilling to take a chance on black playwrights and composers, opting instead for both musicals and dramas created by white artists. Despite this, many great black musical actors and actresses took the stage, and some won awards for their brilliant performances. Pearl Bailey, Diahann Carroll, Juanita Hall, Lena Horne, Harry Belafonte, and Sammy Davis, Jr. are just a few of the artists who captivated both critics and theatergoers during this tuneful decade. At the same time, black dramatic playwrights found greater opportunities in off-Broadway theaters. There, a number of fine African-American dramas were presented throughout the decade, and each one—from *Trouble in Mind* to *Land Beyond the River*—raised issues that were important to the black community.

Then, just a few months before the end of the fifties, *A Raisin in the Sun* opened at the Ethel Barrymore Theatre. This landmark play—brilliantly written, beautifully acted, and wildly successful—demonstrated that a Broadway production could deal seriously with racial problems and still be popular with both black and white audiences. African-American playwrights and performers had made great strides, as had New York theatergoers, who now accepted black casts, mixed-race casts, and integrated audiences. Despite these significant changes, as the sixties dawned, few could imagine the cultural and political turmoil that lay ahead and the many ways it would affect the American theater.

Considered an American classic, Lorraine Hansberry's *A Raisin in the Sun* has been produced many times and in many forms since its 1959 debut. A film version was released in 1961, and *Raisin*—a musical adaptation—premiered in 1973. In 1989, a made-for-TV movie aired, and Tony Award-winning revivals of the original drama ran on Broadway in 2004 and 2014.

The Motown Record Company was established in January 1959 by songwriter Berry Gordy, Jr. The most successful black owned and operated record company in the country, Motown— with its distinctive and much-imitated Motown Sound—would launch the careers of countless artists and bring black music into the homes of white Americans.

On March 11, 1959, Lorraine Hansberry's *A Raisin in the Sun* opened at the Ethel Barrymore Theatre, becoming the first play written by an African-American woman to land on Broadway. A resounding success, the black-centered drama garnered several Tony Award nominations and drew substantial numbers of black theatergoers to the Great White Way.

# STARRING
## IN ORDER OF
## APPEARANCE

| | |
|---|---|
| Diahann Carroll | Ben Vereen |
| Langston Hughes | James Earl Jones |
| Ossie Davis | Louis Gossett, Jr. |
| Helen Martin | Cicely Tyson |
| Godfrey Cambridge | Maya Angelou |
| Ruby Dee | Roscoe Lee Browne |
| Beah Richards | LeRoi Jones |
| Sammy Davis, Jr. | (Amiri Baraka) |
| Leslie Uggams | Robert Hooks |
| Lillian Hayman | James Baldwin |
| Diana Sands | Al Freeman, Jr. |
| Pearl Bailey | Rosetta LeNoire |
| Cab Calloway | Douglas Turner Ward |
| Billy Daniels | Lonne Elder |
| Morgan Freeman | Joseph A. Walker |
| Melba Moore | Charles Fuller |
| Leata Galloway | Charles Gordone |

# 6.
## The Turbulent Sixties

Throughout the sixties, New York theater reflected the sweeping social changes of the decade not only through the themes it explored—including racism and civil rights—but also through inventive staging and nontraditional casting.

In the 1950s, black playwrights and performers had made lasting changes in the theater world. Now, many Broadway theatergoers more than accepted black themes and African-American actors; they welcomed them. During the sixties—a tumultuous decade that saw the rise of the antiwar movement, the hippy counterculture, the Greensboro sit-ins, and Dr. Martin Luther King Jr.'s "I Have a Dream" speech—black theater would undergo further transformation, especially in the less-commercial venues of off-Broadway. No longer would African-American-written dramas simply reflect the racial problems of the times. Increasingly, their unflinching portrayals of a racist society would demand reform. Moreover, beginning in the mid- to late sixties, new black theater companies such as the Black Arts Repertory Theatre would emerge to ensure that the voice of African-American artists would be heard.

Of course, even in a decade of protest and reform, the New York theater was not all about political and social change. Broadway is, in large part, about business, and musicals—while costly to produce and involving great risk—are generally the most profitable of the industry's business ventures. Fortunately, many musicals would feature great African-American performers, and some, like *Golden Boy* and *Hallelujah, Baby!*, would even focus on black subjects. At the same time, the sixties' atmosphere of change was infectious and would be reflected in a number of Broadway's musical offerings.

In February 1960, four students from the Agricultural and Technical College of North Carolina sat down at the "whites-only" lunch counter of their local Woolworth store. When the students asked to be served and were refused, they launched a protest that would inspire demonstrations throughout the South.

President Dwight Eisenhower signed the Civil Rights Act of 1960 in May of that year. The second piece of federal civil rights legislation of the twentieth century, it was aimed at increasing protection for African Americans at the polls. Like the Civil Rights Act of 1957, this act had little effect but helped pave the way for stronger legislation that was to come.

# BREAKING THE RULES IN MUSICALS AND COMEDIES

If 1960s Broadway musicals and comedies could be characterized by any trend, it would be a movement toward unconventional productions and nontraditional casting. Writers, composers, and directors were ready to experiment, and New York audiences were eager to embrace change.

## *No Strings*

Richard Rodgers' *No Strings* exemplified the concepts of both nontraditional staging and inventive casting. The orchestra was shifted backstage, and several musicians were brought onstage to accompany the performers. In keeping with the name of the show, the string section was removed from the orchestra. Cast members moved props and scenery in full view of the audience. But these were minor modifications compared with the casting of Diahann Carroll and Richard Kiley as a biracial couple at a time when year-long protests were needed simply to integrate buses in the South.

Like many of the plays produced in the 1960s, *No Strings* was unconventional in a number of ways. Instead of the orchestra playing in a pit, it was largely situated backstage. Instead of scenery being shifted by a stage crew, cast members moved it in full view of the audience. But most daring for the year 1962 was that the musical centered on a biracial couple.

The script of *No Strings* makes no mention of race, and the plot in no way implies a biracial relationship. But after seeing Diahann Carroll perform on television, Richard Rodgers—who wrote both the lyrics and music for the show—decided to build a play around the lovely and talented young actress. Richard Kiley was later chosen to play opposite Carroll.

One of the most experienced individuals to ever work on Broadway, Richard Rodgers assembled a remarkable team for *No Strings*. This photo, taken during rehearsals, shows (from left to right) actress Diahann Carroll, composer and lyricist Richard Rodgers, writer Samuel A. Taylor, and actor Richard Kiley.

The 1962 musical *No Strings* tells the story of a fashion model named Barbara Woodruff (Carroll) who meets and falls in love with an expatriate writer named David Jordan (Kiley) while in Paris. After a brief romance, the two realize that they must part—with "no strings" attached. Although *No Strings* didn't address racial issues, it generated controversy simply by pairing a black woman with a white man. Rodgers made it clear that the story was about the couple's relationship and not about race, but when Carroll and Kiley left the show, they were replaced by another interracial couple, Barbara McNair and Howard Keel. Despite the initial commotion, or perhaps because of it, *No Strings* became a major box office hit, running for 580 performances before heading out on national tour. It garnered three Tony Awards: Best Performance by a Leading Actress in a Musical (Carroll), Best Score (Rodgers), and Best Choreography (Joe Layton). Richard Rodgers also won a Special Award for all his achievements in theater.

In 1960, six-year-old Ruby Bridges became the first black child to attend an all-white elementary school in the South. Surrounded by federal marshals, Ruby entered William Frantz Elementary School in New Orleans, Louisiana on November 14. Her experience was captured by the Norman Rockwell painting *The Problem We All Live With*, which appeared in *Look* magazine in 1964.

At the end of 1960, in *Boynton v. Virginia*, the Supreme Court ruled that passengers traveling from one state to another on bus or rail should be served without discrimination or segregation. Although this was an important step in the civil rights movement, it would soon become apparent that the law was not being enforced in the Deep South.

# Black Nativity
# A Holiday Tradition

The holiday season of 1961 marked the off-Broadway debut of Langston Hughes' *Black Nativity,* a retelling of the Christmas story from an Afrocentric perspective. Hughes called the show a "Gospel-Song Play" because it combined black spirituals and original songs with narration about the birth of Jesus Christ. The show opened in December at New York City's Forty-First Street Theatre and ran for 57 performances.

For more than half a century, Hughes' exuberant celebration of music, dance, and Scriptures has been presented in various locations around the country. The National Center of Afro-American Artists in Boston, Massachusetts has staged the show annually since 1969, and theaters in Atlanta, Columbus, Chicago, Seattle, and Washington, DC, bring the show back seasonally. Universities, schools, and churches, as well, offer the holiday classic.

In 2004, a long-overdue gospel Christmas album entitled *Black Nativity—In Concert: A Gospel Celebration* was recorded at the Immanuel Baptist Church in Portland, Maine. To nobody's surprise, it was a bestseller.

Premiering in 1961 at off-Broadway's Forty-First Street Theatre, *Black Nativity*—Langston Hughes' retelling of the Christmas story with a black perspective—is now presented annually all across America.

Playwright/actor Ossie Davis wrote the comedy *Purlie Victorious* "to point a mocking finger at racial segregation and laugh it out of existence." While the show didn't achieve Davis's ambitious goal, it was highly popular—so popular that it would eventually give birth to a film adaptation (1963) as well as the hit musical *Purlie* (1970).

## *Purlie Victorious*

Like many other theater professionals of the time, Ossie Davis broke the rules when he decided that instead of approaching the serious topic of racial inequality in a dramatic manner, he would write and star in a comical presentation. In Davis's words, "The purpose of *Purlie Victorious* is to point a mocking finger at racial segregation and laugh it out of existence."

Premiering at the Cort Theatre in September 1961, the play tells the story of the flamboyant self-ordained preacher Purlie (Ossie Davis) who, accompanied by the lovely Lutiebelle (Ruby Dee), returns to Georgia to claim an inheritance from the ruthless plantation owner (Sorrell Brooke) he once served. Purlie wants the money to open his own church. Although the initial plan goes awry, with some help from the plantation owner's son, Charlie—played by Alan Alda in his breakthrough Broadway role—Purlie emerges victorious. Godfrey Cambridge and Beah Richards were also featured in the show, and Cambridge's performance garnered a Tony Award nomination.

While *Purlie Victorious* did not knock racial prejudice out of existence, the popular show was an innovative, humorous attack on bigotry at a time when the civil rights movement was in full swing. It ran for 261 performances. In 1963, a film version was made with most of the original cast, and in 1970, a musical version called *Purlie* opened on Broadway to great critical acclaim.

Ossie Davis assembled a fabulous cast for 1961's *Purlie Victorious*. Here, we see (from left to right) Ossie Davis, Helen Martin, Godfrey Cambridge, Ruby Dee, Beah Richards, and Sorrell Booke. The play also featured Alan Alda in his breakthrough Broadway role.

Worlds apart from the relatively lightweight musicals of the season, *Golden Boy* tackled tough issues such as racial discrimination. Dr. Martin Luther King, Jr., who saw the show soon after it opened, praised the production's unflinching picture of black life in America.

## Golden Boy

In 1964, as the civil rights movement was reaching its peak, another important play was made into a musical. An adaptation of a 1938 Clifford Odets drama, *Golden Boy* featured the music of Charles Strouse and the lyrics of Lee Adams. Originally, Odets had planned to write the book for the musical, but his death in August 1963 halted production until William Gibson, who had penned the stage version of *The Miracle Worker*, stepped in to finish the job.

Although the original drama—also called *Golden Boy*—had an Italian-American protagonist, the revamped plot told the story of a young black man named Joe Wellington, who escapes ghetto life through prizefighting and, in the process, loses his soul and, ultimately, his life. Included in the story line is an interracial romance. Sammy Davis, Jr., played the title role, and the cast also featured Louis Gossett, Jr., Billy Daniels, Paula Wayne, and a twenty-year-old newcomer named Lola Falana.

*Golden Boy* opened in October 1964 at the Majestic Theatre. Davis carried a heavy load, singing nine songs and making his way through a carefully choreographed prizefight. He was also the target of death threats because of his on-stage kiss with Paula Wayne, who took the role of his white mistress. Add to this the show's serious subject matter and urban jazz score, and it's easy to see that *Golden Boy* was a far cry from the other musical offerings of the season, like *Hello, Dolly!* and *Funny Girl*. Yet it became one of the biggest hits of 1964, running for 569 performances and receiving nominations for four Tony Awards.

At the height of the civil rights movement—and despite death threats, from which producer Hillard Elkins tried to shield star Sammy Davis, Jr.—*Golden Boy* opened in October 1964 at the Majestic Theatre. It was a hit, running for **569** performances and receiving four Tony Award nominations.

On March 6, 1961, President John F. Kennedy issued Executive Order 10925, which stated that government contractors must "take affirmative action to ensure that applicants are employed, and employees are treated ... without regard to their race, creed, [or] color." Kennedy also formed the President's Committee on Equal Employment Opportunity.

On May 4, 1961, the first of the Freedom Riders—400 black and white volunteers—set out for the South to test compliance with the Supreme Court's 1960 banning of segregated interstate travel facilities. When Riders met with physical violence and imprisonment, the country's outrage pressured the government into enforcing the anti-segregation laws.

# Sammy Davis, Jr.
# A True Pioneer, A Great Talent

If ever there was a consummate performer, it was Sammy Davis, Jr. Known for his singing, dancing, acting, celebrity impressions, and humor, Davis was often billed as "the greatest living entertainer in the world."

Born on December 8, 1925 in Harlem, by the age of three, Davis was tap dancing with his dad, a vaudeville entertainer, in the Will Mastin Trio. Both Mastin and Davis's father tried to shield him from prejudice, but when he served in the Army during World War Two, the performer was awakened to the intense racism that faced most African Americans. Fortunately, he was assigned to an integrated entertainment unit, where his talents changed the white GIs' perception of him. "My talent was the weapon, the power," Davis wrote.

After the war, Davis returned to the Will Mastin Trio, but soon began working solo on the Las Vegas circuit, playing hotels at which he was not allowed to stay because he was black. As his star rose, Davis drew the attention of both Broadway and Hollywood. His Broadway debut in the 1956 musical *Mr. Wonderful* showcased his many abilities and led to film roles in features such as *Anna Lucasta* (1959), *Porgy and Bess* (1959), the original *Ocean's Eleven* (1960), *Robin and the Seven Hoods* (1964), *Sweet Charity* (1968), and *Tap* (1989). He also won roles in popular TV shows, including the *The Mod Squad* and *All in the Family;* sang the theme song of the hit TV show *Baretta;* and was a regular guest and occasional host on late-night talk shows.

A member of the famous Rat Pack—which also included Frank Sinatra, Dean Martin, Joey Bishop, and Peter Lawford—Davis was known for his partying lifestyle. He also drew attention when he married May Britt, a beautiful blond-haired Swedish-born actress, at a time when interracial marriages were forbidden by law in over thirty states.

Davis's Broadway career would peak in 1964 with his starring role in Clifford Odets' *Golden Boy*, which garnered him a Tony nomination for Best Performance by a Leading Actor in a Musical. He would return to the New York stage just two more times, once for a special two-week engagement titled *Sammy* (1974), and again in 1978, for the revival of *Stop the World—I Want to Get Off* staged at the New York State Theatre.

Hit songs like "I've Gotta Be Me" and "Candy Man," and numerous appearances on television, film, and stage, transformed Sammy Davis, Jr. into a show business icon. Like so many of his peers, he overcame prejudice and discrimination not only to make his own way but also to clear a path for others. His refusal to appear in clubs that were racially segregated spurred the integration of several venues in Las Vegas and other cities. Record producer Quincy Jones said that Davis was "a true pioneer who traveled a dirt road so others, later, could follow on the freeway."

During his long career, Sammy Davis, Jr. moved from the ▶ vaudeville stage to success on the Las Vegas circuit, Broadway, the silver screen, and television. And every step of the way, Davis encountered—and overcame—racial discrimination.

FEHL

## *Hallelujah, Baby!*

Like *Golden Boy*, the 1967 musical *Hallelujah, Baby!* dealt with race, but this light, bubbly show was a complete turnaround from Sammy Davis, Jr.'s drama-based hit. The story chronicles sixty years in the life of Georgina, a talented, lovely African American who is determined to build a singing career. The audience sees Georgina move from the Great Depression through the Second World War to the beginning of the civil rights movement, and also watches her choose between two suitors, black boyfriend Clem and white admirer Harvey.

In *Hallelujah, Baby!*, main character Georgina (Leslie Uggams, right) and her mother (Lillian Hayman) are employed as maids, but Georgiana dreams of a career as an entertainer. Both Uggams and Hayman won Tonys for their performances in this 1967 musical.

The Albany Movement was launched in November 1961 by residents of Albany, Georgia. Intended to eliminate segregation, it attracted national attention when Martin Luther King, Jr. joined the protest. Although the movement failed to integrate the community, it was an important learning experience for King and other civil rights advocates.

In December 1961, Langston Hughes' play *Black Nativity* opened off-Broadway. A retelling of the Christmas story from an Afrocentric perspective, this "Gospel-Song Play" has since been staged all over the country. The National Center of Afro-American Artists in Boston, Massachusetts has produced the show annually since 1969.

The play was originally conceived and written for star Lena Horne. With music by Jule Styne, lyrics by Adolph Green and Betty Comden, and book by Arthur Laurents, it was meant to be a bit intense and edgy. When Horne declined the role, it was reworked for Leslie Uggams, who was far younger and had a softer personality. Opening at the Martin Beck Theatre in April 1967, *Hallelujah, Baby!* received mixed reviews but ran for nearly 300 performances and won five Tony Awards out of nine nominations, including the award for Best Musical. Uggams, who was making her Broadway debut after years of honing her skills in television, won the Tony for Best Performance by a Leading Actress in a Musical.

*Hallelujah, Baby!* was originally written with Lena Horne in mind, but was reworked for Leslie Uggams when Horne declined. The result was a bright and bubbly musical in which Leslie Uggams' talents shined.

Determined to understand the lives of black people, in 1959, white Texas native John Howard Griffin darkened his skin and posed as a black man while traveling through the Deep South. The account of his travels, entitled *Black Like Me* (1962), provided readers with a harrowing view of the racially segregated states of Louisiana, Mississippi, Alabama, and Georgia.

In the spring of 1963, police arrested black Freedom Rider Mary Hamilton at an Alabama protest. At her hearing, Hamilton refused to answer the judge when he insisted on calling her "Mary" instead of the more respectful "Miss Hamilton." Eventually, in *Hamilton v. Alabama*, the Supreme Court decided that everyone in court deserves a title of courtesy.

# Leslie Uggams
# From the Apollo to the Great White Way

It's rare that a child star grows up to be a successful adult entertainer, but Leslie Uggams' extraordinary combination of talents and effervescent personality has allowed her to attract great roles and enthusiastic audiences for over six decades.

Born on May 25, 1943 in New York City, Uggams came from a family with show business in its blood. Her mom danced at the famed Cotton Club in Harlem, and her dad sang with the Hall Johnson Choir before leaving show business. But it was her aunt Eloise, also from the Hall Johnson Choir, who was the family's first Broadway star. Uggams explains, "My Aunt Eloise was in the *Blackbirds of 1928* and later with Pearl Bailey in *St. Louis Woman* before doing *Porgy and Bess*. She taught me spiritual music because my grandfather was a Presbyterian minister. She would also teach me new songs that she enjoyed, and my mother would play them for us on the piano."

Among Uggams' earliest show business memories is that of being taken to an audition by her aunt. Recalling one such audition, she says, "The script had the 'H' word in it and so I wouldn't read it. I told them, 'My mommy says I can't say that word.'" Uggams stood on her principles and missed out on the part, but that didn't mean that she was out of show business. By age eight, she had begun acting school, and by twelve, she had started singing lessons. She also became friends with Mary Martin's daughter, Heller Halliday, which gave her the opportunity to see the Broadway shows *Peter Pan* and *The Sound of Music* when she was a teenager.

In the 1950s, when Uggams began her career, there were few roles for children and even fewer for black children, which made auditions very competitive. Uggams says, "I remember once showing up late for an audition because the mother of the only other black girl auditioning for the part told us the wrong time. I got the part anyway."

As a child, Uggams opened for headliners such as Louis Armstrong at the Apollo Theater, and made appearances on *Your Show of Shows* and *The Milton Berle Show*. Her big break came in 1958, when she was a contestant on the popular quiz show *Name That Tune*. After telling the host that she enjoyed singing, she was allowed to perform "He's Got the Whole World in His Hands" and other songs. "Mitch Miller saw me on the program and brought me down to Columbia Records, where I ended up with a recording contract," says Uggams, who was also made a regular on Miller's TV program *Sing Along With Mitch*.

Although Uggams was on the road to stardom, her path was not without obstacles. Television stations in the South refused to carry Miller's show because of Uggams' race. "The sponsors were having problems because the South would not air the show. Nat King Cole had a similar problem with a show that he could not get a sponsor for because he was black," adds Uggams. Miller was asked to do the show without Uggams, but he declined. In time, the southern stations began to pick up *Sing Along With Mitch,* and Leslie Uggams started receiving fan mail from viewers throughout the South.

By the 1960s, Uggams and other black performers could see that times were changing. "I remember as a teenager, I was thrilled because Diahann Carroll was on Broadway with Richard Kiley and she was going to play a love interest. Wow, that was really something," says Uggams, referring to the musical *No Strings,* which was one of several shows of the time that featured interracial relationships.

Leslie Uggams' Broadway breakthrough would come in the late 1960s with Arthur Laurents' *Hallelujah, Baby!* (See page 156 for more about the show.) Already a household name, Uggams was now a Broadway star, as well, and her first Broadway show yielded a Tony Award for Best Performance by a Leading Actress in a Musical. While studying with the great Stella Adler, with whom she became good friends, Uggams continued to land important Broadway roles. She was featured in *Blues in the Night* (1982), starred in *Jerry's Girls* (1985), and played the role of Reno Sweeney in the 1988 revival of *Anything Goes*. Then in 2003, Leslie joined the cast of *Thoroughly Modern Millie,* and in 2005, she costarred with James Earl Jones in *On Golden Pond*.

In addition to her work on the New York stage, Uggams has always remained active in television. From appearing on *Your Show of Shows* at the age of eleven to her role as Kizzy Reynolds in the groundbreaking mini-series *Roots* (1977), Uggams has an extensive list of TV credits. In 1969, she even had her own variety show—*The Leslie Uggams Show*—which made her the second African-American variety show host.

Throughout her decades-long career, Leslie Uggams has been sure to support the African-American community. "I did a lot of work at the Apollo when I was young, and always had some gig in my black community," says Uggams. She is not about to retire, but promises to continue taking on new roles and new challenges.

In April 2003, Leslie Uggams assumed the role of wealthy but grounded ▶ Muzzy in Broadway's hit show *Thoroughly Modern Millie*. In Act One, Uggams wowed the audience with her sizzling rendition of "Only in New York."

## *The Owl and the Pussycat*

Midway through this decade of rule breaking, the Bill Manhoff comedy *The Owl and the Pussycat* premiered, again challenging established Broadway conventions. Starring white actor Alan Alda and black actress Diana Sands, it was a two-person comedy about a stuffy unpublished writer, Felix, and his neighbor, Doris, an actress and part-time hooker. After Felix gets Doris evicted from her apartment, Doris insists on moving in with him, and they end up fighting their way into an unlikely relationship. While the comedy featured an interracial couple, like *No Strings*, it had not been written about race. Nonetheless, there was the usual controversy.

After making her Broadway debut in 1959's *A Raisin in the Sun*, actress Diana Sands was in great demand—on the New York stage, on the silver screen, and in television—until her untimely death in 1973.

Although 1964's *The Owl and the Pussycat* was not the first show of the decade to feature an interracial couple—that honor belonged to 1962's *No Strings*—it did manage to spark some controversy with its pairing of Diana Sands and Alan Alda. Despite this controversy, or perhaps because of it, the comedy had a run of over 400 performances.

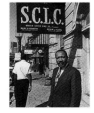

A 1963 movement, the Birmingham Campaign was organized by the Southern Christian Leadership Conference to challenge Birmingham, Alabama's system of racial segregation. The nonviolent campaign elicited a violent response from local authorities, as well as the arrest of Martin Luther King, Jr. But by July, most of Birmingham's segregation ordinances had been overturned.

Delivered at the August 1963 March on Washington for Jobs and Freedom, Martin Luther King's "I Have a Dream" speech was a defining moment of the civil rights movement. King's dream—of a country of freedom and equality arising from slavery and hatred—inspired Americans by explaining the need for change and offering hope for a better future.

Critics applauded the talents of playwright Bill Manhoff and actor Alan Alda, but reviewer Caldwell Titcomb said that the success of *The Owl and the Pussycat* was largely due to Diana Sands, who "can take a run-of-the-mill phrase or line and make you double over." Sands' sparkling portrayal of freewheeling actress and part-time hooker Doris W. garnered a Tony nomination for Best Performance by a Leading Actress in a Play.

*The Owl and the Pussycat* opened at Greenwich Village's ANTA Theatre in November 1964, and ran there until September 1965, when it was transferred to the Royale Theatre. All told, the public enjoyed 427 performances of the comedy. Sands received a Tony nomination for Best Performance by a Leading Actress in a Play, demonstrating that although some theatergoers were uncomfortable with the interracial casting, most found the color-blind show highly entertaining. The story was so popular that in 1970, the movie version appeared featuring George Segal and Barbra Streisand in the title roles.

In 1964, Sidney Poitier accepted the Academy Award for Best Actor for his performance in the film *Lilies of the Field*, becoming the first African-American male actor to win in this category. Poitier had received his early training in New York's American Negro Theater Company and had attracted Hollywood's attention through his work on Broadway.

The Economic Opportunity Act of 1964 was the first step in the War on Poverty. The Act stated, "It is the policy of the United States to eliminate the paradox of poverty in the midst of plenty in this nation by opening, to everyone, the opportunity for education and training, the opportunity to work, and the opportunity to live in decency and dignity."

## *Hello, Dolly!*

By the mid-sixties, the Golden Age of Broadway musicals—characterized by big-budget lavish productions—was only a memory, although a recent one. But no one could convince producer David Merrick that the musical extravaganza was dead. Merrick would uncover a story that had been presented under a variety of names and with varying degrees of success over the years. He would then have a new version created with lyrics and music by Jerry Herman and book by Michael Stewart. With Carol Channing taking the role of matchmaker Dolly Gallagher Levi, *Hello, Dolly!* premiered at the St. James Theatre in January 1964. The show enjoyed rave reviews and swept the Tony Awards, winning in ten categories.

Over the run of the show, Channing was followed by a long succession of significant Dollys, including Ginger Rogers, Martha Raye, Betty Grable, and, eventually, Ethel Merman in her second-to-last Broadway show. But perhaps the most remarkable reinvention of Dolly Levi was that of Pearl Bailey.

In the fall of 1967, David Merrick made the bold move of closing down production for a month and then re-opening *Hello, Dolly!* with an all-black cast. Pearl Bailey stepped into the coveted role of Dolly Levi, and Cab Calloway played her eventual suitor, Horace Vandergelder. The cast also included Billy Daniels and, in his Broadway debut, Morgan Freeman. The new production drew rave reviews, and less than a week after opening night, the cast recorded a new album for

In 1967, after *Hello, Dolly!* had run on Broadway for over 1,500 performances, producer David Merrick decided to replace the all-white cast with an all-black cast led by Pearl Bailey. Big Band great Cab Calloway took the role of Dolly's beau, Horace Vandergelder, and to no one's surprise, *Hello, Dolly!* packed the house.

RCA Records. This was an unusual move, as recordings of Broadway musicals are usually made with the original cast only—not with successive sets of performers. By the time *Hello, Dolly!* closed in late December of 1970, the musical had run for six years and 2,844 performances. The show would be remembered not only as one of Broadway's greatest all-time musicals but also as a major show that switched casts midstream without missing a beat or losing its audience. It seemed that African-American productions had become not just popular but also entirely mainstream.

Our nation's benchmark civil rights legislation, the Civil Rights Act of 1964 prohibited discrimination on the basis of race, color, religion, gender, or national origin. Signed into law by President Lyndon B. Johnson, it ended racial segregation in schools, the workplace, and public facilities, and outlawed unequal voter registration requirements.

In December 1964, in recognition of his nonviolent campaign against racism, thirty-five-year-old Martin Luther King, Jr. became the youngest man to receive the Nobel Peace Prize. When King learned of his selection, he announced that every penny of the prize money—which amounted to about $54,000—would be turned over to the civil rights movement.

# Cab Calloway
## Legendary Jazz Man Who Spanned Generations

Known to many as the "Hi De Ho Man," Cab Calloway was among the royalty of the Big Band Era. Born on Christmas Day of 1907 in Rochester, New York, Calloway showed musical talent at an early age and began taking lessons in music and voice. Despite his parents' protests, he was attracted to jazz and soon began visiting and, eventually, playing in jazz clubs, where he performed as a singer, a drummer, and an emcee. It was during this time that he met Louis Armstrong, who taught him s*cat singing*—vocal improvisation using nonsense syllables instead of words.

In 1930, Calloway took over a band called The Missourians, and in the early 1930s, he replaced Duke Ellington as the bandleader at Harlem's Cotton Club. He would also take his scat singing into the studios to record his biggest hit, "Minnie the Moocher," with which he was forever associated. Many more popular recordings followed, including "The Jumpin' Jive," "Chinese Rhythm," "Moon Glow," "St. James Infirmary," "The Man From Harlem," and "Jitter Bug."

Talented and highly versatile, Calloway was as much in demand in Hollywood as he was in nightclubs. In several films—such as *The Big Broadcast* (1932) and *St. Louis Blues* (1958)—Calloway performed, and many more films featured his music in their soundtrack. In the 1980 cult classic *The Blues Brothers*, the musician, playing himself, sang his trademark song "Minnie the Moocher." This famous scene introduced Calloway to a whole new generation.

After making his triumphant Broadway debut as Sportin' Life in the 1953 Broadway revival of *Porgy and Bess*, Calloway would return to the stage a decade later to star with Pearl Bailey in *Hello, Dolly!* Also on the bill was Calloway's daughter, Chris, who performed with her father's Hi De Ho Orchestra for more than two decades on world tours. Chris would also accompany her father in his next show, *The Pajama Game*, which hit Broadway for a short run in 1973. Cab Calloway's music—stylish and emblematic of the Swing Era—would also be featured in two Broadway revues, *Bubbling Brown Sugar* (1976) and *Uptown . . . It's Hot!* (1986).

Calloway had his own inimitable style that won over fans and music reviewers worldwide. While he became an actor and a dancer, he was first and foremost a jazz man and bandleader. In 1987, he was inducted into the Big Band and Jazz Hall of Fame, and shortly after his death in 1994, the Cab Calloway School of the Arts opened in Wilmington, Delaware.

Cab Calloway's talent and personality were as big as his smile and his outsized zoot suit. It's easy to understand why the "Hi De Ho Man" drew theatergoers to Broadway when he appeared in the 1953 revival of *Porgy and Bess* and 1967's all-black production of *Hello, Dolly!*

## And Then There Was *Hair*

Of all the 1960s musicals that broke the rules, none is more famous than *Hair*. With lyrics and book by James Rado and Gerome Ragni, and music by Galt MacDermot, *Hair* tells the story of a "tribe" of long-haired hippies living in New York City, experimenting with drugs and free love, and fighting against the Vietnam draft. After a 1967 off-Broadway debut, the show opened at the more fashionable Biltmore Theatre in April 1968. Although critics didn't know what to make of this exploration of sixties counterculture, audiences flocked to see it, and the show ran for 1,750 performances.

Race was not a central theme of *Hair*, but the issue was confronted, particularly in the songs "White Boys," which was sung by black women, and "Black Boys," sung by white women. Three African-American performers made their Broadway debuts in the musical. Leata Galloway was one of the original tribe members, as was Melba Moore, who later stepped into a larger role originally played by Diane Keaton. Ben Vereen started out as a replacement before joining the national touring company.

Although race was not a central theme of 1968's *Hair*, the show's biracial cast touched on this issue in the songs "White Boys" and "Black Boys."

Malcolm X, one of the most influential African Americans of the twentieth century, was murdered on February 21, 1965. The leader originally urged black Americans to fight racism "by any means necessary," including violence. Shortly before his death, through, he changed his beliefs, stating, "America is the first country … that can actually have a bloodless revolution."

On March 7, 1965, at the height of the civil rights movement, a march for black voting rights began in Selma, Alabama. When the peaceful demonstrators were brutally attacked by Alabama police, the country was incensed. Within a few days, President Lyndon Johnson responded by presenting a bill that would become the Voting Rights Act of 1965.

# Melba Moore
# Leading Stage Star & Recording Artist

When Melba Moore replaced Diane Keaton in the original Broadway production of *Hair*, little did she know that was on the verge of launching a career that would span five decades and land her four Grammies and a Tony Award.

Born Beatrice Melba Hill on October 29, 1945, Moore was raised first in Harlem, New York, and then in Newark, New Jersey, where she studied music at a performing arts high school. After studying music education at Montclair State University, Moore worked as a music teacher for a time, but she soon decided to try her hand at performing. Her first Broadway role was in the musical *Hair* (1968), and soon after, she played Lutiebelle in the 1970 musical comedy *Purlie*, for which she won a Tony Award for Best Performance by a Featured Actress in a Musical. She would return to Broadway in 1978 in the all-black version of *Kismet* entitled *Timbuktu!*, alongside the legendary Eartha Kitt.

Because her first love had always been music, Moore also used her four-octave vocal range to forge a musical career with a string of popular dance hits that include "This Is It," "Love's Comin' At Ya," and "You Stepped Into My Life." Her vocal talents also landed her on many television shows, including *The Tonight Show Starring Johnny Carson*, *The Flip Wilson Show*, *Soul Train*, and *Solid Gold*. In 1986, she had her own TV show, *Melba*.

But there is nothing quite like Broadway. After a stint in the short-lived comedy *Inacent Black* (1981), for which she wrote some of the incidental music, Moore would step into the long-running musical drama *Les Misérables* (1995), where she became the first African American to play the female lead role of Fantine.

In addition to creating a successful recording career, Melba Moore firmly established herself as a Broadway star in the late sixties, and she has never relinquished the title.

Melba Moore made her Broadway debut in the "American Tribal Love-Rock Musical" *Hair*. Her next role—that of Lutiebelle in 1970's *Purlie*—would win a Tony Award for the rising young star.

In September 1965, Bill Cosby became the first African-American co-star of a network television drama when he appeared alongside Robert Culp in *I Spy*. At first, four television stations, all located in the South, declined to carry the series. Nevertheless, the highly successful series lasted from 1965 to 1968, and Cosby's performance garnered him three Emmy Awards.

Economist Robert Weaver was confirmed as Secretary of President Johnson's new Department of Housing and Urban Development (HUD) in January 1966, making Weaver the first African American to hold a cabinet-level position. Decades earlier, Weaver had been a member of President Roosevelt's "Black Cabinet," where he specialized in housing, education, and employment.

# The Blacks: A Clown Show

In 1961, an English translation of Jean Genet's absurdist drama *The Blacks: A Clown Show* opened at the St. Mark's Playhouse in Greenwich Village. The play concerns a troupe of black performers who must act out the murder of a white woman for the entertainment of a white-masked tribunal, which is then required to judge the blacks for the crime. In its exploration of the struggles of outcasts, *The Blacks* breaks with regular conventions by asking the audience to wear white masks and, sometimes, to participate in the action.

While the drama was far from what many theatergoers may have expected—and it never moved to the Great White Way—it became an avant-garde phenomenon. *New York Times* reviewer Howard Taubman wrote, "This vastly gifted Frenchman uses shocking words and images to cry out at the pretensions and injustices of our world. One of the most original and stimulating evenings Broadway or Off Broadway has to offer."

Featuring an all-black cast that included James Earl Jones, Louis Gossett, Jr., Cicely Tyson, Godfrey Cambridge, Maya Angelou, and Roscoe Lee Browne, *The Blacks* ran for more than 1,400 performances, longer than any off-Broadway nonmusical of the decade.

*The Blacks'* cast was made up of young, talented actors who later became well known. Seen here are Cicely Tyson (far left), Roscoe Lee Browne (center), and Godfrey Cambridge. James Earl Jones, Louis Gossett, Jr., and Maya Angelou also performed in the highly successful show.

# POWERFUL DRAMAS OF THE SIXTIES

While most musicals skirted critical social issues during the sixties, a number of Broadway and off-Broadway dramas approached civil rights problems head-on. These formidable dramas forced the audience to acknowledge the war against civil injustice that was being waged all over America.

## Off-Broadway and the Black Arts Movement

One of the most shocking dramas of the sixties was *Dutchman* by African-American playwright LeRoi Jones. Opening in March 1964 at Greenwich Village's Cherry Lane Theatre, the play tells of a fatal confrontation between a white woman and a black man who meet on a subway in New York City. Lula—manipulative and seductive—seems intent on angering fellow traveler Clay by alternately flirting with him and taunting him with racial stereotypes. Clay is at first polite and intrigued by Lula. But when her taunts grow more cruel and direct, he becomes furious and talks at length about his anger with white people. As emotions escalate, Lula unexpectedly kills Clay by stabbing him in the heart. Just as frightening, Lula, although clearly insane, convinces the other riders to dispose of the body and ignore the incident. Then, like the Dutchman—the legendary ship's captain who brings death to all who encounter him—Lula moves on to her next victim, another young black man.

The jaw-dropping bluntness of the play may have prevented *Dutchman* from reaching Broadway, but did not keep it from winning an Obie. And it was not lost on politically aware theatergoers that the play had emerged just as the civil rights movement was heating up. (See the inset on page 168.)

The anger of the civil rights era erupted in other plays, as well. In April 1964, James Baldwin's *Blues for Mister Charlie* premiered at the ANTA Theatre in Greenwich Village. Based on a real-life incident in which a young African-American man was murdered by Mississippi whites for whistling at a white girl, the play was "dedicated to the memory of Medgar Evers, and his widow and his children, and to the memory of the dead children of Birmingham." The title derived its name from the term "Mister Charlie," which black men applied to the white man, so Baldwin may have been expressing his sadness for the white man's moral crisis as well as for

Perhaps the most famous work of the 1964 off-Broadway season, and certainly one of the most disturbing, *Dutchman* starred Robert Hooks as Clay and Jennifer West as Lula. A few years later, Hooks would help establish the Negro Ensemble Company (NEC), an outlet for America's black theatrical talent.

In May 1966, Stokely Carmichael became national chairman of the Student Nonviolent Coordinating Committee (SNCC). Although he had once believed in nonviolent protest, by this time, Carmichael had adopted a more militant course: "We been saying 'freedom' for six years," he said. "What we are going to start saying now is 'Black Power.'"

The Black Panther Party was founded in 1966 by Huey Newton and Bobby Seale. First called the Black Panther Party for Self-Defense, it was formed to protect black neighborhoods from police brutality. Eventually, it became a militant organization willing to use force to achieve its goals of equality in education, employment, housing, and civil rights.

# The Civil Rights Movement Reaches a Boil

In 1964, after years of nonviolent protest against racial injustice, the Civil Rights Act was signed into law by President Lyndon B. Johnson. This landmark legislation outlawed major forms of discrimination against racial groups, ethnic groups, and religious minorities, ending the "Jim Crow" laws that had upheld racial segregation in the South since the 1800s.

While the Civil Rights Act was a highly significant law, it could not change the attitudes and behavior of white Americans. For many more years, black Americans would have to continue the fight for basic civil liberties, such as the rights to vote in elections, attend good schools, live in a neighborhood of their own choice, and get decent employment for fair pay.

Among the most significant protests of the sixties were Alabama's Selma to Montgomery marches of 1965. Motivated by the exclusion of blacks from the voting process and further spurred by the murder of an unarmed civil rights protestor, these peaceful protests—which were met with violence on the part of the police—marked the emotional and political peak of the country's civil rights movement. Televised footage of lawmen cruelly attacking unresisting marchers provoked public sympathy and, ultimately, resulted in the Voting Rights Act of 1965. To many, it seemed that African Americans were finally achieving full equality. But in reality, most black people saw little if any difference in the way they were treated. They had attained equality in writing only.

Just five days after the Voting Rights Act was signed, the Watts Riots—a six-day uprising—erupted in the poor, largely black Watts neighborhood of Los Angeles, leaving thirty-four people dead and one thousand people injured. Frustration and long-simmering anger were causing peaceful black protests to give way to a violent rebellion against white authority. The next phase of the civil rights movement would be marked by militancy and the call for "black power." Further riots were to follow all over America, including northern cities such as New York and Detroit, as black Americans demanded equality in deed as well as word. The tumultuous decade was also rocked by the assassination of noted civil rights leaders Medgar Evers (1963), Malcolm X (1965), and Martin Luther King, Jr. (1968).

Historians do not agree on the year in which the civil rights movement had its official end. But it is beyond dispute that that the movement had a profound effect on all aspects of American life, including American theater, and that it would leave an indelible mark on the nation's history.

---

the miseries suffered by African Americans. Howard Taubman of *The New York Times* wrote that the play brought "eloquence and conviction to one of the momentous themes of our era." Starring Al Freeman, Jr., Pat Hingle, Rosetta LeNoire, Diana Sands, and Rip Torn, *Blues for Mister Charlie* ran for 148 performances.

Although black playwrights were most certainly making their voices heard, many African Americans felt that more should be done to encourage black art and a sense of ethnic pride. In 1965, following the assassination of Muslim leader Malcolm X, LeRoi Jones, author of *Dutchman*, moved from Greenwich Village to Harlem. There, the playwright—who would eventually change his name to Amiri Baraka—established the Black Arts Repertory Theatre/School (BARTS). The school was designed to provide instruction in all aspects of the dramatic arts and to establish a repertory theater in Harlem.

A drama of energy and passion, 1964's *Blues for Mister Charlie* was "dedicated to the memory of Medgar Evers, and his widow and his children, and to the memory of the dead children of Birmingham."

---

Observed from December 26 through January 1, Kwanzaa—which means "first fruits" in Swahili—was created in 1966 by Dr. Maulana Karenga as the first specifically African-American holiday. With its roots in the black nationalist movement of the sixties, Kwanza is intended to help black Americans reconnect with their African heritage.

In 1958, Mildred Jeter, who was black, married Richard Loving, who was white, in Washington, DC. When they returned home to Virginia, the state jailed them, citing its "miscegenation" laws. The couple fought back, and in 1967, the Supreme Court, in *Loving v. Virginia*, ruled that the state's ban on interracial marriage was unconstitutional.

BARTS became a key institution of the Black Arts Movement (BAM). Although BAM had begun in the 1920s, it was during the 1960s that it gained momentum and visibility, leading to the formation of black theater groups, the publication of black journals, and the creation of black writers groups such as the Harlem Writers Guild. (The Writers Guild is now the oldest African-American writers group in the United States.) BAM also promoted "black power"—a black pride movement that aimed at achieving full political and economic equality with whites, and sometimes advocated armed self-defense.

One important result of the Black Arts Movement was the Negro Ensemble Company, known as the NEC. Founded in 1967 by playwright Douglas Turner Ward, theater manager Gerald Krone, and actor/producer Robert Hooks, the NEC was designed to bring the works of black playwrights to the stage and to provide outlets for black stage performers. In its first season, the NEC produced an evening of black-oriented one-act plays, including a reverse minstrel show in which black performers wore whiteface. These productions were well received and launched the theater group at the St. Mark's Playhouse in Greenwich Village.

Because the Negro Ensemble Company didn't limit itself to plays written by African Americans or to funding by the community, but also worked with white playwrights and accepted money from the Ford Foundation, it drew some criticism from other black groups. Nevertheless, its first-rate productions stood on their own merits and drew interracial audiences. Included among the group's most prominent plays were Lonne Elder, III's *Ceremonies in Dark Old Men* (1969); Joseph A. Walker's *The River Niger* (1972), which went on to Broadway in 1973; and Charles Fuller's *A Soldier's Play* (1981), which was the basis for the 1984 Denzel Washington film *A Soldier's Story*. NEC alumni include notable actors such as John Amos, Angela Bassett, Laurence Fishburne, Sherman Hemsley, Samuel L. Jackson, Cleavon Little, Phylicia Rashad, Esther Rolle, Richard Roundtree, and Denzel Washington.

Born Everett LeRoi Jones, and later known as Amiri Baraka, this poet/playwright gained acclaim through his 1964 play *Dutchman*. Later, he would found the Black Arts Repertory Theatre/School (BARTS), whose mission was to provide instruction in the dramatic arts and build a repertory theater in Harlem.

In the fall of 1967, producer David Merrick made a bold move when he closed down production of *Hello, Dolly!* and, after a month, re-opened the play with an all-black cast starring Pearl Bailey and Cab Calloway. Like the original production, this one was a huge success and contributed to the show's total run of 2,844 performances.

In October 1967, Thurgood Marshall became the first African-American Supreme Court Justice. During his twenty-four-year tenure, Marshall consistently took a liberal stand and supported the protection of individual rights. He is regarded as one of the most important figures of the civil rights movement.

## *The Great White Hope*

Loosely based on the life of black boxer Jack Johnson, 1968's *The Great White Hope* explored the nature of racism in America at the turn of the century.

In October 1968—four years after the success of the musical *Golden Boy*—another show about a black boxer came to Broadway. Howard Sackler's drama *The Great White Hope* had first been produced in a regional theater in Washington, DC, and made its Broadway premiere at the Alvin Theatre in October 1968. The play starred James Earl Jones and Jane Alexander.

Based on the life of boxing champion Jack Johnson, this drama tells the story of Jack Jefferson (James Earl Jones), a powerful man who enjoys a streak of victories in the ring, defeating one white boxer after

Both James Earl Jones and Jane Alexander won Tony Awards for their portrayal of lovers destroyed by a deeply racist society in *The Great White Hope* (1968). The actors would later reprise their roles in a 1970 film adaptation of the story.

When preparing for the role of boxer Jack Jefferson in *The Great White Hope*, James Earl Jones was able to learn from the experiences of his father, ex-boxer Robert Earl Jones. The actor must have done his homework well, because after Muhammad Ali saw the play, the World Heavyweight Champion had high praise for Jones' performance.

another. Soon, the nation's racism fuels a demand for a "great white hope" who will defeat Jefferson in his bid for the heavyweight title. Jefferson wins, becoming the world's first African-American heavyweight champion, but is arrested for crossing a state line with white girlfriend Eleanor Bachman (Jane Alexander). Hounded by the law and rejected by society, the two flee to Havana, but Jefferson's downfall seems inevitable.

According to *New York Times* critic Clive Barnes, *The Great White Hope* "came into the Alvin Theatre . . . like a whirlwind," sweeping the audience along with it. Both Jones and Alexander won great praise, as did the play itself. The drama ran for 546 performances and won Tony Awards for Best Play, Best Actor (Jones), and Best Actress (Alexander). In 1970, it was made into a movie starring Jones and Alexander in the leading roles.

Known for advocating nonviolent direct action as a means of social change, civil rights leader Dr. Martin Luther King, Jr. was assassinated in Memphis, Tennessee on April 4, 1968. When the news of King's death was made public, over a hundred cities experienced an outbreak of violence, and thirty-nine people died.

Commonly called the Fair Housing Act, the Civil Rights Act of 1968 was signed into law by President Lyndon Johnson. Expanding on earlier legislation, this act forbade discrimination concerning the sale, rental, and financing of housing based on race, religion, national origin, or gender. It is considered the final great achievement of the civil rights movement.

# James Earl Jones
# Fifty Years of Captivating America

There are few actors who are as well recognized and respected as James Earl Jones. With a career that spans some six decades, he is known to one generation for his dramatic portrayal of boxer Jack Jefferson in *The Great White Hope*, and another as the voice of Darth Vader in the *Star Wars* film series.

Born on January 17, 1931 in the small town of Arkabutla, Mississippi, Jones grew up with a stutter that rendered him practically mute during his early years. He began to overcome his stutter in high school with the help of a concerned English teacher whom he later referred to as "the father of my voice." The teacher urged him to work on his problem by reading to the class, getting involved in debating, and taking a course in dramatic reading. This not only improved Jones' speech but also gave him the confidence and poise he would need in his life's work.

After high school, Jones pursued a medical career for a time and also enrolled in the Army, but eventually, he decided to study acting in New York City. When he was twenty-one, he became acquainted with his long-estranged father, Robert Earl Jones. A boxer turned actor, Robert took his son on a whirlwind tour of Broadway and off-Broadway, and gave him valuable advice: "Pay attention to the little things actors do."

In 1958, James Earl Jones debuted on Broadway in the role of a valet in Dory Schary's *Sunrise at Campobello*. One night, Jones stuttered in his delivery of a line, but he made it through and never stuttered on stage again.

Jones' commanding stage presence and powerful voice led to other parts in the New York theater. He appeared in Joseph Papp's presentations of Shakespeare's *Henry V* (1960), *A Midsummer Night's Dream* (1961), and *Othello* (1964), and he won a role in Jean Genet's highly acclaimed off-Broadway play *The Blacks* (1961). During this period, the actor also made his film debut in Stanley Kubrick's *Dr. Strangelove or: How I Learned to Stop Worrying and Love the Bomb* (1964).

Jones rose to Broadway fame as boxer Jack Jefferson in 1968's *The Great White Hope*. His father's boxing career, which had included work as a sparring partner for Joe Lewis, was helpful to Jones as he prepared for the part

and went on to win a Tony Award for his performance. Then, after a stint in the Broadway revival of Eugene O'Neill's *The Iceman Cometh* (1973), he would star as Lennie in John Steinbeck's *Of Mice and Men* (1974). Jones considers this his favorite role. In 1978, Jones would continue his line of Broadway successes with a one-man show in which he portrayed outspoken actor Paul Robeson. And in 1987, he took the lead in what would be August Wilson's most famous work, *Fences*.

During the late 1970s, Jones was asked to lend his voice to the notorious Darth Vader in *Star Wars*. While he was not credited on screen, it wasn't long before his role in creating one of film's most recognized villains became known. Jones would perform in a large number of films, including *Conan the Barbarian* (1982), *Soul Man* (1986), *Coming to America* (1988), *Field of Dreams* (1989), *The Hunt for Red October* (1990), *Sneakers* (1992), *Patriot Games* (1992), *The Sandlot* (1993), and *Clear and Present Danger* (1994). He would serve as the narrator in *Beauty and the Beast* (1981) and as the voice of Mustafa in *The Lion King* (1994). He would also appear in a number of television series, ranging from the miniseries *Roots* (1977) and the dramas *Gabriel's Fire* (1990–1991) and *Everwood* (2003–2004), to sitcoms like *Will and Grace* (2003) and *The Big Bang Theory* (2014).

After taking a hiatus from Broadway, Jones returned to play Norman Thayer in the 2005 production of *On Golden Pond*, in which he costarred with Leslie Uggams. He also starred in the revival of Tennessee Williams' *Cat on a Hot Tin Roof* (2008), Alfred Uhry's *Driving Miss Daisy* (2010), and Gore Vidal's *The Best Man* (2012). Jones received Tony nominations for his performances in both *On Golden Pond* and *The Best Man*.

James Earl Jones has won lifetime achievement awards from the Screen Actors Guild, the Academy of Motion Picture Arts and Sciences, and the Drama Desk for being "a commanding force on the stage for nearly half a century." He has also won a National Medal of Arts for his service to American culture. Whether acting on the stage, appearing on the big screen, or simply saying "This is CNN," he continues to delight millions of fans across the nation.

Othello is one of the many Shakespearean roles played ▶
by James Earl Jones at Joseph Papp's Public Theater.
This photo was taken during a 1964 production.

# No Place to Be Somebody

No discussion of black drama in the sixties would be complete without *No Place to Be Somebody* by African-American playwright Charles Gordone. Inspired by Gordone's employment in a Greenwich Village bar, the play explores racial tensions in America through the experiences of a black bartender who finds himself in trouble with white mobsters. Gordone's drama opened at Joseph Papp's Public Theater in May 1969, and after a 250-performance run, was produced at various other off-Broadway venues for a total of 900 performances. In 1971, *No Place* moved to Broadway's Morosco Theatre for 39 performances. More significant than its relatively brief stay on the Great White Way was that the off-Broadway production won a Pulitzer Prize for Drama. This made Gordone the first African-American playwright to receive the award and made *No Place to Be Somebody* the first off-Broadway play to be so honored.

The 1969 play *No Place to Be Somebody*—which explored civil rights through a black bartender's struggles with white mobsters—is memorable for two "firsts." It was the first off-Broadway play to receive a Pulitzer Prize for Drama, and its author, Charles Gordone, was the first African American to receive a Pulitzer in this category.

# THE SIXTIES IN RETROSPECT

Although the decade was coming to a close, the nation would continue to battle racial segregation and seek social reform throughout the seventies and beyond. Broadway, which for many years had promulgated African-American stereotypes, had actually moved ahead of American culture. During the 1960s, it had integrated the stage in shows such as *No Strings, Golden Boy, Blues for Mister Charlie,* and *The Great White Hope.* In some productions, like *No Strings,* it had been delightfully color-blind. In others, like *The Great White Hope,* it had explored important racial issues with brutal honesty.

While there was still work to be done in the nation, the theater had been transformed from a medium that mirrored American culture to one that was leading by example.

In 1968, Shirley Chisholm became the first black woman elected to Congress, where she represented New York State in the House of Representatives for fourteen years. In 1972, she would run in the New York Democratic primary for United States president, establishing another significant first for African-American women.

One in a series of cases that followed historic *Brown v. Board of Education* (1954), *Alexander v. Holmes Board of Education* (1969) addressed the fact that more than a decade after *Brown,* several southern states still had separate schools for whites and blacks. In *Alexander v. Holmes,* the Supreme Court ordered *immediate* desegregation.

# STARRING
# IN ORDER OF
# APPEARANCE

| | | |
|---|---|---|
| Cleavon Little | Vinnette Carroll | Phyllis Hyman |
| Melba Moore | Alex Bradford | Gregg Burge |
| Sherman Hemsley | Micki Grant | Cholly Atkins |
| Virginia Capers | William Hardy, Jr. | Frankie Manning |
| Ernestine Jackson | Salome Bey | Fayard Nicholas |
| Ralph Carter | Mabel Robinson | Ruth Brown |
| Joe Morton | Clinton Derricks-Carroll | Linda Hopkins |
| Debbie Allen | Delores Hall | Carrie Smith |
| Ken Harper | Ashton Springer | Lena Horne |
| Stephanie Mills | Rosetta LeNoire | Whoopi Goldberg |
| Hinton Battle | Avon Long | Ntozake Shange |
| Tiger Haynes | Josephine Premice | Trazana Beverly |
| Ted Ross | Vivian Reed | Joseph A. Walker |
| Dee Dee Bridgewater | Joseph Attles | Douglas Turner Ward |
| André DeShields | Charles "Honi" Coles | Roxie Roker |
| Billy Wilson | Thomas "Fats" Waller | Grenna Whitaker |
| Robert Guillaume | Nell Carter | Frances Foster |
| Norma Donaldson | Armelia McQueen | Graham Brown |
| James Randolph | Charlayne Woodard | Les Roberts |
| Ernestine Jackson | Alan Weeks | Woodie King, Jr. |
| Ken Page | Zoe Walker | August Wilson |
| Ira Hawkins | Ethel Beatty | Theresa Merritt |
| Gilbert Price | Terry Burrell | Charles S. Dutton |
| Obba Babatundé | Leslie Dockery | James Earl Jones |
| Eartha Kitt | Lynnie Godfrey | Mary Alice |
| Ben Vereen | Mel Johnson, Jr. | Lloyd Richards |
| Sheryl Lee Ralph | Lonnie McNeil | Delroy Lindo |
| Jennifer Holliday | Alaina Reed | Angela Bassett |
| Loretta Devine | Jeffrey V. Thompson | Charles Brown |
| Ben Harney | Maurice Hines | Ray Aranha |
| Cleavant Derricks | Gregory Hines | Frankie R. Faison |
| Mbongeni Ngema | Henry LeTang | Courtney B. Vance |
| Hugh Masekela | Duke Ellington | Karima Miller |
| Leleti Khumalo | Judith Jamison | |

# 7.

## The Door Has Opened The 1970s and 1980s

By the 1970s, Broadway was fully integrated. Black and white theatergoers sat together in the audience, and—although people of color may have still been underrepresented on the New York stage—Broadway shows routinely included black performers in their casts.

By the start of the 1970s, the nation had seen the worst of civil rights unrest. Because racist attitudes lingered throughout the country, there were still battles to be fought, but no one could deny that great strides had been made. Legislation had been signed to prevent segregation in schools and housing, and Jim Crow laws were finally off the books. Many aspects of American society were seeing a far greater representation of African Americans than ever before.

Certainly, Broadway had matured in regard to its racial attitudes. Once, New York theaters had presented demeaning caricatures of African Americans in theaters that allowed only white people to attend performances—and that sometimes permitted only white entertainers on the stage. But by the seventies, color was no longer a barrier. Audiences were integrated, and shows routinely had integrated casts, as well. Those productions with all-black casts had mass appeal, and in many cases, they celebrated major African-American stars such as Duke Ellington, Eubie Blake, and Count Basie. Never before had New York theater provided so much opportunity for black performers.

While Broadway was no longer struggling to win the battle of racial tolerance, it was engaged in a fierce battle of a different kind. The 1970s was a time of economic recession, and this could not fail to have its impact on the performing arts. The rising costs of bringing a show to Broadway coupled with declining ticket sales caused dark marquees to dot the formerly vibrant

The New Federal Theatre (NFT) was established in 1970 by Woodie King, Jr. with the goal of bringing people of color and women into mainstream American theater and providing a platform for groundbreaking theater works. Since then, the NFT has served as a venue for numerous African-American performers and launched many important plays, including *For Colored Girls Who Have Considered Suicide When the Rainbow Is Enuf.*

In 1970, Charles Gordone became the first black playwright to receive the Pulitzer Prize for Drama, and his 1969 play *No Place to Be Somebody* became the first off-Broadway play to receive the award. The drama had opened at Joseph Papp's Public Theater in May 1969, and was produced at various other off-Broadway venues before it moved to Broadway's Morosco Theatre.

theater district. Live theater was becoming less affordable for working-class people, who increasingly turned to less expensive forms of entertainment like television. Nervous Broadway producers, eager to find a hit, focused on the always-popular musical, which, while expensive to mount, offered the potential for high profits. Legitimate theater appeared to be an endangered species. Those professionals dedicated to dramatic plays most often turned to off-Broadway, where shows were less costly to stage—and theatergoers could avoid the increasingly grungy and dangerous streets of Times Square.

Yet even in a time of economic trouble, many great productions could be found on the Great White Way as well as the theaters of off-Broadway. In the eighties, Broadway would rebound with new vigor. Just as important, that decade would introduce a new and inventive playwright who would revolutionize the theater with plays designed to chronicle a century of African-American history and culture.

## MUSICALS

While most people consider 1960 to mark the end of the Golden Age of Broadway musicals, it is beyond dispute that the seventies provided a wealth of musicals of different types. Because of hard economic times, some producers chose to play it safe with adaptations and revivals, several of which were designed to showcase African-American performers. As a consequence, the number of original productions dropped to record lows in the early part of the decade. But there were still quite a few new shows from which avid theatergoers could choose, some with all-black casts and some with integrated casts. And then there were the spirited—and wildly popular—musical revues, many of which presented the works of gifted black musicians of the Jazz Age and beyond, introducing an entirely new generation to great American music.

Musical adaptations of books and non-musical plays have long been popular on Broadway. (Think *Kiss Me, Kate* and *South Pacific*.) In the seventies, all-black productions of the adaptations *Purlie*, *Raisin*, and *The Wiz* drew enthusiastic audiences to the Great White Way while garnering a slew of Tony Awards.

## Adaptations and Revivals

The seventies brought to the public a number of nonmusical favorites that were revived and transformed into musical shows, as well as existing musicals that were adapted for black casts. One Broadway hit was even an adaptation of one of the most famous movies of all time. (Or was it a stage adaptation of one of the most popular children's books of all time?) However you interpret the origin of these great shows, it soon became clear that the theater world had fully embraced big-budget large-scale musicals that featured talented black performers—and the public loved it!

During the 1970s, there emerged an African American-centered film genre that became known as *blaxploitation*. At first created specifically for a black urban audience, and eventually appealing to moviegoers of different races and backgrounds, these films were often controversial. Some people felt that the films signified black empowerment, while others believed that they perpetuated negative stereotypes.

President Richard Nixon nominated Judge G. Harrold Carswell to the Supreme Court in 1970. But critics—including the NAACP—soon questioned Carswell's fitness for service. As a lower-court judge, Carswell had shown a marked bias against African Americans, and he had made white surpremacist comments during a 1948 campaign speech. On April 8, 1970, the Senate rejected Carswell's nomination with a 51-48 vote.

## *Purlie*

Based on the 1961 Broadway comedy *Purlie Victorious, Purlie* had a book by Ossie Davis, Phillip Rose, and Peter Udell; lyrics by Udell; and music by Gary Geld. Davis did not actually work on the musical adaptation, but he was credited because so much of his original work was used in the show. Like the play, the musical tells the story of a dynamic preacher who returns to Georgia to claim an inheritance that will enable him to open his own church. The show featured Cleavon Little, Melba Moore, and—in his Broadway debut—Sherman Hemsley, as well as an extended cast of singers and dancers.

*Purlie* opened in March 1970 at the Broadway Theatre, and was later moved to the Winter Garden Theatre and the ANTA Playhouse for a combined run of 688 performances. Drawing critical acclaim, the funny, spirited show made a name for both Little and Moore, and every night, Moore brought the house down with her rousing performance of "I Got Love." *Purlie* was nominated for five Tony Awards and won two—for Best Leading Actor (Little) and Best Featured Actress (Moore). Both stars also garnered Drama Desk Awards.

Based on the 1961 hit comedy *Purlie Victorious,* 1970's musical adaptation *Purlie* treated audiences to the original story along with a score by Gary Geld (music) and Peter Udell (lyrics). The cast included (left to right) Cleavon Little, Melba Moore, John Heffernan, and Sherman Hemsley.

▶ Neither Melba Moore nor Cleavon Little were new to the Broadway stage in 1970. Moore had made her Broadway debut in *Hair* (1968), and Little, in *Jimmy Shine* (1968). But it was *Purlie* that brought the two actors to public attention and garnered them Tony Awards for Best Featured Actress and Best Leading Actor.

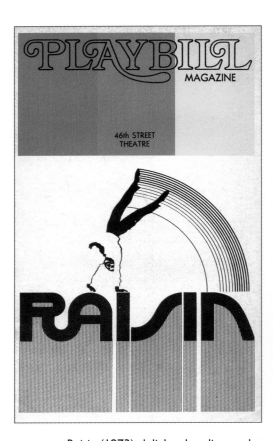

*Raisin* (1973) delighted audiences by masterfully adding musical numbers to Lorraine Hansberry's riveting story of an African-American family. Critics reported that the show inspired nightly ovations at the Forty-Sixth Street Theater.

## *Raisin*

In 1973, the musical *Raisin* opened at the Forty-Sixth Street Theater. Based on Lorraine Hansberry's groundbreaking 1959 drama *A Raisin in the Sun,* it tells the story of the Youngers, an African-American family struggling to find a better way of life in Chicago at the start of the 1950s. The book was written by Robert Nemiroff (Hansberry's ex-husband) and Charlotte Zaltzberg, and the songs were the work of composer Judd Woldin and lyricist Robert Brittan. *Raisin's* cast included Virginia Capers, Ernestine Jackson, Ralph Carter, Helen Martin, Joe Morton, Debbie Allen, and Robert Jackson.

Although the show included music and dance, *Raisin*—like the drama on which it was based—still offered theatergoers the riveting story of the Younger family. Shown here (from left to right) are Joe Morton as Walter Younger, Ernestine Jackson as Ruth Younger, Virginia Capers as Lena Younger, and Debbie Allen as Beneatha Younger. Ralph Carter, who played Travis Younger, is seated.

Critics praised *Raisin's* writers for masterfully adapting Hansberry's work so that the dialogue flowed into the songs without detracting from the story. Clive Barnes of *The New York Times* claimed that it was possibly even better than the original play—"one of those unusual musicals that should not only delight people who love musicals, but might also well delight people who don't." Theatergoers must have agreed, because *Raisin* ran for a total of 847 performances. It was nominated for nine Tony Awards and won two, for Best Musical and Best Performance by a Leading Actress in a Musical (Virginia Capers). Capers, who had begun her Broadway career as an understudy for Adelaide Hall in the 1957 musical *Jamaica*, would reprise her role as the Younger family's matriarch in *Raisin's* national tour.

Among *Raisin's* many musical numbers was an African dance scene inspired by Beneatha Younger's romance with an African exchange student. Here, Walter (Joe Morton) imagines himself a great chief as he dances with his sister, Beneatha (Debbie Allen).

*Swann v. Charlotte-Mecklenburg Board of Education* was an important case in the history of public school integration. In April 1971, the Supreme Court decided that busing was an appropriate means of resolving the problem of racial imbalance in educational institutions. This resulted in the widespread use of busing by federal judges to end segregation.

Throughout the 1950s and 1960s, television station WLBT of Jackson, Mississippi was notorious for its support of racial segregation, and even cut coverage of the civil rights movement from the NBC news feed. NBC and civil rights groups had long complained of WLBT's bias to the FCC. Finally, in 1971, the FCC turned the station's license over to a nonprofit black-majority management company.

# Debbie Allen
# A Boundless Talent, A Versatile Performer

Debbie Allen had her first taste of Broadway when she became a replacement dancer in the chorus of *Purlie*. While seemingly modest, this part would lead to a long, rich career that would include not just dancing but also choreography, acting, directing, and producing. In fact, very few people have enjoyed success in as many different areas of the entertainment field.

Deborrah Kaye Allen was born on January 16, 1950 in Houston, Texas, the third child of award-winning poet Vivian Ayers-Allen and dentist Arthur Allen. Allen soon showed talent, and at the age of five, she was enrolled in dance classes. Although she was at first rejected by the Houston Ballet School, Allen did eventually study there as the only black dancer. After high school, she attended Howard University, where she graduated cum laude with a degree in drama. Throughout college, she continued to dance, both with students from the university and with the dance troupe of choreographer Mike Malone. Allen would later credit Malone with helping her find her path as a dancer.

Soon after graduating from college in 1971, Allen moved to New York City to pursue a career, and within a few months, she became a member of the chorus in the musical *Purlie*. Two years later, Allen won her first major Broadway role as Beneatha Younger in the 1973 musical *Raisin*, and in 1978, she moved on to *Ain't Misbehavin'*. But it was not until her 1980 portrayal of Anita in the Broadway revival of *West Side Story* that she received critical attention as well as a Drama Desk Award for Outstanding Featured Actress in a Musical.

Allen also forged a career in film and, more significantly, in television. In the 1980 film *Fame*, Allan had only a bit part as a dance instructor, but it was enough to win the attention of ABC. When the network created a television series based on the movie, Allen was cast as a teacher and also became the show's choreographer.

This led to an Emmy for Outstanding Achievement in Choreography. She also had featured roles on many television programs, including *Good Times*, *The Love Boat*, *The Cosby Show*, and *Grey's Anatomy*. And from 1987 to 1993, she both produced and directed the *Cosby Show* spin-off *A Different World*.

Allen found time for two more noteworthy Broadway credits. In 1987, she played the title role in the revival of the musical comedy *Sweet Charity,* and in 2008, she directed an all-black revival of *Cat on a Hot Tin Roof,* which featured older sister Phylicia Rashad and James Earl Jones.

Along with acting, directing, and producing, Allen has never lost her love of choreography. She served as choreographer for ten Academy Awards Shows and created dance numbers for a wide range of performers, from Sammy Davis, Jr. to Janet Jackson. In 2001, Allan demonstrated her lifelong commitment to the world of dance when she and husband Norm Nixon opened the Debbie Allen Dance Academy, a nonprofit dance studio that provides instruction to young people in the greater Los Angeles area. Over a decade later, Allen is proud to see some of her students making their way onto the great stages of Broadway.

The multitalented Debbie Allen has enjoyed success not ▶
only as an actress and dancer but also as a director,
a producer, and, perhaps most famously, a choreographer.

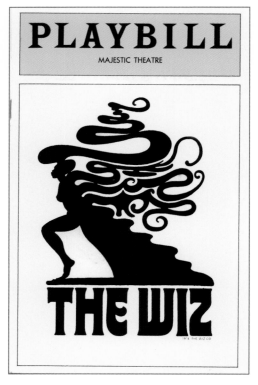

*The Wiz* is one of several musical adaptations that have been made of L. Frank Baum's classic book, *The Wonderful Wizard of Oz*. What sets the 1975 musical apart is that it places Baum's story in the context of black culture.

Just like the Frank Baum book on which it was based, *The Wiz* focuses primarily on Kansas-born Dorothy Gale and her three traveling companions. This photo shows (clockwise from top left) Hinton Battle as the Scarecrow, Ted Ross as the Lion, Tiger Haynes as the Tinman, and Stephanie Mills as Dorothy. Be aware that a young Phylicia Ayers-Allen—later known as Phylicia Rashad—made her Broadway debut in *The Wiz* playing a Munchkin and a field mouse.

## The Wiz

In the early 1970s, Ken Harper was the program affairs director at WPIX Radio when he had the idea of producing a new musical version of L. Frank Baum's book *The Wonderful Wizard of Oz.* Musical adaptations of the children's classic were nothing new. In 1903, a musical extravaganza, with book and lyrics by Baum, has been staged on Broadway, where it ran for 293 performances. And, of course, in 1939, MGM's film *The Wizard of Oz* won praise from both critics and moviegoers, becoming an instant classic. But Harper's version was to be different, for it would place Baum's story in the context of black culture and would add all new music. William F. Brown was signed on to write the book, and music and lyrics would be contributed by Charlie Smalls.

The journey of *The Wiz* to Broadway was fraught with more problems than Dorothy's journey to Oz. Cast members left, the original director had to be replaced in out-of-town tryouts, and as the play moved toward New York, ticket sales were so low that Harper had closing notices ready for posting on opening night. Yet the play did open in January 1975 at the Majestic Theatre, with the original Broadway cast including Stephanie Mills, Hinton Battle, Tiger Haynes, Ted Ross, Dee Dee Bridgewater, and André DeShields.

*The Wiz* received poor reviews from New York critics, and it did not seem that the faltering production could withstand the assault. But shortly after the opening, an editorial appeared in the *New York Amsterdam News*— the oldest black newspaper in the country—urging black theatergoers to

Although *The Wiz* was initially plagued by production problems and poor reviews from New York critics, a robust advertising campaign and support from the black community helped transform it into a hit. The musical ran for nearly 1,700 performances, won seven Tony Awards, and inspired a 1978 film adaptation.

see the play. The editorial explained that white critics might be unable to respond to a story "produced by Blacks, sung by Blacks, and seen predominantly by Blacks on opening night." Mainstream critics also might not understand references to black culture or appreciate the use of black vernacular and the message of black pride. It was therefore up to the people to see and spread the word about this great play.

Spurred by the editorial and subsequent reviews from the black community, as well as by a robust television ad campaign—the second in Broadway history, with the first being the campaign for *Pippin*—sales soared and *The Wiz* became a huge hit, running for 1,672 performances. The show was nominated for numerous Tony Awards and won seven: Best Musical, Best Choreography (George Faison), Best Costume Design (Geoffrey Holder), Best Director of a Musical (Geoffrey Holder), Best Performance by a Featured Actor in a Musical (Ted Ross), Best Performance by a Featured Actress in a Musical (Dee Dee Bridgewater), and Best Original Score (Charlie Smalls). In 1978, a film version would be released starring Diana Ross, Michael Jackson, Lena Horne, and Richard Pryor, and in 1984, Stephanie Mills would reprise her role as Dorothy in a revival of the stage musical. But neither of these productions could rival the success of the 1975 musical, which rocked New York for four years.

In every adaptation of Baum's *The Wonderful Wizard of Oz*, Dorothy learns that she truly belongs in Kansas with Aunt Em and Uncle Henry. Here, we see Stephanie Mills as Dorothy and Tasha Thomas as the caring Aunt Em.

The Congressional Black Caucus (CBC) was established in 1971 as a way for black members of the House of Representatives to collectively work on African-American issues. Through task forces and working groups, the CBC addresses concerns such as civil rights, voter protection, education, energy and environment, health care, poverty, immigration, and justice system reform.

The 1971 publication of Ernest J. Gaines' novel *The Autobiography of Miss Jane Pittman* presented readers with the story of an African-American woman, from her years as a slave to the beginning of the Vietnam War. It has been said that Gaines' book did more than any other book to help white Americans understand the events that led up to the civil rights movement.

The brainchild of director and choreographer Billy Wilson, 1976's all-black revival of *Guys and Dolls* featured the show's original songs—with Motown-style updates—and a cast that included Robert Guillaume, Norma Donaldson, James Randolph, and Ernestine Jackson. While the reviews were good, the musical had a relatively short run.

## *Guys and Dolls*

The original production of *Guys and Dolls* debuted on Broadway in 1950. With music and lyrics by Frank Loesser and book by Jo Swerling and Abe Burrows, the tuneful story of gamblers, gangsters, and other characters in New York's underworld was a major hit. Subsequently, in 1955, 1965, and 1966, New York City Center mounted short runs of the popular show, but not until 1976 was a Broadway revival staged. And this time, there was a twist—the cast was entirely black.

The 1976 show was the brainchild of director and choreographer Billy Wilson, who had envisioned the black revival after staging an all-white production years earlier. The Frank Loesser songs and the Swerling and Burrows book stayed, but the music received Motown-style updates by Danny Holgate and Horace Ott, and the change in ethnicity made it necessary to occasionally alter the lyrics and the dialogue. In a 1976 interview published in *The New York Times,* Wilson compared the process of transforming the original musical into a black musical to the process of "taking chicken soup and making it a little more like gumbo."

The revival opened at the Broadway Theatre in July 1976 with a cast that featured Robert Guillaume, Norma Donaldson, James Randolph, Ernestine Jackson, and Ken Page. The production had a modest run of 239 performances, but it was generally well received by the critics and was nominated for several awards. Ken Page garnered a Theatre World Award.

## *Timbuktu!*

The 1970s saw another all-black revival on the Great White Way. *Timbuktu!* was a resetting of the musical *Kismet*, which had premiered on Broadway in 1953. Like *Kismet*, the play's book was written by Luther Davis, and its songs adapted the music of Alexander Borodin, with lyrics by George Forrest and Robert Wright. The story still concerned a clever poet who arranges for his beautiful daughter to marry a prince, but while *Kismet* was set in Baghdad, *Timbuktu!* was set in the Ancient Empire of Mali, West Africa. In keeping with the new locale, several original songs based on African folk music were written by the *Kismet* lyricists, and new dances, sets, and costumes were created.

*Timbuktu!* starred Melba Moore, Ira Hawkins, Gilbert Price, and Obba Babatundé, who would later costar in *Dreamgirls*. Most exciting was that the cast also featured Eartha Kitt. After Kitt made anti-war remarks at a White House luncheon back in 1968, the doors to the country's entertainment industry had been closed to her, and she had spent several years performing in Europe. This musical marked the actress's return to the Broadway stage.

*Timbuktu!* opened in March 1978 at the Mark Hellinger Theatre. Although the production was lavish, with stunning sets and costumes, the musical was deemed "lackluster" by critics, and generally received poor reviews. The show's run of over 200 performances was probably attributable to the legendary Eartha Kitt, who delivered her usual show-stopping performance.

Although *Timbuktu!* offered lavish sets, gorgeous costumes, and several new songs and dances, this 1978 remake of the musical *Kismet* was poorly received by audiences and reviewers. The fact that it ran for over 200 performances is probably due to the star power of Eartha Kitt, who had returned to the Broadway stage after several years spent abroad.

In 1973, Tom Bradley—the grandson of slaves and the son of sharecroppers—was elected mayor of Los Angeles, making him the first black mayor of a major American city with a white majority. He served as mayor for five terms, until 1993. Among Bradley's accomplishments were completion of the transit system and hosting of the 1984 Olympic Games.

Marian Wright Edelman was the first black woman admitted to the Mississippi Bar. In 1973, inspired by the civil rights movement, Edelman founded the Children's Defense Fund, a nonprofit advocacy and research center that serves as a voice for poor children, children of color, and children with disabilities. Its motto is "Leave No Child Behind."

# Original Book Musicals

While neither 1971's *Jesus Christ Superstar* nor 1972's *Pippin* were "black" musicals, both demonstrated non-traditional casting by choosing actors without consideration of race. The result was that Ben Vereen won powerful roles in two largely white, hugely successful productions.

Although original book musicals were in relatively short supply during the 1970s, there were several that not only were highly successful but also featured great black performers.

## *Jesus Christ Superstar* and *Pippin*

In the early 1970s, two original musicals, *Jesus Christ Superstar* and *Pippin*, captured the attention of critics and theatergoers alike. While neither one was a "black" musical, they both demonstrated color-blind casting, meaning that they cast roles without consideration of the actor's race. The result was that two powerful roles in largely white productions were played by a black actor—Ben Vereen.

Ben Vereen already had several shows to his credit in 1971, when *Jesus Christ Superstar* opened on Broadway, but it took Vereen's portrayal of Judas Iscariot to win the actor both public notice and a Tony nomination for Best Performance by a Featured Actor in a Musical.

Written by Joseph A. Walker, *The River Niger* was first produced by the Negro Ensemble Company (NEC) at the off-Broadway St. Mark's Playhouse. In 1973, when the drama moved to the Brooks Atkinson Theatre, it became the first NEC play to reach Broadway, where it ran for 280 performances and won a Tony Award for Best Play.

On April 8, 1974, Atlanta Braves player Henry "Hank" Aaron hit his 715th home run, breaking Babe Ruth's home run record. Throughout his career, Aaron spoke out for racial equality in baseball—both on the field and in the front office—and after retiring from active play, he became one of the first African Americans to have a position in the major leagues' upper-level management.

Based loosely on the Gospels, the rock opera *Jesus Christ Superstar,* with music by Andrew Lloyd Webber and lyrics by Tim Rice, chronicles the last seven days of Christ's life. After opening at the Mark Hellinger Theatre in October 1971, the musical proved to be controversial but popular, and ran for 711 performances. One of the major roles in the show was that of Judas Iscariot, played by African-American actor Ben Vereen. Although he was not new to the stage (see the inset on page 192), Vereen first received real notice in *Jesus Christ Superstar,* and the rising actor was nominated for a Tony Award for Best Performance by a Featured Actor in a Musical.

In October 1972, *Pippin* opened at the Imperial Theatre. With music and lyrics by Stephen Schwartz and book by Roger O. Hirson, the musical tells the story of Pippin, the son of Charlemagne, through the performance of a magical acting troupe headed by a Leading Player. Fresh from his role as Judas, Vereen took the role of the Player, and once again, he was a hit. After attending a performance of *Pippin, New York Times* critic Clive Barnes described Vereen's performance as "one of the most impressive aspects of the evening." *Pippin* ran for nearly 2,000 performances, and Vereen— although he did not have the title role—won the Tony Award for the Best Performance by a Leading Actor in a Musical.

Already famous for his work in *Jesus Christ Superstar,* Ben Vereen again took the Broadway stage in 1972's *Pippin.* The show was a hit, Vereen's performance was dazzling, and this time, the talented actor took home a Tony.

# Ben Vereen
## Dynamic Star of Stage and Screen

Even a brief review of 1970s musicals and their stars shows that this was the decade of Ben Vereen. But Vereen's career began long before he mesmerized audiences in *Jesus Christ Superstar* and *Pippin*.

The talented performer was born on October 10, 1946. Growing up in Brooklyn, New York, he was drawn to the stage as both a dancer and an actor, and he often appeared in local variety shows. At the age of fourteen, Vereen enrolled in the High School of Performing Arts. There, he studied dance under choreographers Martha Graham, Jerome Robbins, and George Balanchine.

After graduating from high school, Vereen struggled to find stage work, but in 1965, one of his former teachers, Martha Graham, cast him in the musical *The Prodigal Son* at the Greenwich Mews Theatre. Then in 1967, he won a part in Bob Fosse's touring production of *Sweet Charity*. And in 1968, he was cast as a replacement in *Hair* before joining the show's touring company.

In 1971, Vereen had the good fortune to win the important role of Judas Iscariot in the Broadway hit *Jesus Christ Superstar*. Although his dazzling performance earned critical acclaim as well as a Tony nomination, he didn't fully achieve star status until 1972, when he delivered a masterful performance as the Leading Player in *Pippin*. This time, he took home the Tony Award for the Best Performance by a Leading Actor in a Musical.

In addition to his success on the stage, Ben Vereen has forged a career in movies. He made his screen debut in *Sweet Charity* in 1969, and went on to appear in *Funny Lady* (1978), *All That Jazz* (1979), *Why Do Fools Fall in Love* (1998), and a number of other films. Vereen also made his mark on the small screen, where he has appeared in programs ranging from 1975's variety series *Ben Vereen . . . Comin' At Ya* to *How I Met Your Mother* (2010). He is best known, however, for his Emmy-nominated portrayal of Chicken George in the landmark 1977 TV miniseries *Roots*. It was this role that enabled the actor to demonstrate his versatility and dramatic abilities.

Starting in 1987, Vereen suffered a series of personal tragedies culminating in a life-threatening 1992 automobile accident that required extensive physical rehabilitation. Through hard work, Vereen made a full recovery, and in 1993—within a year of the accident—he returned to Broadway as the Chimney Man in *Jelly's Last Jam,* a musical about the life of jazz legend Jelly Roll Morton. Since then, he has been featured in stage productions of *A Christmas Carol* (1995) and *Fosse* (1999), has costarred with Judd Hirsch in *I'm Not Rappaport* (2002), and has played the Wizard of Oz in the Broadway hit *Wicked*. From *Hair* to *Wicked*, through career highs and personal lows, Vereen has remained one of America's most versatile performers for six decades.

After Ben Vereen's career was launched in high-profile musicals, ▶ he enjoyed similar success in both movies and television. But Vereen never forgot his Broadway roots, and he would return to the stage for *Jelly's Last Jam* (1993), *Fosse* (1999), *I'm Not Rappaport* (2002), and *Wicked* (2005).

## *Dreamgirls*

By the start of the 1980s, Broadway was beginning to recover from the recession, and musicals were becoming bigger and better than ever. Director and choreographer Michael Bennett, who had brought *A Chorus Line* to the stage in 1976, had a new project—the story of a black female singing group that rises from poverty to superstardom in the 1960s. Based on the experiences of Motown performers like the Supremes, the show explored the price of success, including the artistic compromises that were made at a time when many young black singers allowed their distinctive rhythm-and-blues sound to be "refined" so they could attract a mainstream audience. *Dreamgirls* had music by Henry Krieger and lyrics and book by Tom Eyen, and its songs—all original—numbered nearly forty. The cast included Sheryl Lee Ralph, Jennifer Holliday, Loretta Devine, Ben Harney, Cleavant Derricks, and Obba Babatundé.

The show opened in December 1981 at the Imperial Theatre and was an instant hit. Critics praised the music, the cast, and the dazzling pro-

The story of a black female singing group that rises from the ghetto to national fame, *Dreamgirls* was a star maker for many of its cast members, most notably, Jennifer Holliday (left). Also shown here are Sheryl Lee Ralph (center) and Loretta Devine (right).

duction, and theatergoers were just as enthusiastic. *Dreamgirls* ran for 1,521 performances and launched the careers of several cast members, most notably, Jennifer Holliday. Not surprisingly, the show was nominated for eleven Tony Awards and won six of them, including Best Book of a Musical, Best Performance by a Leading Actor in a Musical (Ben Harney), Best Performance by a Leading Actress in a Musical (Jennifer Holliday), Best Performance by a Featured Actor (Cleavant Derricks), Best Choreography (Michael Bennett and Michael Peters), and Best Lighting Design (Tharon Musser). The cast album garnered two Grammy Awards, and the signature tune "And I Am Telling You I'm Not Going" became a number-one R&B hit for Holliday in 1982.

*Dreamgirls* had two Broadway revivals, the first in 1987 and the second in 2001. In 2006, it was made into a film starring Beyoncé Knowles, Jamie Foxx, Eddie Murphy, and Jennifer Hudson, who won an Oscar for her performance.

The success of 1981's *Dreamgirls*—which ran for 1,521 dazzling performances and won six Tony Awards—renewed the public's interest in both sixties' girl groups, such as the Supremes, and Motown Records, the small record company that was one of the most influential labels of the time.

## Sarafina!

One of the most unique musicals to surface in the late 1980s was *Sarafina!* Created by South African playwright Mbongeni Ngema, with additional songs by Hugh Masekela, the musical was set during the Soweto Riots of 1976, when 200,000 black students protested the official decree that they had to use Afrikaans—widely viewed as the language of their white oppressors—in their classroom. This struggle marked the beginning of the often violent internal anti-apartheid movement that would last for nearly two decades. But the show didn't entirely focus on the protests. Instead, it followed a high-school class through one term in their Soweto school as they prepare to put on a school program. The cast members were all young people, in their teens and twenties, whom Ngema found through months of auditions held throughout South Africa's black townships.

*Sarafina!* ran in Johannesburg in 1987 before premiering at Broadway's Cort Theatre in January 1988, where it ran for 597 performances. Audiences and critics were intrigued not only by the Mbaqanga music—the street music of South Africa—but also by the story's uplifting message of black pride, hope, and the promise of freedom. The production received nominations for four Tony Awards: Best Musical, Best Performance by a Featured Actress in a Musical (Leleti Khumalo, who played the title role), Best Original Score, and Best Choreography. A 1988 documentary *The Voices of Sarafina!* recounts the story of this amazing presentation, and a movie version of *Sarafina!* was released in 1992.

In 1974, a black feminist group, the Combahee River Collective, was founded in Boston. The collective is best known for creating the Combahee River Collective Statement, which affirmed the group's commitment "to struggling against racial, sexual, heterosexual, and class oppression." Members were active in campaigns against school segregation, police brutality, and violence against women.

Like 1971's *Swann v. Charlotte-Mecklenburg Board of Education, Milliken v. Bradley* was a significant case that occurred in the aftermath of *Brown v. Board of Education.* Although *Swann* had promoted busing to integrate schools, in *Milliken v. Bradley,* the Supreme Court decided that school systems are not responsible for desegregation unless they deliberately created segregation.

# Bringing Broadway Back

Throughout the 1970s, the New York theater community struggled to produce high-quality shows, to keep long-time theatergoers coming back to the theater district, and to attract a new audience. Although the eventual recovery of the economy certainly had a positive impact on the entertainment industry, Broadway also took steps to speed its own revival.

Early in the 1970s, *Pippin* became the first show to advertise on television as a means of drawing people to the theater. Other productions, including *The Wiz*, followed suit. This tactic, which was revolutionary at the time, made more potential theatergoers aware of what was available in New York theaters, and as more people enjoyed the shows, word of mouth continued to increase sales.

At about the same time that TV viewers were enjoying "a free minute from *Pippin*," the Theatre Development Fund, a nonprofit group designed to assist New York City's theater industry, began selling half-price Broadway tickets from a booth that would come to be known as TKTS. Initially, the Times Square booth was greeted with some skepticism by New Yorkers, who were doubtful that any show offering half-price admittance was worth seeing. In time, though, the booth became a boon to the industry, extending the run of many shows and making it possible for millions of people—including many first-time theatergoers—to buy tickets that otherwise would have been prohibitively expensive.

Then, in the early 1980s, a series of highly successful musicals helped reinvigorate the industry. Audience-pleasing hits like *42nd Street, Dreamgirls, Sophisticated Ladies, Woman of the Year*, and *Cats* drew people to Broadway theaters and kept them coming back for more.

## Musical Revues

In the 1970s and '80s, long after Harlem nightclubs had helped introduce black jazz to white America, Broadway offered a number of musical revues that celebrated the great African-American musicians of the Jazz Age.

By the 1970s, Harlem's heyday was long past, and with it had gone the great jazz clubs that had changed American music. Those heady days of the twenties and thirties had not been forgotten, however, nor had the distinctive sound that Harlem had popularized. Beginning in the mid-seventies, Broadway offered several spectacular musical revues that celebrated jazz and the talented black entertainers who had created it.

But not all the revues of seventies were jazz-focused. One production shared stories of children struggling to live in and make sense of the modern-day inner city, and another told the story of Christ through gospel music.

### *The Me Nobody Knows*

In a decade that produced several lavish musical productions, some shows dared to be different. *The Me Nobody Knows* was based on a collection of writings of nearly two hundred students living in poor areas of New York

Founded in December 1975, the National Association of Black Journalists (NABJ) was created for the purpose of providing quality programs and services to and advocating on behalf of black journalists. The largest organization of journalists of color in the nation, the NABJ offers professional development and technical training, and encourages black journalists to become entrepreneurs.

Frank Robinson played for the Cincinnati Reds (1956-1965), Baltimore Orioles (1966-1971), Los Angeles Dodgers (1972), California Angels (1973-1974), and Cleveland Indians (1974-976) before becoming the major leagues' first African-American manager in 1975. In 1982, he was elected to the Baseball Hall of Fame.

City. There was no plot. Instead, the revue presented a series of scenes, each of which combined text with song and dance to represent a ghetto child's experiences, fears, and hopes. The book was written by Robert H. Livingston, Herb Schapiro, and Stephen M. Joseph; the music, by Gary William Friedman; and the lyrics, by Will Holt. The cast of twelve included eight black performers and four white performers.

The musical *The Me Nobody Knows* opened off-Broadway, but in December 1970, it moved to the Helen Hayes Theatre, and in 1971, it found its third home at the Longacre Theatre, running for a total of 378 Broadway performances. Critics gave the show an enthusiastic reception, with Clive Barnes of *The New York Times* calling it a "dark and lovely rock musical." It was nominated for five Tony Awards and garnered the Drama Desk Awards for Outstanding Music and Outstanding Lyrics.

## *Your Arms Too Short to Box With God*

Taking its name from a poem by African-American writer and educator James Weldon Johnson, *Your Arms Too Short to Box With God* followed in the wake of *Jesus Christ Superstar* by telling the story of Christ from his days of preaching to his crucifixion. Conceived by Vinnette Carroll, with music and lyrics by Alex Bradford and Micki Grant, the show was essentially a black gospel revue, comprised of short skits, dance numbers, and solo and group vocal performances. The cast included William Hardy, Jr., Salome Bey, Mabel Robinson, Clinton Derricks-Carroll, and Delores Hall.

The original musical opened at the Lyceum Theatre in December 1976 and ran for 149 performances. The production earned several Tony nominations and won a Tony for Best Performance by a Featured Actress in a Musical (Delores Hall). Broadway revivals were staged in 1980 and 1982, with the 1982 production starring Al Green and Patti LaBelle.

A black gospel revue, 1976's *Your Arms Too Short to Box With God* used song and dance to present the story of Christ as told in the Book of Matthew. Shown here are two members of the original cast—Salome Bey (standing) and Mabel Robinson.

In 1976, *Bubbling Brown Sugar* began a wave of Broadway shows about black composers, lyricists, and performers. *Bubbling Brown Sugar* featured music by a range of artists, *Ain't Misbehavin'* offered the music of Thomas "Fats" Waller, *Eubie!* celebrated composer Eubie Blake, and *Sophisticated Ladies* paid tribute to Duke Ellington.

After its creation in 1926, Negro History Week became increasingly popular. In February 1970, led by Black United Students at Kent State University, Black History Month was celebrated for the first time at Kent State. In 1976 the expansion of Negro History Week to Black History Month was officially recognized by the United States Government.

# Ashton Springer
# Transcending Racial Lines

The 1960s had helped make Broadway more accessible to both black performers and black theatergoers. Yet long after the decade had ended, most of the theater world adhered to the long-held beliefs that black shows were not commercially viable and that, regardless of the quality of the production, African-American theatergoers would never show up in significant numbers. One of the individuals who helped prove them wrong was African-American producer Ashton Springer.

Born on November 1, 1930 in New York City, Springer attended high school in the Bronx and later studied at Ohio State University. After college, Springer became a social worker in the Bronx and also ran a coin-operated laundry in Queens. Improbably, it was the laundry that served as the young entrepreneur's bridge to Broadway. When playwright N. Richard Nash, best known for *The Rainmaker*, decided to become an investor in the business, he and Springer got to know each other. Through this association, Springer gradually became immersed in the theater, and in 1960, he worked as Nash's assistant in the Broadway production of *Wildcat*. He took to his new career like a fish to water, and within a short time, Springer had decided to become a producer—despite the fact that African-American producers were a great rarity during that era.

The first show that Ashton Springer brought to the stage was a 1969 revival of *No Place to Be Somebody,* the play that brought author Charles Gordone a Pulitzer Prize for Drama. Springer is best known, though, as producer of the popular '70s musicals *Bubbling Brown Sugar* (1976) and *Eubie!* (1978), which captivated both black and white theatergoers. All told, he shepherded nearly a dozen Broadway plays in the 1970s and early '80s, becoming the first major black producer on the Great White Way. In 1979, he was called "the hottest black producer out there" by *The Washington Post*.

Ashton Springer is recognized for not just bringing African-American talent to the stage but also bringing African-American audiences to Broadway. Throughout his life, he firmly believed in the need to transcend racial lines and produce great plays that were "not black theater, not white theater. Just theater."

Although his Broadway career was cut short in the eighties by financial problems, Ashton Springer is known as a pioneer who opened the door for future black producers. When Springer died in 2013 at the age of eighty-two, the marquees of Broadway were dimmed in memory of the man who dreamed of a theater that was for everyone, white and black.

## *Bubbling Brown Sugar*

Although billed as a musical history of Harlem, *Bubbling Brown Sugar* was a musical revue with a thin plot, but the lack of story line didn't keep it from being highly entertaining. In fact, this production began a great wave of Broadway shows about notable black songwriters and performers.

Based on a concept by Rosetta LeNoire, the show had a book by Loften Mitchell and featured music by a range of artists from the 1920s, '30s, and '40s, including Duke Ellington, Eubie Blake, Count Basie, Cab Calloway, Fats Waller, Billie Holiday, and many others, with original music by Danny Holgate, Emme Kemp, and Lillian Lopez. Jazz favorites such as "Stompin' at the Savoy," "Sophisticated Lady," "Sweet Georgia Brown," "God Bless the Child," and "It Don't Mean a Thing" were performed by an energetic cast that included Avon Long, Josephine Premice, Vivian Reed, and Joseph Attles. The production also featured veteran tap dancer Charles "Honi" Coles, who offered a clever impersonation of legendary vaudevillian Bert Williams. The dazzling choreography was by Billy Wilson, who was also credited with the musical staging.

*Bubbling Brown Sugar* opened at the ANTA Playhouse in March 1976 and ran for 766 performances. It was nominated for three Tony Awards and won the Drama Desk Award for Outstanding Featured Actress in a Musical (Vivian Reed).

Rosetta LeNoire, who conceived of the idea for *Bubbling Brown Sugar*, had begun her career as an actress and made her Broadway debut in the 1939 hit *Hot Mikado*. Her godfather, legendary performer Bill "Bojangles" Robinson—star of *Hot Mikado*—affectionately called his goddaughter "Brown Sugar."

In 1976, *Bubbling Brown Sugar* began a wave of Broadway musicals about African-American songwriters and performers. The show's sensational dance numbers garnered a Tony Award nomination for choreographer Billy Wilson.

Of all the musical revues that sought to recreate Harlem's golden age, 1978's *Ain't Misbehavin'* was the most successful. A tribute to the life and music of Thomas "Fats" Waller, the show ran for 1,604 performances and won three Tony Awards, three Drama Desk Awards, and two Theatre World Awards.

Nell Carter's dynamic performance in 1978's *Ain't Misbehavin'* won her a Tony Award for Best Performance by a Featured Actress in a Musical. Fame would bring Carter further career opportunities, including a major role in the long-running television show *Gimme a Break!*

## *Ain't Misbehavin'*

The most successful musical revue to bring back Harlem's golden age was 1978's *Ain't Misbehavin'*. Based on a concept by Murray Horwitz and Richard Maltby, Jr., and directed by Maltby, with musical arrangements by Luther Henderson and choreography by Arthur Faria, the show celebrated the life and music of Thomas "Fats" Waller. A stride pianist, composer, singer, and comic entertainer, Waller was known mainly for his compositions and comic persona during his lifetime, but was later recognized for the important role he played in laying the groundwork for modern jazz piano. *Ain't Misbehavin'*—which took its title from a 1929 Waller song—included thirty numbers, most of them composed by Waller and a few of them popularized by Waller. Many of the songs, like "I'm Gonna Sit Right Down and Write Myself a Letter," were standards. The small cast included Nell Carter, Armelia McQueen, Charlayne Woodard, Ken Page, and André DeShields.

*Ain't Misbehavin'* began as an intimate show with a limited run at the Manhattan Theatre Club, but critical acclaim and packed houses prompted a team of producers to transplant the revue to the Longacre Theatre in May 1978. During its 1,604-performance run, it would be relocated two more times, first to the Plymouth Theatre and then to the Belasco. Cast replacements were made as needed, with the most notable addition being Debbie Allen. The revue was nominated for four Tony Awards and won three of them, for Best Musical, Best Performance by a Featured Actress in a Musical (Nell Carter), and Best Direction of a Musical (Richard Maltby, Jr.). It also won three Drama Desk Awards and two Theatre World Awards. Then in 1988, the popular show enjoyed a Broadway revival with the original cast, director, and choreographer.

### Eubie!

The year 1978 also brought the musical *Eubie!* to Broadway. A homage to ragtime composer and pianist Eubie Blake, *Eubie!* was conceived and directed by Julianne Boyd and choreographed by Billy Wilson and Henry LeTang. It offered twenty-four songs, including "Charleston Rag," "Shuffle Along," and "Goodnight Angeline." The talented cast featured Ethel Beatty, Terry Burrell, Leslie Dockery, Lynnie Godfrey, Mel Johnson, Jr., Lonnie McNeil, Alaina Reed, Jeffrey V. Thompson, and—united for the first time in five years—brothers Maurice and Gregory Hines. Every night, the Hines brothers would receive standing ovations as they tapped and sang their way through Blake's classic tunes.

The original opening-night cast of *Ain't Misbehavin'* included Nell Carter, André DeShields, Armelia McQueen, Ken Page, and Charlayne Woodard. But several replacements were made later in the run. This photo of the production shows (left to right) Armelia McQueen, Ken Page, Debbie Allen, Alan Weeks, and Zoe Walker

*Eubie!* ran from September 1978 to October 1979 at the Ambassador Theatre, with the cast giving 439 performances. The spirited revue was nominated for several awards and won three: Maurice Hines and Gregory Hines received Outer Critics Circle Awards, and Gregory Hines won a Theatre World Award. (For more about the Hines brothers, see the inset on page 202.)

Chosen by President James Carter as U.S. Ambassador to the United Nations in 1977, civil rights activist and politician Andrew Young was the first African American appointed to this position. Serving from 1977 to 1979, Ambassador Young supported human rights on a global scale and negotiated an end to white-minority rule in Namibia and Zimbabwe.

United professionally for the first time in five years, brothers Maurice and Gregory Hines—best known for their childhood tap-dancing act—performed together in the 1978 hit musical revue *Eubie!* Both brothers received rave reviews as well as special Outer Critics Circle Awards. Gregory Hines' performance was also honored with a Theatre World Award.

# Maurice and Gregory Hines
# Tapping Through Life

No discussion of 1970s musicals would be complete without the mention of brothers Maurice and Gregory Hines. And their influence has extended far beyond that decade not only because of their long and successful careers but also because of their determination to keep alive the art of tap dancing as it had been practiced by earlier generations of black hoofers.

Maurice Hines (born December 13, 1943) and Gregory Hines (born February 14, 1946) were raised in New York City. Their mother, Alma Hines, encouraged her sons to become entertainers as a means of escaping poverty. She explained that because they were black, they had to work harder and become highly skilled in tap dancing, singing, and other aspects of performing. Grandmother Ora Hines had been a showgirl in Harlem's Cotton Club, so dancing seemed to be in their blood. Certainly, the boys needed little prodding from their mother to develop their skills. Maurice began taking tap-dancing lessons at the age of five and, when he got home from the dance studio, he would eagerly teach his little brother what he'd learned. Soon, both boys were taking lessons with teacher Henry LeTang, who choreographed special dances for the talented duo. When they were only seven and five years of age, Maurice and Greg began appearing at the Apollo Theater's famed Amateur Night, and they made their Broadway debut in the 1954 musical comedy *The Girl in Pink Tights*. They then became a touring act, first as the Hines Kids; later as the Hines Brothers; and, after they were joined by their self-trained drummer father, as Hines, Hines and Dad.

During their many years of performing, the Hines used what they called the "old technique" of tap dancing—the style characteristic of the Berry Brothers and the Nicholas Brothers, who had begun their careers during the Jazz Age. At a time when many black performers refused to learn this African-American form of art because it represented an age of black oppression to them, Maurice and Greg saw its value, and so did their audiences. The act reached national prominence when it made more than three dozen guest appearances on Johnny Carson's *Tonight Show*.

Over many years of working together, the brothers developed different professional interests, and in 1973, Maurice and Gregory Hines went their separate ways. It took the 1978 revue *Eubie!* (see page 201) to bring them together again. Maurice was hired first, and—with the help of both Maurice and the brothers' long-time mentor Henry LeTang—Gregory was added to the cast. The audience loved them, both separately and when they tap-danced together to "Dixie Moon." The brothers also appeared in the 1981 Broadway revue *Sophisticated Ladies*, with Gregory winning the lead in the original cast and Maurice taking over his role when he left the show.

After *Sophisticated Ladies*, Gregory continued his work as an actor and dancer, both on the stage and in dozens of movies. Throughout his life, he was also a tireless advocate for tap. Maurice, too, continued dancing and acting, as well as directing and choreographing musicals and music videos. The brothers appeared together in the 1984 film *The Cotton Club*, playing—not surprisingly—a tap-dancing duo.

Gregory Hines died on August 9, 2003 at the age of fifty-seven. Ten years later, Maurice Hines created the show *Tappin' Thru Life* to honor his younger brother, their life together, and the singers who had inspired their work. Toward the end of each evening, as a means of including Gregory, Maurice performed an early Hines Brothers soft-shoe routine next to an empty spotlight. He also used the production to pass the torch to tap-dancing brothers John and Leo Manzari, helping to ensure that the Hines' brand of dancing would not die.

After many years of working together, ▶
Maurice Hines (left) and Gregory Hines (right)
pursued separate careers for five years.
Then in 1978, they teamed up again for *Eubie!*,
a celebration of jazz great Eubie Blake.

## Sophisticated Ladies

Three years after the debut of *Ain't Misbehavin'* and *Eubie!,* another revue paid tribute to the contributions of an African-American jazz legend. This time, the legend was Edward Kennedy "Duke" Ellington, and the show—named after a 1932 Ellington song—was *Sophisticated Ladies.*

The revue was conceived by Donald McKayle; directed by Michael Smuin; and choreographed by McKayle, Smuin, and Henry LeTang. It offered about three dozen numbers, including "Take the 'A' Train," "It Don't Mean a Thing (If It Ain't Got That Swing)," "Don't Get Around Much Anymore," "Satin Doll," and other Ellington classics. The undisputed star of the show was Gregory Hines, and the cast also featured Judith Jamison, Phyllis Hyman, Hinton Battle, and Gregg Burge, as well as a host of other talented black performers—all of whom were dressed to the nines to befit the play's lavish nightclub setting. As a final elegant and authentic touch, the music was contributed by the Duke Ellington Orchestra, which appeared on a floating bandstand led by Mercer Ellington, the late Duke's son.

*Sophisticated Ladies* offered not only three dozen of Duke Ellington's classic numbers but also wonderfully elegant sets and costumes. Here, stars Gregory Hines and Judith Jamison wear fashions created by Willa Kim, who won a Tony Award for Best Costume Design.

The show opened at the Lunt-Fontanne Theatre in March 1981, and immediately received stellar reviews. *New York Times* reviewer Frank Rich praised the grand scale of the production as well as the talents of Gregory Hines and company. *Sophisticated Ladies* ran for 767 performances, with Maurice Hines—Gregory's older brother—taking over the lead when Gregory left the show. The revue was nominated for eight Tony Awards and won two, for Best Performance by a Featured Actor in a Musical (Hinton Battle) and Best Costume Design (Willa Kim).

## Black and Blue

The last musical revue of the 1980s was *Black and Blue,* a stylish tribute to black American jazz and blues artists like Duke Ellington, Jimmy Lunceford, W.C. Handy, and Fats Waller. The show was conceived and directed by Claudio Segovia and Hector Orezzoli, two Argentine producers who sought to recreate the singing and dancing that had made Harlem nightclubs so popular between the World Wars. Cholly Atkins, Henry LeTang, Frankie Manning, and Fayard Nicholas (of the Nicholas Brothers) provided the choreography, and Sy Johnson and Luther Henderson provided musical supervision, arrangements, and orchestration.

*Black and Blue* featured three stars—well-known blues singers Ruth Brown, Linda Hopkins, and Carrie Smith. These veteran performers were backed by a team of old-time hoofers and a large dance ensemble, as well as a band composed of top jazz musicians. The score of over a dozen numbers included "St. Louis Blues," "I Can't Give You Anything But Love," "Am I Blue?," "Stompin' at the Savoy," and of course, Fats Waller's "Black and Blue."

The revue opened at the Minskoff Theatre in January 1989. Critics compared the production to the type of flamboyant show that Florenz Ziegfeld used to mount, complete with lavish sets and gorgeous costumes. *Black and Blue* ran until January 1991, for 829 performances. The musical was nominated for nine Tony Awards and won three: Best Performance by a Leading Actress in a Musical (Ruth Brown), Best Choreography (Cholly Atkins, Henry LeTang, Frankie Manning, and Fayard Nicholas), and Best Costume Design (Claudio Segovia and Hector Orezzoli).

A tribute to black jazz and blues artists, *Black and Blue* opened at the Minskoff Theatre in 1989. With its lavish sets and costumes, the show was compared to the extravagant productions of Broadway impresario Florenz Ziegfeld.

In the 1970s, Ashton Springer emerged as the first major black producer on the Great White Way. Although he is best known for *Bubbling Brown Sugar* (1976) and *Eubie!* (1978), he shepherded many other shows—both musicals and dramas—including 1969's *No Place to Be Somebody,* the 1976 all-black revival of *Guys and Dolls,* and 1979's *Whoopee!*

Alice Walker's novel *The Color Purple,* with its poignant story of African-American women struggling in rural Georgia, won both the 1983 Pulitzer Prize for Fiction and the National Book Award for Fiction. In 1985, *The Color Purple* was adapted into a film of the same name, and in 2005, a musical adaptation premiered at the Broadway Theatre.

# ONE-WOMAN SHOWS

In addition to the more standard musicals and dramas that were staged on Broadway during the 1980s, two one-woman shows by fine black performers were offered to theatergoers. The first production starred a veteran performer, already well known to stage and screen audiences, while the second brought a relatively new entertainer to the attention of the public.

In 1981, Lena Horne starred in *The Lady and Her Music*—a one-woman show in which the singer-actress performed over two dozen musical numbers and told the story of her career. The stunning production won a Special Tony Award for Horne.

In 1981, the glamorous singer-actress Lena Horne starred in *Lena Horne: The Lady and Her Music.* Produced by Michael Frazier and Fred Walker, the one-woman show featured more than two dozen musical numbers, including Horne's signature "Stormy Weather," as well as "The Lady Is a Tramp," "Just One of Those Things," and many other popular songs. The show also gave the star an opportunity to share the story of her successful but often rocky career on Broadway, in the movies, and in nightclubs.

*The Lady and Her Music* opened at the Nederlander Theatre in May 1981 and closed on Horne's sixty-fifth birthday, June 30, 1982, for 333 Broadway performances. A reviewer for *Rolling Stone* magazine wrote that Horne had "turned the conventions of the one-person extravaganza inside out. . . . Instead of a self-glorifying ego trip, her performance is a shared journey of self-discovery about the human cost (to the audience as well as the singer) of being a symbol." A Special Tony Award was bestowed to honor the outstanding quality of the production and Horne's brilliant contribution to Broadway.

In 1984, a very different one-woman show appeared on a major New York stage starring a very different kind of entertainer. Comedienne Whoopi Goldberg had been playing in fringe clubs and small theaters for three years when director Mike Nichols saw her solo performance of "The Spook Show" at New York's Dance Theatre Workshop. Impressed by Goldberg's original material as well as her comedic and acting skills, Nichols took a risk by bringing a revamped version of her show to Broadway. Called simply *Whoopi Goldberg,* the show premiered in October 1984 at the Lyceum Theatre and played to sold-out audiences through March 1985, for a total of 156 performances. *New York Times* theater critic Mel Gussow said, "Reviewing her show at Dance Theatre Workshop last winter, I suggested that, before long, people would try to compare future comics to the inimitable Whoopi Goldberg. One should add that her time has arrived." In addition to winning the Drama Desk Award for Outstanding One-Person

Although the IRS provides tax exemptions to institutions organized for religious purposes, in 1971, it created a policy denying exemptions to institutions that practice racial discrimination. The IRS thus denied exemptions to two schools—Bob Jones University and Goldsboro Christian School. In 1983's *Bob Jones University v. United States,* the Supreme Court concluded that the IRS had acted properly.

In 1983, Dr. Guion Stewart "Guy" Bluford, Jr. became the first African American to travel into space as a crew member of the Space Shuttle *Challenger.* Bluford would participate in three more Space Shuttle flights and be inducted into the International Space Hall of Fame (1997) and the United States Astronaut Hall of Fame (2010).

Show, Whoopi Goldberg attracted the attention of director Steven Spielberg, who launched the performer's movie career by giving her a leading role in his 1985 film *The Color Purple*.

## DRAMAS

When Lorraine Hansberry's *A Raisin in the Sun* was produced with great success in 1959, many people thought that the time had finally come for the black drama on Broadway. By presenting a riveting story that focused on black issues, Hansberry had attracted not only white theatergoers but also—for the first time—African-American audiences, who were thrilled to see their world represented on stage.

But in the seventies, the deck was stacked against new black Broadway productions. The financial recession and the deterioration of the Broadway area of Manhattan combined to lower ticket sales. Many people couldn't afford the rising prices of Broadway tickets, and the tourists who had formerly flocked to see Broadway shows were now frightened by the rising crime in and around Forty-Second Street. Porno theaters and peep shows now stood where lavish Broadway theaters once drew elegant clientele. The increased presence of police in the theater district indicated that this was not a safe area—especially at ten or eleven o'clock at night, when shows typically let out. Seeing the growing reluctance of people to buy tickets, Broadway producers shied away from backing black dramas, which had always been perceived as being unprofitable.

Fortunately, at the same time that Broadway was experiencing a low point, off-Broadway and even off-off-Broadway theaters were gaining greater respectability in safer neighborhoods. The Off-Broadway Alliance was formed in the early seventies to unify these small, sometimes makeshift theaters. This helped make it possible for the theater community to stay in the city, and enabled the production of shows that might otherwise have been unable to find a venue. Although the growth of off-Broadway at first exacerbated the problems of big-time producers by providing unwanted competition, in time, these alternative theaters would actually help aid Broadway's recovery by allowing original productions to undergo a gestation period, gain momentum, and generate a buzz before moving to the Great White Way.

Eventually, just as Lorraine Hansberry had broken down barriers in the late fifties, in the 1980s, a black dramatist would emerge with plays so powerful that Broadway would once again see productions by and about African Americans. This time around, the playwright would be August Wilson.

Whoopi Goldberg's 1984 one-woman show, aptly titled *Whoopi Goldberg*, won the comedienne-actress the praise of critics and audiences alike. Among the theatergoers was Steven Spielberg, who was so impressed by Goldberg's talents that he gave her the leading role in his 1985 film *The Color Purple*.

---

In the months following the 1968 assassination of Martin Luther King, Jr., Congressman John Conyers, Jr., introduced legislation to make King's January 15 birthday into a national holiday. The King Memorial Center in Atlanta sponsored the first annual observance of King's birthday in 1969, but it was not until 1983 that President Ronald Reagan signed the King Holiday Bill into law.

A leading national advocate for African Americans during the early 1980s, Jesse Jackson urged blacks to work toward self-reliance and to become more politically active. The voter registration drive that he spearheaded was a key factor in the 1983 election of Harold Washington as the first African-American mayor of Chicago. A year later, Jackson ran for the Democratic presidential nomination.

*For Colored Girls Who Have Considered Suicide When the Rainbow Is Enuf* used poetry, music, and dance to convey what it's like to be black and female in America. The play was launched off-Broadway, but in 1976, it was transferred to the Booth Theatre, where it ran for over 700 performances.

## Off-Broadway and Beyond

The growth of off-Broadway did not occur by magic. In addition to the efforts of the Off-Broadway Alliance, several significant groups—including Joseph Papp's Public Theater (see the inset on page 211), the Negro Ensemble Company (see page 169), and the New Federal Theatre (see page 212)—worked hard to bring less-commercial productions to the stage. Some of the dramas that began in off-Broadway venues went on to be successful on Broadway, as well, and in some cases, off-Broadway producers worked in collaboration with one another to deliver an important show to a wider audience. A case in point is Ntozake Shange's *For Colored Girls Who Have Considered Suicide When the Rainbow Is Enuf.*

*For Colored Girls* is composed of twenty poems that express the struggle faced by black women from childhood to old age. The poems are performed—not just read—by seven female characters who are known not by names but by colors, such as "The Lady in Purple." Referred to as a "choreopoem," the unconventional play made its first New York appearance at a Lower East Side bar and was soon transplanted to the New Federal Theatre (NFT). Then, through a collaboration of NFT's Woodie King, Jr. and Joseph Papp, it moved to Joseph Papp's Public Theater. Once at the Public, it ran for 120 performances, always to packed audiences and rave reviews. In September 1976, the Joseph Papp production was transferred to the Booth Theatre on Broadway, where it ran until July 1978 for a total of 742 performances. It received a Tony Award for Best Performance by a Featured Actress in a Play (Trazana Beverley), and was eventually made into a 2010 movie named *For Colored Girls,* starring Janet Jackson, Phylicia Rashad, Anika Noni Rose, and Whoopi Goldberg.

Instead of giving each of *For Colored Girls'* characters a name, playwright Ntozake Shange chose to identify each by color—"The Lady in Blue," for instance—so that their interwoven stories would create a rainbow of life.

Another successful black play that originally had its home in an off-Broadway theater was *The River Niger*. Written by Joseph A. Walker, it was first produced in 1972 by the Negro Ensemble Company (NEC) at the St. Mark's Playhouse. Critics hailed the show as a strong family drama that, although it had roots in the contemporary black experience, was relevant to both black and white theatergoers. Set in Harlem, it concerns a poet father (Douglas Turner Ward) and his air force-dropout son (Les Roberts), who struggle to identify a means of revolution. In doing so, they touch on themes as far-ranging as violence in Harlem and civil rights activism in South Africa. The NEC production won an Obie Award for Best Play.

Complete with the original cast, *The River Niger* was transferred to Broadway's Brooks Atkinson Theatre in March 1973. Again, the production was highly praised. Like the reviewers who had written about the drama in its earlier off-Broadway production, Clive Barnes of *The New York Times* recommended the "remarkable black play" to both white and black theatergoers, but emphatically stated that people in the black community "have to go to the theater more and find out what your black brothers and sisters can do for you up there on stage." Perhaps for the first time, black people made up the majority of the audience. The Broadway production ran for a total of 280 performances and won the Tony Award for Best Play. It also drew nominations for Best Featured Actor (Douglas Turner Ward) and Best Featured Actress (Roxie Roker as Ward's wife). In 1976, a film adaptation was released starring James Earl Jones, Cicely Tyson, and Louis Gossett, Jr.

When 1973's *The River Niger* moved from off-Broadway's St. Mark's Playhouse to Broadway's Brooks Atkinson Theatre, the play retained its original cast, including (clockwise from left), Roxie Roker, Grenna Whitaker, Frances Foster, Douglas Turner Ward, Graham Brown, and Les Roberts.

# Joseph Papp and the Public Theater

Born Joseph Papirofsky in Brooklyn, New York on June 22, 1921, Joseph Papp began staging shows while in the Navy during the Second World War. After the war, Papp was determined to bring affordable theater to New York City. He took a major step toward his goal in 1957, when he obtained a permit to stage productions of Shakespeare's plays in Central Park. Despite objections from some politicians, this program—which became known as the New York Shakespeare Festival or simply Shakespeare in the Park—would become a staple of New York theater. Once the open-air Delacorte Theater was established in the park, Papp searched for an all-year theater. In 1967, in the former Astor Library on LaFayette Street, Papp opened the Public Theater. Between the Public and the Delacorte, Papp was making his dream of affordable theater in the city a reality. "Culture, by itself, was not significant," said Papp, adding that "it had to be always doing something for the masses, for ordinary people, not just servicing an elite."

Papp believed in rainbow casting, and from the beginning, many of his shows—such as 1967's *Hair*, the Public's first non-Shakespeare production—were racially mixed. He also was interested in offering classics with African-American actors. In 1972, for instance, he produced an all-black production of Anton Chekov's play *The Cherry Orchard,* with James Earl Jones cast in the starring role of Lopahin.

By 1979, Papp was close to developing an African-American-Hispanic acting troupe dedicated to producing the plays of Shakespeare. But the first two productions—*Julius Caesar* and *Coriolanus*—were panned by the critics. To make matters worse, black companies were furious that Papp was using money that would otherwise be funneled to black theater organizations, and the Asian-American community condemned Papp for not providing a forum for Asian performers. As a result, plans for the African-American-Hispanic Shakespeare company were abandoned.

Despite the fact that Papp didn't actualize his dream of a racially mixed troupe, the Public Theater produced a number of African-American plays. In 1969, it staged *No Place to Be Somebody* by Charles Gordone, and in 1976, it presented Ntozake Shange's *For Colored Girls Who Have Considered Suicide When the Rainbow Is Enuf.* Like many of the Public's productions, both of these plays ultimately moved to Broadway. This is why Papp, who is best known for providing an affordable and unconventional alternative to Broadway plays, is also viewed as a champion of Broadway. He was responsible for more than forty shows' landing on the Great White Way. And during the bleak days of the 1970s, he not only drew audiences back to the theater but also provided a venue for talented black playwrights and performers.

The open-air Delacorte Theater, shown here under construction in Central Park, allowed Joseph Papp to make the works of Shakespeare and other playwrights accessible to a wide range of people. And from the start, many of Papp's productions had racially mixed casts.

# The New Federal Theatre

In 1970, Woodie King, Jr., a young actor-producer-director, founded the New Federal Theatre (NFT) on the Lower East Side of Manhattan. This undertaking emerged from a theater program designed to provide outlets for youngsters living in poverty. From an inauspicious start in the basement of a local church, the NFT grew quickly, and in 1974, it moved to the Henry Street Settlement's Louis Abrons Arts Center.

Since its inception, the NFT has been dedicated to staging minority drama—not just black drama—and making live theater available to the many people who live on the Lower East Side, as well as anyone interested in first-rate productions. It sponsors a variety of ethnic theater groups and events, and provides emerging playwrights with the opportunity to have their works produced. It also offers training in all aspects of theater, dance, and film.

In the 1970s, perhaps the best-known play the NFT helped bring to the stage was Ntozake Shange's *For Colored Girls Who Have Considered Suicide When the Rainbow Is Enuf,* but it produced many others as well, including 1971's critically acclaimed *Black Girl* by J.E. Franklin. African-American writers whose works have been presented at the NFT include J.E. Franklin, Amiri Baraka, Damien Leake, Laurence Holder, Ron Milner, Ed Bullins, and Alexis De Veaux. Performers who have appeared in NFT productions include Morgan Freeman, Denzel Washington, Leslie Uggams, Debbie Allen, Phylicia Rashad, Samuel L. Jackson, Ruby Dee, Laurence Fishburne, and Garrett Morris. The theater has, to date, staged over 180 theatrical productions.

## August Wilson Hits Broadway

Although a few black dramas had made their way to Broadway by first establishing their commercial worth through off-Broadway runs, for the most part, it was still believed that black dramas were of little interest to mainstream audiences. This would begin to change when the works of August Wilson came to New York.

August Wilson was born on April 26, 1945 in the Hill District of Pittsburgh, Pennsylvania, a largely black neighborhood. Later, his family would move to a white working-class area, where they became victims of racial prejudice. Young Wilson encountered prejudice in school, as well, and eventually, he dropped out. But this did not end his education. While working at odd jobs, Wilson schooled himself by reading black writers like Richard Wright, Ralph Ellison, and Langston Hughes. Although he was learning the harsh realities of a largely white world, he was also learning to value his African-American heritage and to see what could be accomplished through talent and hard work.

Remarkably, when August Wilson dropped out of school at the age of fifteen, he did not abandon his studies. Instead, he began educating himself at the Carnegie Library of Pittsburgh, where he immersed himself in the works of black writers. In 1999, the Library created a diploma especially for their very famous "graduate."

In October 1984, *Ma Rainey's Black Bottom* opened at the Cort Theatre, introducing Broadway audiences to the first of August Wilson's Pittsburgh Cycle of plays about the African-American experience in the twentieth century. Directed by Lloyd Richards, Wilson's play captured a slew of awards, including the New York Drama Critics' Circle Award for Best Play.

Airing from 1984 to 1992, *The Cosby Show* is regarded as one of the defining shows of the decade. Although praised by many people for breaking racial stereotypes with its depiction of an upper-middle-class African-American family, it was criticized by others for implying that racism was a problem of the past. Nevertheless, it presented black themes and often promoted black culture.

At an early age, Wilson knew that he wanted to be a writer and spent a good deal of time observing the people in his Pittsburgh neighborhood, listening not only to the stories they told but also to the way they expressed themselves. At the same time, he became involved in the Black Power movement and began to see himself as a black nationalist. Wilson devoted himself to writing poetry at first, but eventually, he became interested in drama. In 1968, in the hopes of presenting dramatic productions dealing with the plight of African Americans, Wilson and his friend Rob Penny founded the Black Horizon Theater in the Hill District. It was there, in the neighborhood in which Wilson had grown up, that his first dramas were staged.

Unlike most dramatists, Wilson developed a master plan. After completing his first three plays, he decided that he wanted to write ten plays, each of which would chronicle both the hopes and struggles of African Americans in one decade of the twentieth century. Because, with one exception, the plays were set in the Hill District, the dramas—which were not created in chronological order—would become known collectively as the Pittsburgh Cycle. Ultimately, they would be regarded as one of the finest achievements in contemporary drama.

The first of August Wilson's plays to reach Broadway was *Ma Rainey's Black Bottom*. Set in 1927 in a Chicago recording studio—this is the one Wilson "Cycle" play that does not take place in Pittsburgh—it tells the story of a Paramount-label session in which singer Ma Rainey and four musicians attempt to record "Ma Rainey's Black Bottom" and other songs. As the characters exchange stories, it becomes apparent that all of them are victims of white racism. Those musicians who are successful have had to compromise their art in order to succeed. Those who insist upon naming their own terms are doomed to failure. Entertainment is a white man's game, and the rules are rigged.

Influenced by literary greats like Langston Hughes and by the injustice around him, playwright August Wilson wrote the Pittsburgh Cycle, a series of plays that chronicle the experience of African Americans during the twentieth century.

In 1986, Debi Thomas became the first black athlete to win the women's title at the United States Figure Skating Championships. Two years later, in Calgary, Canada, she was the first African-American Olympian to win a medal at the Winter Olympics. Even while skating competitively, Thomas pursued higher education, and in 1997, she received her medical degree from Northwestern University Medical School.

When the Chicago-based talk show that Oprah Winfrey hosted was renamed *The Oprah Winfrey Show* and was then syndicated, Winfrey became the first African-American woman to host a successful national daytime talk show. In 1986, Winfrey would form her own television production company, Harpo Productions, and four years later, she would launch her own magazine, *O, The Oprah Magazine*.

The play opened at the Cort Theatre in October 1984 starring Theresa Merritt and Charles S. Dutton. For the most part, the reviews were good. Frank Rich of *The New York Times* lauded the cast and observed that the electricity at the theater must be equal to that of the first production of Lorraine Hansberry's *A Raisin in the Sun.* Perhaps most significant, he stated that Wilson's play "sends the entire history of black America crashing down upon our heads." *Ma Rainey's Black Bottom* ran until June 1985 for 276 performances. Despite its relatively modest stay on Broadway, it was nominated for three Tony Awards and won the New York Drama Critics' Circle Award for Best Play.

The next of August Wilson's plays to reach Broadway was *Fences,* which would become the most famous work of the playwright's career. Set in 1957, it focuses on a former Negro-league baseball player, Troy Maxson. Although years have passed since the end of his sports career, Troy remains bitter because the color barrier kept him from winning a spot on a major-league team. Now, Troy is a garbage collector, and he is still fighting racial discrimination as he tries to become the first black driver of a garbage truck. But the story's major conflict is between Troy and his son, Cory. Cory has a chance to attend college on a football scholarship, but his father refuses to give permission because he doesn't want his son to suffer the same racial discrimination that he experienced as a baseball player. Troy's anger wreaks havoc on the lives of everyone for whom he cares, erecting fences around him.

*Fences* made its Broadway debut in 1987 at the Forty-Sixth Street Theatre, with James Earl Jones in the leading role. The show ran for over 500 performances and was a success both critically and commercially, bringing in $11 million in its first year of production. This was a record for a nonmusical play. *Fences* also won numerous Tony Awards, including Best Play, Best Performance by a Leading Actor in a Play (James Earl Jones), Best Performance by a Featured Actress in a Play (Mary Alice), and Best Direction of a Play (Lloyd Richards). Moreover, the moving drama earned Wilson his first Pulitzer

THEY COULD MAKE A WHOLE PLAY
ABOUT THE DAY WE RECORDED

# Ma Rainey's Black Bottom

Ivan Bloch   Robert Cole   Frederick M. Zollo   present
The Yale Repertory Theatre production of
Ma Rainey's Black Bottom
by August Wilson
Starring Charles S. Dutton, Leonard Jackson, Robert Judd, Joe Seneca
Lou Criscuolo, John Carpenter, Aleta Mitchell, Scott Davenport-Richards, Christopher Loomis
and Theresa Merritt
Costumes by Daphne Pascucci   Setting by Charles Henry McClennahan   Lighting by Peter Maradudin   Musical Direction by Dwight Andrews
Sound by Jan Nebozenko   Casting by Meg Simon/Fran Kumin   General Management Kingwill & Goossen   Production Stage Manager Mortimer Halpern
Associate Producers Bart Berman   Hart Productions   William P. Suter
Directed by Lloyd Richards
Ⓣ CORT THEATRE 48th Street, East of Broadway, N.Y.C.

Opening at the Cort Theatre in 1984, *Ma Rainey's Black Bottom* was the first of August Wilson's Pittsburgh Cycle of plays to reach Broadway. The drama received good reviews and was nominated for three Tony Awards.

In November 1986, the First National Symposium on Non-Traditional Casting was sponsored by Actors' Equity. A gathering of about five hundred theater professionals from around the country, the symposium's goal was to promote "the casting of ethnic, minority and female actors in roles where race, ethnicity, or sex is not germane to character or play development."

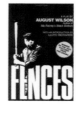

In 1987, African-American playwright August Wilson won his first Pulitzer Prize for Drama for what would be the most famous work of his career, *Fences.* The show also won the Drama Desk Award for Outstanding New Play, the New York Drama Critics' Circle Award for Best Play, the Tony Award for Best Play, and the Outer Critics Circle Award.

Prize. As a testament to its enduring themes, *Fences* was revived on Broadway in 2010, with Denzel Washington in the lead, and again it garnered several Tony Awards.

Before the end of the eighties, one more August Wilson play would reach Broadway. In March 1988, while *Fences* was still running at the Forty-Sixth Street Theatre, *Joe Turner's Come and Gone* opened at the Ethel Barrymore Theatre. Set in 1911, it chronicles the hardships of former slaves who had migrated to the North in search of jobs and a better life, only to face further discrimination. The cast included Delroy Lindo and Angela Bassett.

The show opened to rave reviews, and the producers expected that the next day, there would be a line of people waiting outside the theater to buy tickets. This didn't happen, and the new August Wilson drama closed after only 105 performances. Nevertheless, it was nominated for the Tony Award for Best Play, and it won the New York Drama Critics' Circle Award for Best Play. More than twenty years later, in 2009, David Rooney wrote in *Variety*, "There's relatively little traditional plot . . . but with its rivers of talk, discursive stories, wild flights of imagination and bone-chilling visions, this is a vibrant canvas in which every character makes a distinctive contribution to Wilson's throbbing mosaic of life."

A firm believer in black drama that provides a realistic examination of African-American life, August Wilson had made a lasting mark on the Broadway stage while bringing important issues to the attention of both black and white theatergoers. In the decades to follow, all but one of his Pittsburgh Cycle plays would appear on the Great White Way, and the talented playwright would continue to win awards for his groundbreaking dramas.

## LOOKING BACK

The recession of the 1970s had hit Broadway hard, causing the lights in many theaters to go dark. But Broadway, as always, was resilient. A constant stream of dazzling musicals kept drawing people to the theater district. And with so many award-winning productions featuring music by great black musicians as well as performances by talented black entertainers, more African Americans than ever before were able to find shows that were both entertaining and inspiring. In fact, it was during this decade that the black Broadway audience began to increase.

Then in the 1980s, a small but important revolution occurred. August Wilson came to New York, and within a few years, thousands of people had seen his plays. Light-hearted black musicals had been appreciated for several decades. Now it was clear that the public was also eager to view dramas that took an unblinking look at African-American life.

*Fences* (1987), the most famous of August Wilson's plays, had a stellar cast, including James Earl Jones, Charles Brown, Ray Aranha, Mary Alice, Frankie R. Faison, Courtney B. Vance, and Karima Miller. The show ran for over 500 performances, setting a record for nonmusical plays, and both Jones and Alice won Tony Awards for their performances.

On February 10, 1989, former Supreme Court lawyer Ronald H. Brown was elected chairman of the Democratic Party National Committee. The first black American to hold the top position in a major political party of the United States, Brown helped secure the 1992 election of Bill Clinton, and in 1993, he became the country's first African-American secretary of commerce.

A native of Harlem, New York, Colin Luther Powell became Chairman of the Joint Chief of Staffs in 1989 during the administration of President George H.W. Bush. Powell was the first African American to achieve that position, the highest military post in the Department of Defense. In 2001, he would become the first African American to be appointed Secretary of State.

# STARRING
## IN ORDER OF APPEARANCE

| | | |
|---|---|---|
| Rosa Guy | Tommy Hollis | Brandon Victor Dixon |
| LaChanze | Lou Myers | Charl Brown |
| Jerry Dixon | Laurence Fishburne | Bryan Terrell Clark |
| Doug Eskew | Cynthia Martells | Valisia LeKae |
| Milton Craig Nealy | Anthony Chisholm | Leslie Uggams |
| Kevin Ramsey | Al White | Stephen McKinley Henderson |
| Jeffrey D. Sams | Roscoe Lee Browne | Monté Russell |
| Glenn Turner | Sullivan Walker | Lloyd Richards |
| George C. Wolfe | Chuck Patterson | Suzan-Lori Parks |
| Gregory Hines | Viola Davis | Mos Def |
| Tonya Pinkins | Keith David | Phylicia Rashad |
| Savion Glover | Michele Shay | Anthony Chisholm |
| Ken Ard | Ruben Santiago-Hudson | John Earl Jelks |
| Adrian Bailey | Tommy Hollis | Harry Lennix |
| Brenda Braxton | Roger Robinson | James A. Williams |
| Toni Braxton | Rosalyn Coleman | Debbie Allen |
| Ann Duquesnay | Langston Hughes | James Earl Jones |
| Vincent Bingham | Zora Neale Hurston | Terrence Howard |
| Jared Crawford | Alice Walker | Stephen Byrd |
| Jimmy Tate | Kingsley Leggs | Alia Jones-Harvey |
| Dulé Hill | Felicia P. Fields | Kenny Leon |
| Raymond King | Anika Noni Rose | Samuel L. Jackson |
| Baakari Wilder | Harrison Chad | Angela Bassett |
| Jeffrey Wright | Veanne Cox | Lydia R. Diamond |
| Lebo M. | Chandra Wilson | Mekhi Phifer |
| Brian Stokes Mitchell | Fela Anikulapo-Kuti | Condola Rashad |
| Audra McDonald | Sahr Ngaujah | Tracie Thoms |
| August Wilson | Kevin Mambo | Cicely Tyson |
| S. Epatha Merkerson | Lillias White | Blair Underwood |
| Charles S. Dutton | Saycon Sengbloh | Nicole Ari Parker |
| Rocky Carroll | Gelan Lambert | Daphne Rubin-Vega |
| Apryl R. Foster | Montego Glover | Wood Harris |
| Carl Gordon | Patina Miller | Cuba Gooding, Jr. |
| LisaGay Hamilton | Berry Gordy | Vanessa Williams |

# 8.

## Broadway Now and Tomorrow

The 1990s marked a new beginning for Times Square and the theater district. For some twenty years, the area had been overrun with crime and the home of peep shows and sex shops. Although Broadway never stopped staging great productions, many potential theatergoers had stayed away, viewing the area as both unsafe and unsightly. Redevelopment proposals had been submitted in the 1980s but were not implemented until the beginning of the next decade, when the arrival of upscale hotels, theme stores, and restaurants began to change the face of the area. In 1995, when rezoning chased out any unsavory businesses that remained, the pace of change quickened.

At about the same time that rezoning laws were making Times Square safer, Disney Theatrical Group—the stage play and musical production arm of the Walt Disney Company—signed a ninety-nine-year lease to the New Amsterdam Theatre. Once the home of the Ziegfeld Follies, the New Amsterdam had since become dilapidated and fallen into disuse. With government subsidies, Disney restored the theater's original grandeur. When the New Amsterdam reopened in April 1997 to great fanfare, Mayor Rudy Giuliani called it the "turning point" in the revitalization of Times Square. And it wasn't just the New Amsterdam that was getting much-needed attention. In 1990, New York State had taken possession of six historic theaters on Forty-Second Street and appointed a nonprofit organization to supervise their restoration. The city was reclaiming the Great White Way.

Mayor Rudy Giuliani called the 1997 reopening of the New Amsterdam Theatre a "turning point" in the renewal of Times Square. Governor George Pataki echoed this sentiment, predicting that the theater district, once restored, would be "the number one tourist attraction in America."

Politician Lawrence Douglas Wilder led a life of many firsts. In 1969, he became the first black member of the Virginia Senate since Reconstruction. In 1985, he became the first black man to be elected Lieutenant Governor of Virginia. And in 1989, he was the first African American to be elected governor of any state, serving as the Governor of Virginia from 1990 to 1994.

In the early 1990s, Frederik Willem de Klerk, the last president of apartheid-era South Africa, announced the release of political prisoner Nelson Mandela and began the dismantling of apartheid, a system of white-ruled segregation. South Africa's first democratic elections were held in 1994, and a Government of National Unity was formed with Nelson Mandela as president.

As Broadway was undergoing revitalization, new shows continued to emerge on the scene. There was still a belief that all-black plays—and especially black dramas—were greater financial risks than shows with white casts. Nevertheless, the 1990s would bring with it a variety of fine African-American musicals and dramas. At the same time, color-blind and non-traditional casting would continue to feature black performers in roles that customarily had been filled by white actors. (See the inset on page 220.)

## MUSICALS OF THE 1990s

If there had ever been questions about the ability of black musicals to attract an enthusiastic audience, those doubts had been quieted in the 1970s and 1980s, when shows like *Dreamgirls, Ain't Misbehavin'*, and *Sophisticated Ladies* became favorites with both theatergoers and critics. In the 1990s, Broadway continued to present musicals that featured remarkable black performers and music. And toward the end of the decade, a lavish Disney production with a largely black cast would became one of the longest-running musicals in Broadway history.

### *Once on This Island*

The first major black musical to appear in the 1990s was *Once on This Island,* a romantic fantasy based on the novel *My Love, My Love* by Trinidad-born Rosa Guy. Featuring book and lyrics by Lynn Ahrens and music by Stephen Flaherty, the show used musical numbers to tell the story of a magical but ill-fated romance between a dark-skinned peasant girl from a Caribbean island and a handsome *grand homme*—a lighter-skinned resident from the "right" side of the island. *Once on This Island* starred LaChanze as the young girl and marked the Broadway acting debut of director and composer Jerry Dixon.

*Once on This Island* filled the Booth Theatre with dance and movement for ninety enchanting minutes. Here, LaChanze (center) shines as peasant girl Ti Moune in one of the dances created by choreographer Graciela Daniele.

After initially being staged at off-Broadway's Playwrights Horizons theater, the musical moved to the Booth Theatre, where it ran from October 1990 to December 1991, for a total of 469 performances. The critics loved it, with Frank Rich of *The New York Times* applauding the lush music, the full-voiced cast, and the "fantastical atmosphere." *Once on This Island* was nominated for eight Tony Awards.

In 1991, almost sixty years after it was written and twenty years after the death of its most famous author, Langston Hughes' and Zora Neale Hurston's play *Mule Bone* was produced for the first time. As a work of two great writers of the Harlem Renaissance, *Mule Bone* was much anticipated. Unfortunately, the play proved disappointing and ran for only 63 performances.

Signed into law on November 21, 1991, by President George H.W. Bush, the Civil Rights Act of 1991 was created to strengthen and improve federal civil rights legislation in cases of employment discrimination. It allowed an employee who proved intentional discrimination to seek injunctive relief, attorney's fees, and costs from the employer.

# Non-Traditional Casting

In 1986, an Actors' Equity Association survey revealed that during the previous four years, over 90 percent of all United States professional theater had all-white casts—despite the fact that African Americans and other racial minorities made up about 17 percent of the population. In other words, minorities were being underrepresented on Broadway and in theaters across the country. Moreover, major New York productions were found to hire a lower percentage of minority actors (6 percent) than regional theaters (a little under 12 percent).

The theater community's response to this study was the First National Symposium on Non-Traditional Casting, which was held in November 1986. Sponsored by Equity, the symposium was co-produced by the Non-Traditional Casting Project (NTCP), a not-for-profit advocacy organization dedicated to finding solutions to racism and exclusion in the theater, film, and television. The gathering included over 1,000 actors, directors, producers, and other professionals. Its goal was to promote non-traditional casting, which, according to Equity's collective bargaining agreement with Broadway producers, is "the casting of ethnic minority and female actors in roles where race, ethnicity, or sex is not germane."

The issue of non-traditional casting is not without controversy. While many people support the practice because it increases minority employment and creates a richer, more diverse theater experience, others strongly believe that it is not in the best interest of African Americans. Perhaps not surprisingly, some of the greatest resistance has come from black playwrights. In a 1996 speech, Pulitzer Prize-winning playwright August Wilson denounced color-blind casting as a form of "assimilation" that denies black performers their unique heritage and identity. Instead of casting black people in roles originally written for whites, he demanded that theaters help develop black plays. Lonne Elder, III, who wrote the play *Ceremonies in Dark Old Men,* stated, "It [non-traditional casting] might be fine for employment parity, but it would be deadly for the theater."

Despite the naysayers, non-traditional casting is not only here to stay but seems to be gaining in popularity. In 2008, Morgan Freeman was cast opposite Frances McDormand in Clifford Odets' *Country Girl.* That same year, S. Epatha Merkerson recreated the part that Shirley Booth had originated in William Inge's *Come Back, Little Sheba.* And in 2013, an all-black production of Horton Foote's *The Trip to Bountiful* was launched—and won a Tony Award for leading actress Cicely Tyson. No one can argue that non-traditional casting continues to provide African-American actors with a range of great roles and to offer entertainment that appeals to all theatergoers, regardless of their race and ethnic background.

In 1991, professor and educator Henry Louis Gates, Jr.—a leading scholar of African-American literature, history, and culture—became Harvard University's Director of the W.E.B. DuBois Research Institute. At the heart of the institute is the Fellows Program, which annually appoints scholars who conduct individual research on subjects related to African and African-American studies.

In 1987, Mae C. Jemison became the first black woman to be admitted into the astronaut training program, and on September 12, 1992, she boarded the Endeavour with six other astronauts and became the first African-American woman to travel into space. Prior to her career with NASA, Jemison had obtained her medical degree from Cornell University Medical College.

## *Five Guys Named Moe*

In 1992, the 1940s jazz/pop music of Louis Jordan was celebrated in the revue *Five Guys Named Moe*. The show had its start in London's West End before being transported across the pond to Broadway's Eugene O'Neill Theatre. Produced by Cameron Mackintosh—whose credits include *Cats, Phantom of the Opera,* and *Les Misérables*—*Five Guys Named Moe* was light on story but offered about two dozen songs by Jordan, as well as dancing and comedy. The cast featured Jerry Dixon (from *Once on This Island*), Doug Eskew, Milton Craig Nealy, Kevin Ramsey, Jeffrey D. Sams, and Glenn Turner.

*Five Guys Named Moe* opened in March 1992 and, despite poor reviews, it ran for 445 performances, closing in May 1993.

During the 1940s, singer-saxophonist Louis Jordan and his Tympany Five launched fifty-seven singles onto the Rhythm and Blues charts, including 1943's "Five Guys Named Moe." Called "the King of the Jukebox," Jordan was popular with both black and white audiences.

A celebration of the songs of Louis Jordan, 1992's *Five Guys Named Moe* offered . . . well . . . five guys named Moe, who used Jordan's hits to provide advice for a broken-hearted character named Nomax. The cast of six, pictured here, included (from left to right) Jeffrey D. Sams, Kevin Ramsey, Doug Eskew, Milton Craig Nealy, Glenn Turner, and Jerry Dixon (seated).

A pioneer in the field of journalism, ABC News anchor Carole Simpson became the first African American and the first woman to moderate a United States presidential debate in 1992. Held at the University of Richmond, the debate included then-President George H.W. Bush, Democratic candidate Bill Clinton, and independent candidate Ross Perot.

From 1993 to 2004, African-American playwright and director George C. Wolfe served as artistic director of New York City's Public Theater. During his tenure, Wolfe's most notable success was the musical *Bring in 'Da Noise, Bring in 'Da Funk,* which premiered at the Public Theater in 1995 and moved to Broadway's Ambassador Theatre in 1996.

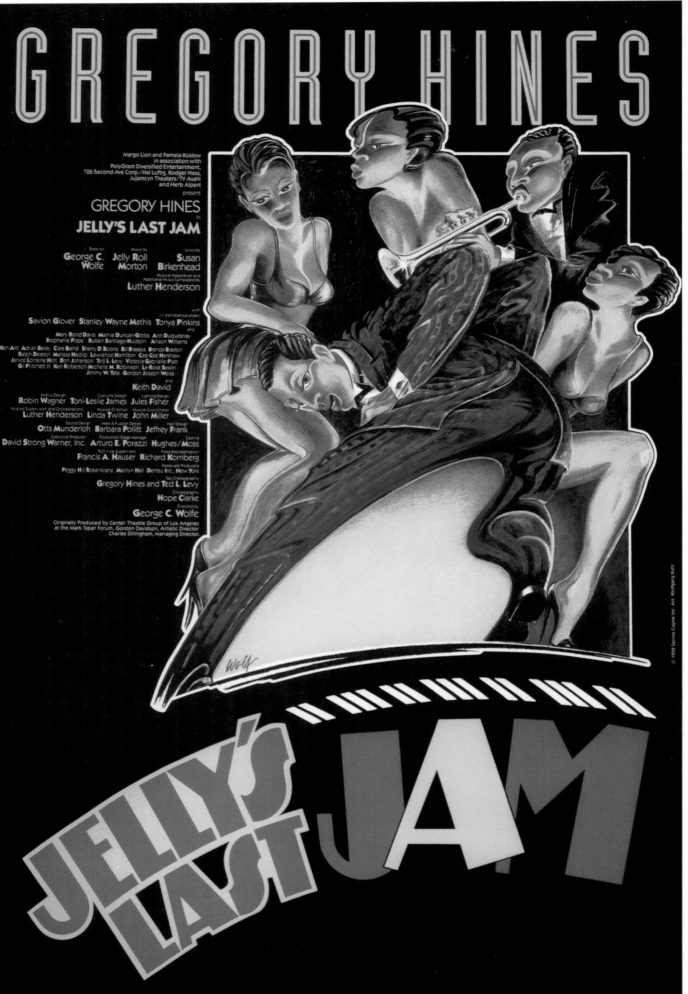

## *Jelly's Last Jam*

Also opening in 1992, and more successful than *Five Guys Named Moe*, was *Jelly's Last Jam*, which brought the life of New Orleans jazz musician, composer, and ragtime pioneer Jelly Roll Morton to the stage. With a book by George C. Wolfe, who also was director; music by Jelly Roll Morton; lyrics by Susan Birkenhead; and additional music by Luther Henderson, the show starred Gregory Hines as Jelly Roll Morton and featured Tonya Pinkins as a nightclub proprietor and Morton's love interest. Savion Glover played the jazz musician as a young man.

A departure from upbeat African-American revues, *Jelly's Last Jam* is set at the Jungle Inn—"a lowdown club somewhere's 'tween Heaven 'n' Hell"—on the night of Morton's death. The musical numbers are presented as a Judgment Day inquisition into Morton's life, which allows the characters to explore not only the story of American jazz but also the experience of African Americans. Because Jelly Roll Morton was a light-skinned Creole who reportedly denied his black ancestry, the show has an unusual focus on breaks and tensions within the black community itself.

*Jelly's Last Jam* opened at the Virginia Theatre in April 1992 and met with glowing reviews. *The New York Times'* Frank Rich—who by now had earned the title "Butcher of Broadway" for his often harsh commentary—lauded Gregory Hines' multiple talents; the high-voltage performance of the singers and dancers, including tap-dancing sensation Savion Glover; and the ingenious crafting of Morton's compositions. He also singled out the contributions of writer and director George C. Wolfe and advised "anyone who cares about the future of the American musical" to see the show. Theatergoers must have taken heed, because the popular revue ran for 569 performances, closing late in 1993.

*Jelly's Last Jam* won the Drama Desk Award for Outstanding Book of a Musical. It was also nominated for ten Tony Awards and won three: Best Performance by a Leading Actor in a Musical (Gregory Hines), Best Performance by a Featured Actress in a Musical (Tonya Pinkins), and Best Lighting Design (Jules Fisher). John Simon of *New York* magazine referred to Hines as "the consummate leading man," and many felt that his portrayal of Morton was the crowning achievement of his career. *Jelly's Last Jam* was also the last Broadway show in which Gregory Hines would appear.

*Jelly's Last Jam's* stylized musical numbers combined biographical flashbacks with boisterous entertainment. In this scene, Morton (played by Gregory Hines) joins a New Orleans jazz celebration.

◀ This poster for *Jelly's Last Jam* evokes the mood of the musical, which explored the tumultuous life of New Orleans-born jazz musician Jelly Roll Morton.

# George C. Wolfe
# A Passion for the Performing Arts

Born in Frankfort, Kentucky on September 23, 1954, George C. Wolfe first took an interest in the theater during high school—and his passion for the performing arts never cooled. After graduation, Wolfe pursued a bachelor of arts in theater at Pomona College in Claremont, California. He then earned a master of fine arts in writing and musical theater at New York University.

A writer and director since the 1980s, George Wolfe did not attract national attention until the 1992 debut of his award-winning musical *Jelly's Last Jam*. Since then, he has served as artistic director of the Public Theater (1993 to 2004), and has continued to direct critically acclaimed plays, including *Bring in 'Da Noise, Bring in 'Da Funk* (1996), *Topdog/Underdog* (2002), and *Caroline, or Change* (2004).

During the 1980s, Wolfe directed several off-Broadway productions, including two plays that he had authored—*The Colored Museum* (1986), his skewering of black stereotypes, and *Spunk* (1989), an adaptation of three stories by Harlem Renaissance author Zora Neale Hurston. Although *Spunk* won an Obie for best director, Wolfe didn't attract national attention until the debut of *Jelly's Last Jam* (see page 223), which he also wrote and directed. The stunning musical revue received a string of Tony Award nominations and won Wolfe the Drama Desk Award for Outstanding Book of a Musical. This opened the door for Wolfe to direct Tony Kushner's *Angels in America: Millennium Approaches* (1993). Again, Wolfe was nominated for a Tony for Best Director, and this time, he took the coveted prize home.

In 1993, Wolfe also took the reins of the Public Theater, which had long been run by the legendary Joseph Papp. The Public continued to flourish under Wolfe, who remained artistic director and producer until 2004. His most notable success was the musical *Bring in 'Da Noise, Bring in 'Da Funk,* which in 1996 moved to Broadway, where it earned Wolfe his second Tony Award.

After leaving the Public, Wolfe continued to be active in both Broadway and off-Broadway theater. His directorial credits include *Caroline, or Change* (2004), *Mother Courage and Her Children* (2006), *A Free Man of Color* (2010), and *The Normal Heart* (2011). He also directed films, including *Lackawanna Blues* (2005), and even worked in front of the camera in *The Devil Wears Prada* (2006). Wolfe once said, "If there's something that intrigues me or fascinates me, or I don't know how to do it, then I should do it."

In fact, nothing seems to faze George Wolfe. In 2009, he was named the Chief Creative Officer of Atlanta's National Center for Civil and Human Rights, which is dedicated to honoring the struggle for black freedom. Doug Shipman, the Center's Executive Director, said, "We look forward to seeing how his strengths in storytelling will fuel new discussions on civil rights lessons and human rights issues." When the CCHR opened in June 2014, the positive response of visitors showed that the Center had exceeded expectations and become a vital addition to the fabric of America.

## *Smokey Joe's Café*

One of the most impressive box office hits of the first half of the nineties came from the successful team of Jerry Leiber (composer) and Mike Stoller (lyricist). White songwriters Lieber and Stoller were strongly influenced by a shared love of black pop music, and beginning in the 1950s, the talented duo bridged racial barriers by writing for mostly black singers, including The Coasters, The Drifters, and The Clovers. *Smokey Joe's Café* showcased thirty-nine of their hit songs, including rock 'n' roll and rhythm and blues. With some additional tunes by folks like Phil Spector, the musical was a strict revue, with no unifying theme or dialogue. The strong cast was led by three Broadway veterans, Ken Ard, Adrian Bailey, and Brenda Braxton, whose combined credits of more than twenty Broadway shows ranged from *Jelly's Last Jam* and *Sophisticated Ladies* to *Cats* and *Chicago*.

    *Smokey Joe's Café* opened at the Virginia Theatre in March 1995. Although it received only tepid reviews—critic Ben Brantley accused it of "sanitizing peppiness"—it was a hit with audiences, who were thrilled to hear long-time favorites like "Fools Fall in Love" and "Love Potion No. 9." The show ran for 2,036 performances, making it Broadway's longest-running musical revue. It received seven Tony Award nominations and won the 1996 Grammy Award for Best Musical Show.

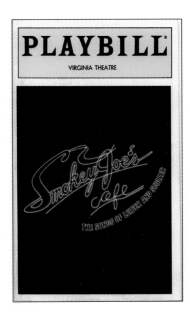

With songs by the successful team of Jerry Leiber and Mike Stoller, and a cast of veteran performers, including Ken Ard, Adrian Bailey, and Brenda Braxton, *Smokey Joe's Café* delivered a record-breaking 2,036 performances.

# A New Belle for *Beauty and the Beast*

On September 9, 1998, rhythm and blues singer Toni Braxton made her Broadway debut by taking on the role of Belle in Disney's long-running hit *Beauty and the Beast*. This fulfilled Braxton's lifelong dream of performing on the Broadway stage, and just as important, it marked the first time that an African-American woman would play a leading Disney character on the Great White Way. Over the years, Disney had received its fair share of criticism for having no black "princess" roles in its classic animated films. This unconventional casting silenced some of Disney's critics.

    The show's creators took steps to customize the role for the thirty-one-year-old husky-voiced star. Alan Menken wrote a new song, "A Change in Me," for Braxton, and Belle's wardrobe was given a "Braxton-esque" style, with barer shoulders and back. Everyone knew that the artist would bring her own unique approach to the part. "Let's just say Belle is like a big ol' glass of milk and I'm adding Nestle chocolate syrup to it," Braxton explained. She remained with *Beauty and the Beast* until February 1999, when Andrea McArdle took over the role.

In 1995, educator Ruth Simmons made history when she took the reins of Smith College, becoming the first black female president of a major college. In 2001, Simmons became the first black woman president of an Ivy League university when she was elected president of Brown. Simmons focused much of her energy on increasing diversity in higher education.

Organized by Louis Farrakhan, the controversial leader of the Nation of Islam, the Million Man March took place on October 16, 1995 in Washington, DC, to promote African-American unity and instill family values. Most of the marchers—over a million, by some estimates—were black men, and speakers included Jesse Jackson, Rosa Parks, and Maya Angelou.

## Bring in 'Da Noise, Bring in 'Da Funk

In 1992, when George C. Wolfe directed *Jelly's Last Jam* and worked with brilliant young dancer Savion Glover, he realized the power of tap as a black folk tradition. Thus, the seed was planted for a new show—*Bring in 'Da Noise, Bring in 'Da Funk*—which would tell the story of African Americans, from slavery to the present, through tap.

At the Public Theater, Wolfe brought together a team to turn his idea into a show. Poet Reg E. Gaines wrote the book and lyrics; Daryl Waters, Zane Mark, and Ann Duquesnay composed the music; and the talented Savion Glover signed on as choreographer. The musical debuted off-Broadway at the Public Theater in November 1995, and was transferred to Broadway's Ambassador Theatre in April 1996. The opening-night cast included Glover, Duquesnay, Vincent Bingham, Jared Crawford, Dulé Hill, Raymond King, Jimmy Tate, Baakari Wilder, and Jeffrey Wright.

Critics could not have been more impressed by *Bring in 'Da Noise.* They applauded the exuberant dancing, the unique means of delivering a political message, and the powerful performances. After attending opening night, Ben Brantley of *The New York Times* promised, "Its rhythms will continue to pulse in your bloodstream long after the show is over."

*Bring in 'Da Noise, Bring in 'Da Funk* ran on Broadway for 1,135 remarkable performances, closing in January 1999. It was nominated for nine Tony Awards and received four. Ann Duquesnay won for Best Performance by a Featured Actress in a Musical; Jules Fisher and Peggy Eisenhauer, for Best Lighting Design; Savion Glover, for Best Choreography; and George C. Wolfe, for Best Director.

In one high-energy number after another, *Bring in 'Da Noise, Bring in 'Da Funk* choreographer Savion Glover told the story of black American history through tap dancing. Here, the cast—including Jimmy Tate, Vincent Bingham, Raymond King, Baakari Wilder, Savion Glover, and Jared Crawford—performs "Industrialization."

The spare scenery created by Riccardo Hernandez provided a perfect canvas for *Bring in 'Da Noise, Bring in 'Da Funk's* dancers. This scene simply features Savion Glover surrounded by mirrors.

## *The Lion King*

In 1994, Disney had enjoyed enormous success when it brought a stage adaptation of its animated film *Beauty and the Beast* to Broadway. It was not surprising when just a few years later, with *Beauty and the Beast* still packing the house at the Palace Theatre, Disney transferred another of its celebrated movies to the New York stage. The show was *The Lion King,* and this time around, Disney decided to hire experimental director-designer Julie Taymor to create a more artistic and adventurous adaptation. Moreover, the cast of this exciting new musical would be mostly African-American.

The book for Broadway's *The Lion King* was written by Roger Allers and Irene Mecchi. In addition to the songs that had been created by Elton John (composer) and Tim Rice (lyricist) for the movie, new music and lyrics were composed by Lebo M., Mark Mancina, Jay Rifkin, Julie Taymor, and Hans Zimmer. Because Lebo M. is a South African musician, the Broadway score became an extraordinary blend of American pop music and vibrant African melodies and rhythms. Julie Taymor not only directed the play but also designed the costumes and collaborated on the mask designs with Michael Curry.

*The Lion King* tells the story of a lion cub's journey to adulthood. At the start of the play, Simba idolizes his father, Mufasa—the king of all creatures on the African Savanna—but shirks his duties as a prince. When Simba's wicked uncle, Scar, takes Mufasa's life, Simba flees his home, the Pride Lands, and finds new animal friends. But ultimately, Simba must face his enemy and reclaim the kingdom that he is destined to rule. The original cast included Jason Raize as Simba, John Vickery as Scar, and Samuel E. Wright as Mufasa.

When *The Lion King* made its Broadway debut in November 1997 at Disney's flagship New Amsterdam Theatre, the audience was immediately captivated by the exotic African "animals" that paraded down the aisles at the start of the show. All of the animals were played by actors who wore fabulous masks and costumes that defined the creatures they portrayed while still enabling the audience to see their faces. Like the audience, the critics roared unanimous approval of this visually dazzling production. Vincent Canby of *The New York Times* said that Julie Taymor's transformation of the Disney cartoon into a major Broadway event was "magical," and that *The Lion King* was "one of the most memorable, moving and original theatrical extravaganzas in years." Greg Evans of *Variety* called it "a marvel, a theatrical achievement unrivaled in its beauty, brains, and ingenuity." The show was nominated for eleven Tony

*The Lion King* opened at Disney's flagship New Amsterdam Theatre in November 1997, and moved to the Minskoff Theatre in June 2006. With its colorful African theme, a mostly African-American cast, and a score that blends American pop with authentic African rhythms, this production has become one of the longest-running musicals of all time.

In 1997, when Eldrick "Tiger" Woods won his first Masters at Augusta National Golf Club, he became the first person of color to win the Masters, one of pro golf's four major championships. Lee Elder, who in 1975 had been the first African American to play at the Masters, said, "No one will turn their head when a black man walks to the first tee after this."

The Million Woman March of October 25, 1997 united up to 2 million people, mostly African-American women, in Philadelphia, Pennsylvania. The daylong program of prayer, music, and inspirational speeches was designed to show solidarity and to spotlight issues—including AIDS, abuse, and addiction—that are often ignored by mainstream women's groups.

Awards and won six: Best Musical, Best Direction of a Musical (Julie Taymor), Best Choreography (Garth Fagan), Best Scenic Design (Richard Hudson), Best Costume Design (Julie Taymor and Michael Curry), and Best Lighting Design (Donald Holder). The show also received three Drama Desk Awards.

*The Lion King* appeared at the New Amsterdam until June 2006, when it moved to the Minskoff. So far, it has run for well over 6,000 Broadway performances, making it one of the longest-running musicals of all time.

## Ragtime

Two years before the close of the decade, the musical *Ragtime* opened on Broadway. With a book by Terrence McNally, lyrics by Lynn Ahrens, and music by Stephen Flaherty, the show was based on the best-selling 1975 novel of the same name by E.L. Doctorow. Neither an all-black musical nor a musical that unconventionally cast black actors in a smattering of "color-blind" roles, *Ragtime* wove the history of black Americans into the tapestry of the country's history by telling the story of three different groups— African Americans, Eastern European Jews, and the white upper-class—that lived in the United States at the turn of the century. Blacks were included in the cast because they were an integral part of the national experience.

The African-American thread of *Ragtime* concerns Coalhouse Walker, a charismatic ragtime pianist, and his lover, Sarah, who has given birth to Coalhouse's child. Although Coalhouse and Sarah hope to build a life together, circumstances—including rampant racism in the country—are against them, and eventually, their optimism turns to anger and their dreams end in catastrophe. Their story is the most tragic of the three that make up this sweeping musical.

*Ragtime* opened in January 1998 at the Ford Center for the Performing Arts. The cast included Brian Stokes Mitchell as Coalhouse Walker and Audra McDonald as Sarah. The reviews were mixed. While the performances were lauded, critics felt that the production's overuse of theatrical technology got in the way of the story. Nevertheless, *Ragtime* ran for over 800 performances, not closing until the start of the new millennium. It was nominated for thirteen Tony Awards and won four: Best Book of a Musical (Terrence McNally), Best Original Score (Stephen Flaherty and Lynn Ahrens), Best Orchestrations (William David Brohn), and Best Performance by a Featured Actress (Audra McDonald). (See the inset on page 234 to learn about Audra McDonald.)

Neither an all-black musical nor an unconventionally cast white musical, *Ragtime* included people of color in the cast because it wove the history of black Americans into that of turn-of-the-century America. The show's stars included Brian Stokes Mitchell and Audra McDonald, who won a Tony for Best Performance by a Featured Actress.

In 1998, Mark Whitaker was named editor of *Newsweek*, making him the first African American to lead a national news magazine. During his tenure, which ended in 2006, *Newsweek* won four National Magazine Awards. Later, Whitaker became Senior Vice President and Washington Bureau Chief for NBC News, and Executive Vice President for CNN Worldwide.

In the wake of the 9/11 terrorist attacks, attendance at Broadway plays dropped by 80 percent, and several shows were forced to close. Both the city and the state of New York came to the theater district's aid by purchasing thousands of give-away tickets and creating a promotional campaign. By March 2002, box office numbers had returned to normal.

## DRAMAS OF THE 1990s

In the 1980s, Broadway had been awed by the talents of emerging play-wright August Wilson, whose Pittsburgh Cycle of plays explored black history in a new way by presenting a decade-by-decade chronicle of the African-American experience during the twentieth century. Three Wilson works had been produced on Broadway during the 1980s—*Ma Rainey's Black Bottom* (1984), *Fences* (1987), and *Joe Turner's Come and Gone* (1988). All of these remarkable dramas had garnered awards, with *Fences* winning the Pulitzer Prize for Drama. The nineties would see three more productions by the now-famous writer. Moreover, the decade would bring to the Great White Way a play by two legendary artists of the Harlem Renaissance movement.

### *The Piano Lesson*

Opening in April 1990 at the Walter Kerr Theater, August Wilson's *The Piano Lesson* focused on the black experience in 1930s America. The production—which starred S. Epatha Merkerson and Charles S. Dutton—was nominated for several Tony Awards and earned August Wilson his second Pulitzer Prize for Drama.

Set in the 1930s, *The Piano Lesson* focuses on the Charles family's dispute over what should be done with a piano. The imposing instrument has been associated with their family since their great-grandfather, a slave, lost his wife and son when they were traded for the piece. Berniece, a young widow, believes that the piano—which bears carved images of the family's ancestors—must be saved as a reminder of their tragic past. But Boy Willie, Berniece's brother, has a very different view of the musical instrument. He is determined to sell the piano so that he can purchase the land on which his ancestors have long toiled, first as slaves and then as sharecroppers. The quarrel within the Charles family highlights the long shadow that slavery has cast over them, as well as the struggle between honoring the past and moving ahead to the future.

*The Piano Lesson* made its Broadway debut at the Walter Kerr Theatre in April 1990, with S. Epatha Merkerson playing Berniece and Charles S. Dutton (who had starred in *Ma Rainey's Black Bottom*) taking the role of Boy Willie. Also in the cast were Rocky Carroll, Apryl R. Foster, Carl Gordon, LisaGay Hamilton, Tommy Hollis, and Lou Myers. The critics praised Wilson's skills as a writer, Lloyd Richards' expertise as a producer, and the mesmerizing cast, with *New York Times'* Frank Rich calling *The Piano Lesson* a "joyously African-American play." Running for a total of 328 performances, it was nominated for several Tony awards and won the Drama Desk Award for Outstanding New Play and the New York Drama Critics' Circle Award for Best Play. Most impressive, the play—which is the fourth in the Pittsburgh Cycle—garnered playwright August Wilson his second Pulitzer Prize for Drama.

August Wilson's 1990 play *The Piano Lesson* was inspired by the ▶
Romare Bearden painting of the same name, which is seen in
the center of the *Playbill* cover. The subject of Bearden's work
is thought to be jazz pianist Mary Lou Williams.

THE PIANO LESSON
BY August Wilson
DIRECTED BY Lloyd Richards
© 1990 SERINO COYNE
Details from works by painter Romare Bearden courtesy of The Nanette Bearden Contemporary Dance Theatre and Nanette Bearden.
LLOYD RICHARDS, YALE REPERTORY THEATRE, CENTER THEATRE GROUP/AHMANSON THEATRE, GORDON DAVIDSON AND THE JUJAMCYN THEATERS with BENJAMIN MORDECAI, EXECUTIVE PRODUCER
in association with Eugene O'Neill Theatre Center, Huntington Theatre Company, Goodman Theatre and Old Globe Theatre present CHARLES S. DUTTON in THE PIANO LESSON by AUGUST WILSON
with ROCKY CARROLL APRYL R. FOSTER CARL GORDON LISA GAY HAMILTON TOMMY HOLLIS S. EPATHA MERKERSON LOU MYERS Scene Design by E. DAVID COSIER, JR
Lighting Design by CHRISTOPHER AKERLIND Costume Design by CONSTANZA ROMERO Musical Director/Composer DWIGHT D. ANDREWS Sound Design G. THOMAS CLARK Production Stage Manager KAREN L. CARPENTER
General Manager LAUREL ANN WILSON Casting MEG SIMON/FRAN KUMIN Associate Producer STEPHEN J. ALBERT Directed by LLOYD RICHARDS Presented in New York in association with the MANHATTAN THEATRE CLUB
WALTER KERR THEATRE, 219 WEST 48TH STREET

# TWO TRAINS RUNNING

## BY August Wilson · DIRECTED BY Lloyd Richards

YALE REPERTORY THEATRE, STAN WOJEWODSKI, JR., ARTISTIC DIRECTOR, CENTER THEATRE GROUP/AHMANSON THEATRE, GORDON DAVIDSON, PRODUCING DIRECTOR and JUJAMCYN THEATERS with BENJAMIN MORDECAI, EXECUTIVE PRODUCER
in association with Huntington Theatre Company, Seattle Repertory Theatre and Old Globe Theatre present LLOYD RICHARDS' YALE REPERTORY THEATRE PRODUCTION of TWO TRAINS RUNNING by AUGUST WILSON
with ROSCOE LEE BROWNE   ANTHONY CHISHOLM   LARRY FISHBURNE   CYNTHIA MARTELLS   CHUCK PATTERSON   SULLIVAN WALKER   AL WHITE   Scene Design by TONY FANNING   Costume Design by CHRISI KARVONIDES
Lighting Design by GEOFF KORF   Production Stage Manager KAREN L. CARPENTER   General Manager LAUREL ANN WILSON   Casting MEG SIMON CASTING   Directed by LLOYD RICHARDS

## WALTER KERR THEATRE
### 219 WEST 48TH STREET

## Two Trains Running

Another chapter of the Pittsburgh Cycle opened in 1992 with the debut of *Two Trains Running*, August Wilson's account of the 1960s. Although the drama takes place at the height of the civil rights movement, surprisingly, it largely ignores the turbulence of the era. The lunch counter regulars who gather in the Hill District diner do not speak of the Vietnam War, the Freedom Riders, or the Selma to Montgomery March. They mention Martin Luther King, Jr. only once. For the most part, these men are interested not in distant leaders dreaming of change, but in the day-to-day challenges of their lives. The diner's owner wonders how much money he'll get for his building, which is being bought by the city for demolition. The patrons complain about a mentally disturbed man who comes by every day in hopes of food. A retired house painter is bitter about white men who exploit black labor, and about "niggers" who don't fight back. In fact, everyone is discontented, and all talk about the problems of dealing with the white man. At the same time, they view arguments that "black is beautiful" as the desperate talk of people who are "trying to convince themselves." In *Two Trains Running*, the disparity between the legal victories being won through the civil rights movement and the social indifference faced by average African Americans is all too clear.

The August Wilson drama opened at the Walter Kerr Theatre in April 1992, featuring Laurence Fishburne (billed as Larry Fishburne and making his Broadway debut), Cynthia Martells, Anthony Chisholm, Al White, Roscoe Lee Browne, Sullivan Walker, and Chuck Patterson. Like all of August Wilson's previous plays, *Two Trains Running* was directed by the playwright's mentor, Lloyd Richards. (The two would part company in 1996, after Wilson's *Seven Guitars* was produced.)

Critics praised Wilson's musical language and his skillful use of storytelling to reveal a world hidden to outsiders. Frank Rich wrote, "The play rides high on the flavorsome talk that is a Wilson staple." But many people thought that *Two Trains Running* was out of character for Wilson because it presented no dramatic confrontations. The show closed in August 1992 after 160 performances. It was, however, nominated for several Tony Awards—including Best Play, Best Featured Actor, and Best Featured Actress—as well as the Pulitzer Prize for Drama. Laurence Fishburne took home the Tony for Best Featured Actor in a Play, and *Two Trains* also won two Theatre World awards and the Drama Desk Award for Outstanding Featured Actor in a Play (Fishburne).

◀ Set in the 1960s, *Two Trains Running* illustrates the disparity between the legal victories won by the civil rights movement and the injustice facing black Americans in their daily lives. Its 1992 opening was also the Broadway debut of actor Laurence Fishburne.

# Audra McDonald
# A Once-in-a-Generation Performer

On October 2, 2012, The Drama League of New York announced that five-time Tony Award winner Audra McDonald would be the honoree of The Drama League's 29th Musical Celebration of Broadway. Drama League Executive Director Gabriel Shanks said, "Audra McDonald, in my view, is the once-in-a-generation performer of our time." To those who had been following her career, this honor came as no great surprise.

Audra Ann McDonald was born on July 3, 1970 and was raised in Fresno, California. She began to study acting at the age of nine, and by the age of twelve, she was already performing in Roger Rocka's Dinner Theater. Clearly talented and already an experienced performer, McDonald attended the Roosevelt School of the Arts during high school and then studied classical voice at New York's Juilliard School, graduating in 1993.

Audra McDonald's breakthrough role came in 1994, when—in a famous instance of non-traditional casting—she landed the part of Carrie Pipperidge in a revival of *Carousel*. Her portrayal won her a Tony Award for Best Performance by a Featured Actress in a Musical.

While she was still at Juilliard, McDonald made her Broadway debut as a replacement in *The Secret Garden*. Her breakthrough role, however, came in a 1994 revival of the Rodgers and Hammerstein musical *Carousel*. Despite fainting at the audition, she not only landed the part of Carrie Pipperidge but also walked away with a Tony Award for Best Performance by a Featured Actress in a Musical.

In 1995, McDonald moved on to a featured role in Terrence McNally's *Master Class*. Again, the young actress was rewarded with a Tony, as was her costar, Broadway veteran Zoe Caldwell. In 1998, Audra was back on stage, this time with Brian Stokes Mitchell in *Ragtime*. Attracting outstanding notices in a musical that received only mixed reviews, McDonald became the youngest actress to win three Tony Awards and the only performer to collect three Tonys within five years.

Like many accomplished Broadway stars, McDonald has also tried her hand at acting on the silver screen and the small screen. Her first film role came in 1996, when she was cast in the motion picture *Seven Servants* with Anthony Quinn. Other films include *The Object of My Affection* (1998) and *Cradle Will Rock* (1999). But McDonald didn't make her presence felt off the New York stage until 2007, when she played Dr. Naomi Bennett on the ABC television series *Private Practice*. She has also sung regularly with several major American orchestras—including the Los Angeles Philharmonic, the Boston Symphony, and the San Francisco Symphony—and has won two Grammy Awards for her recordings.

Despite McDonald's success in many venues, Broadway is clearly her home. Since 2000, she has appeared as Lady Percy in *Henry IV* (2003), as Ruth Younger in *A Raisin in the Sun* (2004), as Olivia in *Twelfth Night* (2009), and as Bess in *Porgy and Bess* (2012). During this time, she received two more Tonys—one for the drama *A Raisin in the Sun* and the other for the musical *Porgy and Bess*. Unparalleled in versatility, Audra McDonald continues to win fans and accolades both on and off the Great White Way.

## Seven Guitars

The last August Wilson drama staged in the '90s was *Seven Guitars*. Taking place in the late 1940s, it begins after the funeral of charismatic blues musician Floyd Barton, who is being waked in the backyard of a Pittsburgh tenement. Through flashbacks, jokes, gossip, and squabbles, the characters construct the events that led to the funeral while describing a world in which the system is undeniably stacked against the black man.

*Seven Guitars* opened in March 1996 at the Walter Kerr Theatre. It marked the Broadway debut of film actress Viola Davis and also featured Keith David, Michele Shay, Ruben Santiago-Hudson, Tommy Hollis, Roger Robinson, and Rosalyn Coleman. The play received generally good reviews, with *The New York Times'* Vincent Canby calling Wilson's newest contribution "as funny as it is moving and lyrical." *Seven Guitars* ran for 188 performances and won the New York Drama Critics' Circle Award for Best Play.

Actress Viola Davis made her Broadway debut in August Wilson's *Seven Guitars* in 1996, and later appeared in two other Wilson plays—*King Hedley II* (2001), for which she received a Tony Award, and the 2010 revival of *Fences*. Davis has also made a name for herself on the silver screen, appearing in such films as *Doubt* (2008) and *The Help* (2011).

Opening in 1996, *Seven Guitars* featured Keith David, Michele Shay, Ruben Santiago-Hudson, Tommy Hollis, Roger Robinson, Rosalyn Coleman, and Viola Davis.

## *Mule Bone*

In 1991, nearly twenty years after the death of its most famous coauthor and almost sixty years after it was written, a new black play opened on Broadway. The work was *Mule Bone* and the writer was Langston Hughes.

*Mule Bone* had been completed in 1930 by Hughes and Zora Neale Hurston—key literary figures of the Harlem Renaissance. The process of writing the work had culminated in a falling out between the authors, and the play had remained unproduced for several decades. During that time, *Mule Bone* still managed to cause controversy because, in their efforts to bring the authentic language of African Americans to the Broadway stage, Hughes and Hurston had written the dialogue using black vernacular. It was feared that if it were ever staged, audiences would hear not the poetry and music of the language, but reminders of minstrelsy and vaudeville.

Based on a black folktale, the play concerns two men who are fighting for the affection of the same lady. When one of the men knocks the other out with the hock-bone of a mule, the result is a trial that turns on an issue of biblical interpretation. If the Bible does not say that a mule bone is a weapon, was a crime actually committed?

*Mule Bone* opened at the Ethel Barrymore Theatre in February 1991. Unfortunately, the story of the play's creation proved to be more riveting than the show itself, in part, because the script had been watered down through revisions. Reviewers panned the production, calling it bland and amateurish, and the long-awaited Hughes-Hurston effort ran for only 68 performances.

## THE NEW MILLENNIUM

During the twentieth century, African-American performers had made enormous progress in the theater world. Once relegated to black-only plays performed in makeshift theaters, they had slowly become accepted, first in musicals and later in dramas. By the last decades of the century, talented African Americans were dazzling audiences in serious productions written by and about African Americans, in big-budget shows that honored great black musicians, and even in dramas and musicals that had been originally written for white performers, but now featured actors and actresses of color. As more black performers made their way to the stage, the audiences, too, began to include more African Americans. As late as the 1930s, Broadway theaters had excluded black theatergoers or limited them to the balcony. Now, both casts and audiences were integrated.

Langston Hughes and Zora Neale Hurston's exclusive use of black vernacular in the play *Mule Bone* long provoked debate and anxiety. Could audiences accept the dialogue as written? When the decision was finally made to mount the play in 1991, it was heavily edited to make it less "embarrassing." Unfortunately, the revised work was found to be dull, and *Mule Bone*, though long anticipated, ran for only 68 performances.

◀ *Mule Bone* was the result of a collaborative effort by two giants of the Harlem Renaissance—Langston Hughes and Zora Neale Hurston. It was based on "The Bone of Contention," a folktale that Hurston—an anthropologist—had discovered in her hometown of Eatonville, Florida.

But while racial barriers had come crashing down in many areas of the theater—acting, writing, directing, choreography, and more—there was still one area in which there was little participation by African Americans, and that was producing. Keli Goff, writing in *The Root,* once declared that black producers are "Halley's Comet rare" on the Great White Way. In the new millennium, all this would begin to change. Stephen Byrd and Alia Jones-Harvey would become full-time producers, and celebrities like Oprah Winfrey, Whoopi Goldberg, and Alicia Keys would recognize the need to back African-American productions. This would result in a wide selection of shows for New York audiences.

## MUSICALS OF THE NEW MILLENNIUM

Like the decade before it, the first years of the twenty-first century produced a variety of Broadway musicals starring great black performers and, in many cases, exploring important African-American issues. Among the first was an adaptation of a successful film that portrayed African-American life in the early twentieth century.

### *The Color Purple*

In 1985, Alice Walker's Pulitzer Prize-winning novel *The Color Purple* was made into a movie starring Whoopi Goldberg, Danny Glover, and Oprah Winfrey. It told the story of Celie Harris, a poor African-American woman whose life in rural Georgia is marred by abuse from her stepfather and her husband, but who eventually learns her own worth through the women around her. The emotionally charged movie won both critical and popular acclaim, and in 2005, a musical version of the story was launched on Broadway.

The stage version of *The Color Purple* featured a book by Marsha Norman and music and lyrics by Brenda Russell, Allee Willis, and Stephen Bray. Interestingly, the producers of the musical included Oprah Winfrey. Winfrey—who had long been a champion of the story—invested in the play and served as one of the producers not only to help get Walker's tale to the New York stage, but also to increase the musical's visibility and accessibility. The marquee read: *Oprah Winfrey Presents: The Color Purple,* and everyone took notice. Discounted tickets were offered as a means of attracting people who had previously found Broadway shows unaffordable.

The musical opened at the Broadway Theatre in December 2005, with a cast that included LaChanze, Kingsley Leggs, and Felicia P. Fields. The reviews, while not entirely positive—the play was criticized for having a

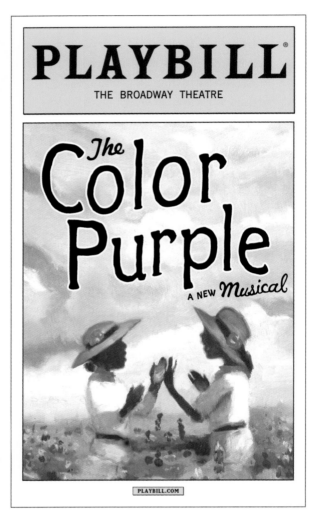

Produced by Oprah Winfrey, who offered discounted tickets to provide an affordable Broadway experience, *The Color Purple* (2005) ran for over 900 performances and drew both black and white theatergoers to the Great White Way.

In the years after Martin Luther King, Jr. was killed, reports surfaced that the U.S. Government was destroying documents related to the murder case. In 2002, politician and activist Cynthia McKinney introduced for the first time the Martin Luther King, Jr., Records Collection Act, which would release government records pertaining to King's life and death. It was proposed anew in 2010.

In 2002, playwright Suzan-Lori Parks was awarded the Pulitzer Prize for Drama for *Topdog/Underdog,* which explored the conflict between two brothers. This made Parks the first African-American woman to be so honored. At the time, Parks had already won several other major awards, including a 1996 Obie for her play *Venus* and the coveted "Genius Grant" prize of the MacArthur Foundation.

hurried, event-packed pace—praised the actors' spirited performances and promised an exhilarating theater experience. More important, the shows were packed—*The Color Purple* had recouped its investment by the end of 2006—and more than half of the audience was black. The musical ran until February 2008 for a total of 910 performances. It was nominated for eleven Tony Awards and received one for Best Performance by a Leading Actress in a Musical (LaChanze).

## Caroline, or Change

Described by *The New York Times'* Ben Brantley as a "solemn singing show with a social conscience," *Caroline, or Change* had both book and lyrics by Tony Kushner, who is best known for the Pulitzer Prize-winning play *Angels in America*. Jeanine Tesori composed the music, which combined blues, Motown, spirituals, classical music, and Jewish dance tunes. It starred Tonya Pinkins in the title role and also featured Anika Noni Rose, Harrison Chad, Veanne Cox, and Chandra Wilson.

The story concerns a black maid, Caroline, who works for a Jewish family in Louisiana during the civil rights movement of the sixties. The family's young son, Noah, has a strong emotional bond to Caroline, who provides stability for the young boy during difficult times. Then Noah's stepmother

In 2004's *Caroline, or Change*, title character Caroline Thibodeaux—played by Tonya Pinkins—spends her days doing her employers' laundry while playing the radio for company. Here, the radio is personified by three singers—Ramona Keller, Tracy Nicole Chapman, and Marva Hicks; the washing machine, by Capathia Jenkins.

comes up with a plan designed to teach Noah a lesson about his careless habit of leaving change in his pockets. Caroline is to keep the young boy's nickels and dimes in lieu of a desperately needed raise. When the arrangement goes very wrong, Noah's relationship with Caroline is ruptured.

The "solemn" musical—which contains no spoken words, but over fifty songs—was developed at the Public Theater by director George C. Wolfe. After a short run at the Public, *Caroline, or Change* was transferred to the Eugene O'Neill Theatre, where it ran from May 2004 until August 2004, for a total of 136 performances. While it had a relatively short life on Broadway, both the story and the performances received high praise. According to Jesse McKinley of *The New York Times,* the problem seemed to be that it lacked "a certain dramatic oomph." Lack of oomph notwithstanding, the show was nominated for six Tony Awards, including Best Musical, and won a Tony for Best Performance by a Featured Actress in a Musical (Anika Noni Rose).

## *Fela!*

An original Broadway musical is always a daring venture with a questionable chance of survival. But that didn't stop celebrity producers Shawn Carter (better known as Jay Z), Will Smith, and Jada Pinkett Smith from getting behind the story of Nigerian-born Fela Anikulapo-Kuti, a world-renowned musician and political activist.

*Fela!* was conceived by Bill T. Jones, Jim Lewis, and Stephen Hendel. While most of the score was the work of Fela, additional music was composed by Aaron Johnson and Jordan McLean, with lyrics by Jim Lewis. The book was written by Lewis and Jones, and Jones also provided direction and choreography. Actors Sahr Ngaujah and Kevin Mambo alternated in playing the title role, and the cast also featured Lillias White, Saycon Sengbloh, Ismael Kouyaté, and Gelan Lambert.

Originally staged off-Broadway, *Fela!* moved to the Eugene O'Neill Theatre in November of 2009, and the lavish production was greeted by wildly enthusiastic reviews. Ben Brantley of *The New York Times* praised the powerful performers, the eye-opening set, the pulsating music, and most of all, the exuberant dancing. According to Brantley, "By the end of this transporting production, you feel you have been dancing with the stars." Celebrities flocked to see the show, with high-profile audience members including Beyoncé, Denzel Washington, Harry Belafonte, Ben Stiller, Mick Jagger, Sting, Michelle Obama, and Spike Lee, who reportedly attended eight times. Enjoying a run of 463 performances, *Fela!* was nominated for eleven Tony Awards and won three: Best Choreography (Bill T. Jones), Best Costumes (Marina Draghici), and Best Sound (Robert Kaplowitz). After the show closed in January 2011, tours played on both sides of the Atlantic, and in 2012, a new production had a limited engagement at the Al Hirschfeld Theatre.

*Fela!*—which had its Broadway debut in November of 2009—is a celebration of the life and music of Nigerian pop star and political activist Fela Anikulapo-Kuti. After a successful run, the show toured both sides of the Atlantic before returning to Broadway in 2012.

In 2003, actor Brian Stokes Mitchell—whom *The New York Times* dubbed "The Last Leading Man"—became Chairman of the Board of The Actors Fund of America, a nonprofit organization that assists American entertainment and performing arts professionals. Mitchell is known for his leading roles in a range of Broadway productions, including *Ragtime* (1998) and *King Hedley II* (2001).

In 2004, following the resignation of Colin Powell, Condoleezza Rice became the first African-American woman to serve as United States Secretary of State. During her tenure, Rice advocated for "Transformational Diplomacy," which sought to relocate American diplomats to areas of severe political and social trouble and address issues such as disease, drug smuggling, and human trafficking.

# September 11 and Broadway

When two terrorist-piloted planes destroyed the Twin Towers of the World Trade Center on September 11, 2001, the nation was devastated, and nowhere were the effects more keenly felt than New York City. As smoke from the attack filled the air, city streets emptied, and tourists stayed home in fear, Mayor Rudy Giuliani gave a press conference about rescue attempts at Ground Zero. Seemingly out of the blue, the Mayor said, "The best thing you can do for our city is take in a Broadway show." Later, a representative from City Hall would explain that as long as Broadway theaters were dark, the city itself would look dark—and defeated—to the rest of the world.

Certainly, the situation in the theater district was grim. By the end of September, attendance had dropped by 80 percent, $5 million in ticket sales had been lost, and five shows had permanently closed. While the Mayor's decree didn't instantly turn the tide, it did inspire the theater community to reach out to its audience. Many shows re-opened just days after the attacks, and small crowds watched shaken performers do their best to provide a brief respite from the tragedy. Then, on September 28, 450 actors gathered in Times Square to sing "New York, New York." Performers like Bernadette Peters, Matthew Broderick, Nathan Lane, and Bebe Neuwirth said that they had banded together to tell people that there was no need to be afraid. New York was a safe place that continued to produce great entertainment.

While the Times Square gathering was a good start, clearly, it would take more than a song to rescue the Great White Way. So Broadway travelled to City Hall and Albany to ask for help—and came away with millions of dollars. An amazing 50,000 theater tickets were purchased by the city for $2.5 million. Nearly 30 percent of the tickets were given to the families of the victims, as well as firefighters and other rescue workers, while the remaining tickets went to a variety of New York organizations in the hopes of filling Manhattan's theaters. The state, following the city's lead, invested another $1 million on a promotional campaign. In addition, the Broadway community stepped up to support the relief efforts. Many producers donated $5 from every ticket sale to the Twin Towers Fund, raising about $750,000 in all. In most of the shows, performers took up collections after the final curtain, forwarding the money to downtown relief efforts. And in several theaters, the cast asked theatergoers to join them in singing "God Bless America" to boost morale.

It took time, but by March of 2002, Broadway box office numbers were back up to the previous year's levels of $12.1 million a week. In fact, Broadway was so successful that producers were obliged to give back $1 million to the city. The Mayor redirected the returns to nonprofit arts organizations, some of which were able to help off-Broadway theaters, which had not received financial aid during the original Broadway effort.

Having begun her career on Broadway, Phylicia Rashad continued to work on the New York stage even when playing Clair Huxtable in TV's *The Cosby Show*. Then, in 2004, Rashad's portrayal of Lena Younger in a Broadway revival of *A Raisin in the Sun* made her the first black woman to win a Tony Award for Best Performance by a Leading Actress in a Play.

On October 16, 2005—fourteen days after the death of playwright August Wilson—the Virginia Theatre was renamed the August Wilson Theatre, making it the first Broadway theater to be named after an African American. Wilson is best known as author of the Pittsburgh Cycle, a series of plays that chronicle the black experience in twentieth-century America.

## *Memphis*

Loosely based on the experiences of Memphis disc jockey Dewey Phillips, who was among the first white DJs to play black music, *Memphis* has a book by Joe DiPietro, music by David Bryan, and lyrics by Joe DiPietro and David Bryan. It tells the story of white DJ Huey Calhoun, whose love of music crosses race lines, and of Felicia Farrell, an aspiring young black singer who can't break out of Memphis's segregated clubs of the 1950s. Huey and Felicia meet and fall in love, and both their relationship and their careers are marked by frustration and sometimes violence because of the time and place in which they live.

*Memphis* had an extensive pre-Broadway run—from 2003 to 2009—during which the show went through many rewrites while always retaining the same two leading actors, Chad Kimball as Calhoun and Montego Glover as Farrell. In October 2009, the show made its Broadway debut at the Shubert Theatre. Critics applauded both the performers and the production, with John Simon praising its "rousing music and singing, spectacular dancing, and witty, moving story." *Memphis* ran until August 2012 for 1,165 performances. It was nominated for an array of Tony Awards and won four: Best Musical, Best Book of a Musical (Joe DiPietro), Best Original Score (David Bryan and Joe DiPietro), and Best Orchestrations (Daryl Waters and David Bryan).

## *Sister Act*

In 2011, six years after *The Color Purple* opened at the Broadway Theatre, another musical adaptation of a popular movie debuted on the Great White Way—again, with a celebrity producer. This time, the show was *Sister Act*

*Sister Act*, 2011's stage adaptation of the successful 1992 film of the same name, and *Memphis* (2009), the story of one of the first white DJs to play black music, both presented musical numbers within the context of well-drawn plots. While 2013's *Motown: The Musical* offered only a thin story line, it delighted audiences with its dynamic performance of more than fifty Motown hits.

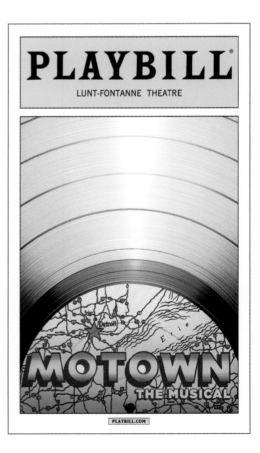

and the roster of producers included Whoopi Goldberg, who had starred in the 1992 film version of the story.

*Sister Act* has a book by Bill and Cheri Steinkellner, with additional material by Douglas Carter Beane, music by Alan Menken, and lyrics by Glenn Slater. The story concerns Deloris Van Cartier, a lounge singer whose life takes an unexpected turn when she witnesses a murder and, on police orders, ends up hiding in a convent that has fallen on hard times. Deloris helps the ailing convent by breathing life into the choir, and at the same time, she finds the sisterhood that was lacking in her life.

Productions of *Sister Act* were staged in both Pasadena, California (2006) and London (2009) before a revised adaptation opened at the Broadway Theatre in April 2011. Patina Miller, who had originated the role of Deloris Van Cartier in London, headed the integrated cast. Miller received splendid reviews, as did the cast in general, but otherwise, the critics' reactions were mixed. *Sister Act* ran for 561 performances, closing in August 2012, and was nominated for five Tony Awards.

## *Motown: The Musical*

Spirited musical revues have almost always been popular on Broadway, especially when the scores include pop classics that audiences have known and loved for decades. It's no wonder that theatergoers were delighted when Berry Gordy, the founder of legendary Motown Records, produced a show that told the story of his life while presenting dozens of the hits that helped make his company a cultural icon. Gordy himself wrote the book, basing it on his autobiography *To Be Loved: The Music, the Magic, the Memories of Motown.* The original cast included Brandon Victor Dixon as Berry Gordy, Charl Brown as Smokey Robinson, Bryan Terrell Clark as Marvin Gaye, Valisia LeKae as Diana Ross, and a host of other highly gifted performers.

*Motown: The Musical* debuted in April 2013 at the Lunt-Fontanne Theatre. Amazingly, the show featured more than fifty hits, from "ABC" and "Ain't No Mountain High Enough" to "Signed, Sealed, Delivered I'm Yours." Virtually all of Motown's great artists—Diana Ross and the Supremes, The Miracles, The Marvelettes, The Temptations, Martha and the Vandellas, The Jackson Five, and more—were represented in this nonstop celebration of the Motown Sound. Because the revue incorporated so many songs, it did skimp on storytelling. Even major figures like Smokey Robinson made only brief appearances to leave room for musical numbers. But while critics remarked on the thin story line and shorthand dialogue, audiences were clearly delighted by dynamic performances of the tunes that helped shape American music.

*Motown: The Musical* may have scrimped on storytelling—in large part, because it's impossible to tell the story of every major Motown artist in a single show—but it did not scrimp on music. Charles Sherwood of *The New York Times* called *Motown* a "musically vibrant trip back to the glory days of Detroit," and theatergoers tapped their toes to every number, from "I Heard It Through the Grapevine" to "Ain't No Mountain High Enough."

Spearheaded by a coalition of African-American leaders, the Millions More Movement was launched on October 15, 2005, the tenth anniversary of the Million Man March. Open to men, women, and children, the movement was created to unite black individuals and groups and mobilize them to change the policies that keep so many people of color in poverty.

On October 31, 2005, the body of Rosa Parks was flown to Washington, DC, where it would lie in honor in the Capitol Rotunda. Parks—who has been described as the mother of the civil rights movement—was the first woman and the second African American to receive this distinction, which is generally reserved for presidents, politicians, and soldiers.

# DRAMAS OF THE NEW MILLENNIUM

Shortly after the dawn of the twenty-first century, August Wilson—by far, the most celebrated African-American playwright to date—saw another of his Pittsburgh Cycle works staged in a New York theater. The Great White Way was still cautious about productions that centered on black issues or featured predominantly black casts, believing that they could never make back the high cost of staging a show on Broadway. Nevertheless, Wilson's drama would soon be followed by several other important African-American plays, some of which would explore the lives of prominent people of color or provide a new perspective on the black experience. Moreover, because of two determined black producers, several classic dramas that had been written for white performers would now boast African-American or multiracial casts.

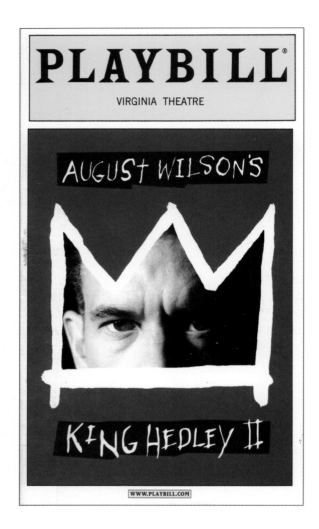

One of the darkest of August Wilson's Pittsburgh Cycle plays, *King Hedley II* had a star-studded cast that included Brian Stokes Mitchell, Charles Brown, Leslie Uggams, and Viola Davis. Davis, who had made her Broadway debut in another Wilson play, took home both a Tony Award and a Drama Desk Award for her stunning performance.

## *King Hedley II*

August Wilson's play *King Hedley II* is the ninth in his ten-part Pittsburgh Cycle. Set in the 1980s, it tells the story of King, a black man who plans to overcome a life of hardship and oppression and create a better life for himself, his wife, and his mother, by buying a video store with money he's made selling stolen refrigerators. While King longs for a brighter future, he struggles with a difficult past, which includes abandonment by his mother and time spent in jail. The conflict between big dreams and cruel legacies leads to a tragic finale.

Considered one of the darkest of August Wilson's Cycle, *King Hedley II* debuted at the Pittsburgh Public Theater. It then played in other regional theaters before opening at Broadway's Virginia Theatre in May 2001. Its star-studded cast included Brian Stokes Mitchell, Charles Brown, Leslie Uggams, Viola Davis, Stephen McKinley Henderson, and Monté Russell. For the first time, a Broadway production of an August Wilson play was directed not by Lloyd Richards, but by Marion Isaac McClinton.

Although the three-hour drama received mixed reviews, the performances were praised, as were Wilson's fine monologues. The play ran for 72 performances, closing in less than three months, but earned six Tony nominations and four Drama Desk Award nominations. For her dazzling portrayal of Hedley's wife—a woman fighting for the right to abort a pregnancy—Viola Davis took home both a Tony Award and a Drama Desk Award for Best Featured Actress. For his performance, Charles Brown also won a Drama Desk Award.

With the goal of opening Broadway to people who had never before seen a show on the Great White Way, Oprah Winfrey not only made a sizeable investment in 2005's *The Color Purple* but also placed her name on the marquee—"*Oprah Winfrey Presents: The Color Purple.*" In addition, she offered steeply discounted tickets that made the show affordable to people with lower incomes.

Since 1954's landmark case *Brown v. Board of Education,* many battles have been fought over the integration of public schools. On June 28, 2007, in *Parents Involved in Community Schools v. Seattle School District No. 1,* the Supreme Court invalidated programs in Seattle, Washington and Louisville, Kentucky that sought to create or maintain diversity by using race to help determine admissions and transfers.

# Lloyd Richards
# Championing Playwrights for Five Decades

The person chiefly responsible for bringing the plays of August Wilson to the Broadway stage was pioneering director Lloyd Richards. In fact, during his decades-long career, Richards championed generations of young and talented playwrights, both black and white, helping to shape American theater.

Lloyd George Richards was born on June 29, 1919 in Toronto, Ontario, and was raised in Detroit, Michigan. He began his college education by studying law at Detroit's Wayne University. Eventually, though, the young man—greatly influenced by a class on Shakespeare—shifted his focus to theater arts. After graduating from Wayne, he worked as an actor, first in Detroit and later in New York. He also taught acting and directed off-Broadway plays.

In the 1950s, Richards accepted the task of directing Lorraine Hansberry's *A Raisin in the Sun.* For a time, it seemed doubtful that the drama—written by an African-American woman and centering on the African-American experience—would receive the financial backing it needed to be produced on Broadway. But it did, and when it opened in March 1959, Richards became the first black director of a Broadway play. More important to Richards, he had helped the actors deliver riveting performances that were true to Hansberry's vision. The play was a groundbreaking success.

After *A Raisin in the Sun,* Richards directed further Broadway productions. As his reputation grew, he also became the head of actor training at New York University's School of the Arts; Professor of Theater and Cinema at Hunter College; Dean of the Yale University School of Drama; and, in 1981, head of the National Playwrights Conference at the Eugene O'Neill Theater Center. It was in this last capacity that he received a submission by a then unknown playwright named August Wilson. Richards was impressed, and after helping Wilson refine *Ma Rainey's Black Bottom,* he steered it through the Yale Repertory Theatre and directed its 1984 production at Broadway's Cort Theatre. Between 1984 and 1996, Richards would collaborate on and direct five additional Wilson plays, including 1987's *Fences,* which won a Tony Award for Best Director.

As head of the Playwrights Conference, Richards helped develop the careers of many writers, including Lee Blessing, David Henry Hwang, Wendy Wasserstein, and Christopher Durang. He was known as a writer's director, for he wanted the playwright's vision to be realized with as little tampering as possible. He was also known for steering his actors with a gentle hand, helping them make wise choices in the creation of their characters. When Richards died at the age of eighty-seven, a year after August Wilson's death, veteran actor Charles S. Dutton said, "Lloyd had only two sons, but he had a lot of children." Through these "children," Lloyd Richard's legacy lives on in theaters throughout the country.

From his direction of Lorraine Hansberry's *A Raisin in the Sun* to his work on August Wilson's Pittsburgh Cycle plays, Lloyd Richards helped bring the works of African-American writers to the stage. Richards was also Professor of Theater and Cinema at Hunter College, Dean of the Yale University School of Drama, and head of the National Playwrights Conference at the Eugene O'Neill Theater Center.

Stephen C. Byrd and Alia Jones-Harvey brought their first production—an all-black revival of *Cat on a Hot Tin Roof*—to the stage in 2008. The only African-American Broadway producers at the time, Byrd and Jones-Harvey then set about creating other all-black and multiracial shows as a means of attracting people of color to the New York theater district.

On July 30, 2008, the United States House of Representatives issued an unprecedented apology to African Americans for the institution of slavery and the subsequent Jim Crow segregation laws that reduced black Americans to second-class status for many years. The apology was drafted by Representative Steve Cohen, a Democrat from Tennessee.

## *Topdog/Underdog*

In 2002, a play by another talented black writer, Suzan-Lori Parks, hit Broadway. The two-man comic drama *Topdog/Underdog* tells the story of a pair of African-American brothers in their thirties who hustle on the streets playing three-card monty. Named Lincoln and Booth by a father with an unusual sense of humor, they were long ago abandoned by their parents and have had to rely on each other to survive in hopes of finding a way out of poverty. Yet their frustrations and sibling rivalry lock them in an ongoing battle.

Directed by George C. Wolfe, *Topdog/Underdog* received critical acclaim at the Public Theater in 2001 before moving to the Ambassador Theatre in April 2002. It starred actor and hip-hop artist Mos Def, in his

Suzan-Lori Parks' first full-length play, *Imperceptible Mutabilities in the Third Kingdom*, won off-Broadway's Obie Award for Best New Play when it was produced in 1989. Park's had also won a second Obie as well as a MacArthur Foundation "genius award" by the time 2001's *Topdog/Underdog* garnered the Pulitzer Prize for Drama.

*Topdog/Underdog* explores the complex relationship between two brothers, Booth (played by Mos Def) and Lincoln (Jeffrey Wright). In this scene, Booth tries to convince Lincoln to join him in a three-card monty con game.

Broadway debut, and Jeffrey Wright, who had appeared in *Bring in 'Da Noise, Bring in 'Da Funk.*

Ben Brantley, theater critic for *The New York Times*, greeted the new production with accolades for the brilliant script, the masterful direction, and the vibrant performances of the actors—especially Jeffrey Wright. Praising the work of director George C. Wolfe, Brantley called *Topdog/Underdog* "the most exciting new home-grown play to hit Broadway since Mr. Wolfe's production of Tony Kushner's *Angels in America.*" Not all of the reviewers were as enthusiastic, but all expressed admiration for what they considered to be the playwright's greatest achievement to date. For her dazzling work, Suzan-Lori Parks—who had already won two Obies as well as a MacArthur Foundation "genius award"—became the first African-American woman to receive the Pulitzer Prize for Drama. *Topdog/Underdog* attracted a diverse audience and ran until August 2002, delivering 144 performances.

## Gem of the Ocean

Three years after the debut of *King Hedley II*, another August Wilson play was produced on Broadway. *Gem of the Ocean* had first been staged in Chicago's Goodman Theatre in 2003. Then, in December 2004, it opened at New York's Walter Kerr Theatre under the direction of relative newcomer Kenny Leon. The cast included Phylicia Rashad, LisaGay Hamilton, Anthony Chisholm, Ruben Santiago-Hudson, and John Earl Jelks.

Although this was one of the last works written by August Wilson, *Gem of the Ocean* takes place in 1906, making it the first of the Pittsburgh Cycle. It tells the story of Aunt Ester (Phylicia Rashad), a 285-year-old former slave and spiritual healer who holds in her memory the complete history of Africans living in America. When drifter Citizen Barlow (John Earl Jelks) turns to Aunt Ester to absolve him of guilt for committing a crime, she launches the fugitive on a mystical ocean journey aboard the slave ship *Gem of the Ocean*, enabling him to come to terms with his wrongdoings so he can start life anew and use the freedom his people were granted more than a century ago.

This soul-stirring drama was regarded by many as one of the finest works in the ten-play series and an essential key to understanding the Pittsburgh Cycle. Although it had a short run of 72 performances, it was nominated for five Tony Awards and has since been revived in theaters all over the country.

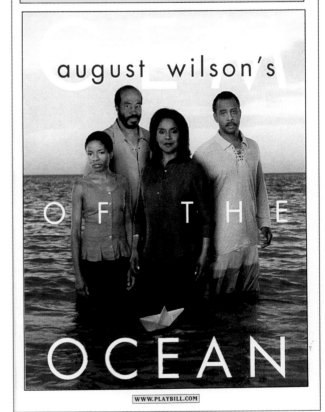

Starring (left to right) LisaGay Hamilton, Anthony Chisholm, Phylicia Rashad, and Ruben Santiago-Hudson, 2004's *Gem of the Ocean* presented what is chronologically the first story of August Wilson's Pittsburgh Cycle. Many regard it not only as one of Wilson's finest works, but also as the key to understanding his ten-play masterpiece.

At the 2008 Democratic National Convention in Denver, Colorado, Barack Obama accepted the Democratic nomination for President of the United States. Although other black leaders—such as Shirley Chisholm (1972)—had been presidential candidates, Obama was the first African American to win the nomination of a major party in a presidential election.

On January 20, 2009, Barack Obama was sworn in as the forty-fourth President of the United States. The first African American to become president, President Obama acknowledged the precedent and referred to himself as a "man whose father less than sixty years ago might not have been served at a local restaurant" because of his race.

# Phylicia Rashad
# Breaking Ground on the Great White Way

Although much of the world will always know her as Clair Huxtable of the TV sitcom *The Cosby Show,* Phylicia Rashad has also enjoyed a highly successful career on Broadway. In fact, the talented actress's initial training was for the theater, and she has made history on the Great White Way.

Born on June 19, 1948 as Phylicia Ayers-Allen, she was the second child of poet Vivian Ayers-Allen and dentist Arthur Allen. Inspired by her mother, Phylicia studied fine arts at Howard University, graduating magna cum laude in 1970. Her next step was to move to New York and pursue a career in acting.

The young actress got her first break on Broadway in *The Wiz* (1975 to 1979), in which she played a Munchkin and a field mouse. While she was thrilled to be on stage, her theater career was not moving forward as she hoped. Fortunately, the entertainment industry offered other options. In 1983, Phylicia joined the cast of the soap opera *One Life to Live,* and just a year later, she landed the role of a lifetime as an attorney, wife, and mother of five on one of television's most celebrated series, *The Cosby Show.* This was to be her home until 1992.

By the time *The Cosby Show* ended, Phylicia Ayers-Allen—now Phylicia Rashad—was well known within both television and the theater. Because *Cosby* had been filmed in New York City, from 1987 to 1989, Rashad had been able to perform in Stephen Sondheim's Broadway hit *Into the Woods.* She also appeared in *Jelly's Last Jam* (1992 to 1993). But it was not until the 2004 revival of *A Raisin in the Sun* that the actress enjoyed her long-awaited breakthrough in a leading stage role. Playing Lena Younger, the matriarch of the Younger family, Rashad became the first black woman to win a Tony Award for Best Performance by a Leading Actress in a Play.

After her triumphant run in *A Raisin in the Sun,* Rashad starred in August Wilson's prestigious *Gem of the Ocean* (2004). This was followed by Broadway roles in *Cymbeline* (2007) and *August: Osage County* (2007). Then, in 2008, Rashad played opposite James Earl Jones in an all-black version of *Cat on a Hot Tin Roof.* (See page 251 for more about this production.) In addition to having a star-studded cast, *Cat* had the distinction of being directed by Rashad's younger sister, Debbie Allen.

Phylicia Rashad has also pursued a film career, appearing in such movies as *For Colored Girls,* a 2010 adaptation of the stage play *For Colored Girls Who Have Considered Suicide When the Rainbow Is Enuf.* In 2009, Rachad reprised her award-winning role of Lena Younger in a made-for-TV film version of *A Raisin in the Sun.* For this, she won the 2009 NAACP Image Award for Outstanding Actress in a Television Movie, Mini-Series or Dramatic Special. Explaining her importance to the African-American community, Ayuko Babu, founder of the Pan African Film Festival, said, "Over the years she has had parts that give insight into who we are, from August Wilson's *Gem of the Ocean* to *The Cosby Show.* She speaks to us and lets the world know who we are."

When Phylicia Rashad was playing Clair Huxtable in TV's *The Cosby Show,* the series was filmed in New York City rather than Los Angeles. This unusual arrangement allowed Rashad to also work on Broadway, so from 1987 to 1989, the versatile actress portrayed the witch in Stephen Sondheim's *Into the Woods.*

## *Radio Golf*

The last two original productions of August Wilson's plays—*Gem of the Ocean* (2004) and *Radio Golf* (2007)—were directed by Kenny Leon. Ben Brantley of *The New York Times* praised Leon for giving *Radio Golf* an "engaging snap" and keeping "things moving at enough of a clip so that even what are essentially economics lessons have a theatrical zest."

These *Playbills* illustrate the diversity of black drama offered during the first few years of the twenty-first century. *Radio Golf* (2005)—whose Playbill bears a photo of author August Wilson—completed Wilson's ten-play exploration of the African-American experience. The 2008 production of *Cat on a Hot Tin Roof* was a classic American drama with an all-black cast. And 2008's *Thurgood* told the story of Thurgood Marshall, the first black man to become a justice of the Supreme Court.

Completed months before August Wilson's October 2, 2005 death, *Radio Golf* is the final chapter of Wilson's Cycle. Set in 1997, it's the story of Ivy League-educated Harmond Wilks, an African American who finds himself at a crossroads. A real estate developer, Wilks has done well in business and is poised to run for mayor of Pittsburgh. He should be happy—but he's not. If his latest project to revitalize the Hill District is to be completed as planned, a house must be torn down—the same house that was inhabited by former slave Aunt Ester in Wilson's *Gem of the Ocean*. Wilks begins to ponder the price of success and assimilation. Should his rich heritage, symbolized by Aunt Ester's house, be sacrificed to make way for Starbucks, Whole Foods, and the blandness of white society? That is the central question posed in this coda to Wilson's historic series of works.

Like *Gem of the Ocean, Radio Golf* was produced and developed in other theaters before making its May 2007 Broadway debut at the Cort—the same theater where Wilson's first play, *Ma Rainey's Black Bottom*, had opened in 1984. The cast included Harry Lennix (as Wilks), Anthony Chisholm, John Earl Jelks, Tonya Pinkins, and James A. Williams. Directed by Kenny Leon, it was recognized by critics as a thoughtful ending to Wilson's saga. The play ran for 64 performances, closing in July 2007. It was nominated for a string of awards, including four Tonys, and won the New York Drama Critics' Circle Award for Best American Play.

On October 16, 2005—two weeks after Wilson's death—New York's Virginia Theatre was re-named the August Wilson Theatre, making the two-time Pulitzer Prize winner the first African American to have a theater named in his honor. Since *Radio Golf's* short run in 2007, revivals of Wilson's plays *Joe Turner's Come and Gone* (2009) and *Fences* (2010) have both appeared

on Broadway. Most of Wilson's series continues to be staged throughout the country. Moreover, the full ten-play Pittsburgh Cycle has been performed several times as a tribute to Wilson's contribution to African-American theater. In 2006, the John F. Kennedy Center for the Performing Arts offered each play in staged readings with costumes and scenery. In 2013, *August Wilson's American Century Cycle* presented full dramatic readings of the plays through New York Public Radio recordings.

August Wilson's *Radio Golf* portrays the 1990s as a soul-sapping era for black Americans. Having at last been allowed to enter the white man's world, the lead character finds it bland and sanitized—devoid of the richness and meaning of his African-American heritage.

## Cat on a Hot Tin Roof

First staged in 1955, Tennessee Williams' *Cat on a Hot Tin Roof* has been a frequent visitor to Broadway. In 2008, the fifth Broadway production was launched, this time, with an important difference—an all African-American cast. Moreover, *Cat* had black producers Stephen C. Byrd and Alia M. Jones-Harvey and was directed by Debbie Allen.

*Cat on a Hot Tin Roof* opened at the Broadhurst Theatre in March 2008, starring James Earl Jones, Phylicia Rashad, Terrence Howard, and Anika Noni Rose. Although the reviews were not entirely positive, the show had a large audience, which, according to Stephen Byrd, was 70- to 80-percent African-American. It ran until June 2008 for 125 performances. (To read more about *Cat* and about Byrd and Jones-Harvey, see the inset on page 252.)

## Thurgood

In 2008, a unique one-man drama had a limited run on Broadway. *Thurgood* was written by George Stevens, Jr. and starred Laurence Fishburne in the title role of Thurgood Marshall. Although Marshall is best known as the first African American to be confirmed as a justice of the Supreme Court, the play covered Marshall's entire career, illuminating a lifetime of commitment to ensuring the equal treatment of individuals—and especially minorities—by the government.

*Thurgood* opened at the Booth Theatre in April 2008. Although it was essentially a first-person documentary on American history, Fishburne's performance was so compelling that the show was deemed "surprisingly absorbing, at times even stirring" by *The New York Times*. In addition to providing an evening's entertainment, the solo drama reminded people of the country's legacy of sanctioned racism. It also reminded them of a progressive era in which dedicated individuals won civil-rights victories that forever changed our country for the better.

*Thurgood* closed in August 2008 after 126 performances. Following its New York production, the play ran at the Geffen Playhouse in Los Angeles (2010) and the Kennedy Center in Washington, DC (2010). In 2011, a tape of the Kennedy Center performance aired on HBO.

Only ten days after Barack Obama became the first black President of the United States, Michael Steele, former Lieutenant General of Maryland, was elected the first African-American Chairman of the Republican National Committee. After holding the post for a two-year tenure marked by controversy and party debts, Steele was replaced by Reince Priebus.

To commemorate the 100-year anniversary of the NAACP, in 2009, the U.S. Postal Service issued commemorative stamps bearing the images of twelve civil rights pioneers, including Ella Baker, Daisy Gatson Bates, J.R. Clifford, Medgar Evers, Fannie Lou Hamer, Charles Hamilton Houston, Ruby Hurley, Mary White Ovington, Joel Elias Spingarn, Mary Church Terrell, Oswald Garrison Villard, and Walter White.

# Stephen Byrd and Alia Jones-Harvey
# Hitting the Sweet Spot on Broadway

Unlike many people in the theater world, Stephen Byrd did not devote his early years to the arts. He did not study acting, stage management, or producing. He was to take a more roundabout route to Broadway.

Byrd earned degrees in economics and finance from Temple University and the Wharton School of the University of Pennsylvania, respectively. His professional life began at Goldman Sachs and he went on to spend more than twenty years as an investment banker. Then Byrd's interest turned to the field of entertainment, and he became CEO of the American Cinema Group, which raised capital for television and film products. But Byrd became frustrated with Hollywood—he once said, "In Hollywood, you can die of hope"—and began exploring the possibility of producing Broadway shows. He decided to bring a new audience to Broadway, a black audience. But rather than presenting black-themed plays, he would modernize classic plays by using predominantly African-American casts. With this goal, he formed Front Row Productions, Inc.

For Byrd's first project, he decided to bring Tennessee Williams' *Cat on a Hot Tin Roof* to the Broadway stage, and he chose friend Alia M. Jones-Harvey, who worked in financial services, to join him. Now partners, the two embarked on their first venture.

It wasn't easy. In fact, Byrd and Jones-Harvey encountered great resistance to the idea of staging the American classic with an all-black cast. At first, the estate of playwright Tennessee Williams was reluctant to give them the rights to produce the work. But when Byrd signed on James Earl Jones to play Big Daddy, the Williams estate agreed, and Front Row began to secure investors. Although the process was challenging, the fledgling producers persevered, and the play opened on Broadway in 2008. Within twelve weeks, the production had recouped its investment—in great part, because black audiences turned out in droves. Although *Cat* ran for just over 100 performances, it was the highest-grossing play of the 2008 season. By combining a proven dramatic work with star appeal, Byrd and Jones-Harvey had created an "event" for black Americans.

Determined to bring African-American theatergoers to Broadway, producers Stephen Byrd and Alia Jones-Harvey offer all-black revivals of American classics such as *Cat on a Hot Tin Roof* (2008), *A Streetcar Named Desire* (2012), and *The Trip to Bountiful* (2013).

For Front Row's second project, Byrd and Jones-Harvey chose Tennessee Williams' *A Streetcar Named Desire*. *Streetcar's* highly talented multiracial cast included Blair Underwood of *L.A. Law* fame, Nicole Ari Parker, Daphne Rubin-Vega, and Wood Harris. In an interview, Underwood said that he was thrilled to be part of the show because he wanted to "push the door open further" for other minority actors. He also explained that the multiracial cast attracted a new segment of theatergoers by making them feel "included in this slice of American pie."

Although *A Streetcar Named Desire* did not sell out the house, it did well. This encouraged Byrd and Jones-Harvey to plan future projects, including an all-black revival of Horton Foote's *The Trip to Bountiful* (see page 258) and a multiracial production of Shakespeare's *Romeo and Juliet*.

Stephen Byrd once said that his shows are designed to appeal to theatergoers whose tastes run somewhere between Tyler Perry and August Wilson. "That's the sweet spot," he explained. Byrd and Jones-Harvey continue to hit the sweet spot with high-quality productions that speak to a new group of theatergoers.

## The Mountaintop

Written by Katori Hall and directed by Kenny Leon—director of the Tony-winning 2010 revival of August Wilson's *Fences*—*The Mountaintop* is a two-character fictional depiction of the last night of Martin Luther King, Jr.'s life. The play starred Samuel L. Jackson as King and Angela Bassett as a chambermaid named Camae. The story is set in a shabby motel, where King, who has just delivered his "I've Been to the Mountaintop" speech, is waiting for the return of associate Reverend Ralph Abernathy. When Abernathy is slow in arriving, King spends his time chatting with the maid who delivered his coffee. King and Camae talk, flirt, smoke cigarettes, and argue about the effectiveness of King's nonviolent methods for achieving racial equality.

First staged in London, where it received an Olivier Award for best new play, *The Mountaintop* made its Broadway debut at the Bernard B. Jacobs Theatre in October 2011. While some reviewers praised the show, calling it brilliant and moving, others criticized Bassett for being too effusive and "cute." Still, *The Mountaintop* ran until January 2012, when it closed after 117 performances.

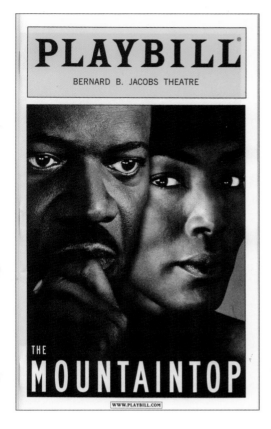

## Stick Fly

Written by Lydia R. Diamond and directed by Kenny Leon, *Stick Fly* tells the story of the conflicts within an African-American family. What makes the play very different from so many others—like Wilson's *Piano Lesson* or Parks' *Topdog/Underdog*—is that the LeVay family is well-to-do. This distinction inspired rhythm and blues singer Alicia Keys to become one of the producers of the comedy-drama. Keys explained that the play "portrays black America in a way that we don't often get to see in entertainment." And for the most part, the show explores conflicts that can occur in *any* family, regardless of ethnic background. As veteran actor Ruben Santiago-Hudson observed, the characters are "regular people with regular people's problems."

*Stick Fly* opened in December 2011 at the Cort Theatre. In addition to Santiago-Hudson, the original Broadway cast included Rosie Benton, Dulé Hill, Mekhi Phifer, Condola Rashad, and Tracie Thoms. The play met with enthusiastic audiences and mostly positive reviews, with the critics especially praising newcomer Condola Rashad, who was called "quietly captivating" and "a powerful presence" by Charles Isherwood of *The New York Times*. *Stick Fly* ran until February 2012, delivering 93 performances, and Rashad—the daughter of actress Phylicia Rashad—was nominated for the Tony for Best Featured Actress in a Play.

# Cicely Tyson
# A Lifetime of Pursuing Excellence

Not many actresses win the lead in a Broadway play at the age of eighty—and then walk away with a Tony Award for their performance. But then, Cicely Tyson is not just any actress.

Tyson was born on December 19, 1933 in Harlem, and grew up in New York. When she was still in her teens, she became a fashion model and appeared on the cover of top magazines such as *Vogue* and *Harper's Bazaar*. But Tyson was not satisfied with a career in modeling, so when she caught the eye of black character actress Evelyn Davis, who thought that the young woman would be perfect in an upcoming film, Tyson eagerly pursued this new possibility. Although the Davis film was never produced, Tyson had found a path that would bring her a lifetime of fulfilling work.

Tyson studied in various acting schools, and in 1959, the young actress appeared in an off-Broadway revival of Vinnette Carroll's *The Dark of the Moon*. This began a string of roles in New York productions, including Jean Genet's controversial *The Black*s (1961), in which she worked with James Earl Jones and Maya Angelou; *Moon on a Rainbow Shawl* (1962); *Tiger, Tiger, Burning Bright* (1962); *The Blue Boy in Black* (1963); and *Carry Me Back to Morningside Heights* (1968). Although Tyson was determined to work in a wide range of plays, she generally refused roles in musicals because she wished to break away from the stereotypical image of African Americans as natural singers and dancers who have no place in serious productions.

During the 1960s and '70s, Tyson began her career in television. She played a continuing role in George C. Scott's series *East Side/West Side* and became a frequent guest star in series such as *Naked City, I Spy,* and *The Bill Cosby Show*. At about the same time, she began working in films. Because the actress wanted to portray strong and positive women of color, it was not easy for her to find suitable parts in an era of "blaxploitation" films. Fortunately, Tyson was asked to play Rebecca Morgan in *Sounder* (1972), a movie noteworthy for its sensitive portrayal of a black sharecropper family. Tyson's performance met with critical acclaim, and she soon landed the title role in the television drama *The Autobiography of Miss Jane Pittman* (1974). A fictional account of the struggles of African Americans as seen through a black woman who lives from the time of slavery to the civil rights movement, the movie required Tyson to age ninety years. Again, the critics were dazzled, and Tyson won an Emmy for the Best Lead Actress in a Drama. When she wasn't starring in a movie or TV series, she was working on behalf of arts in the black community, helping to create further opportunities for African Americans. One of Tyson's greatest achievements was the Dance Theater of Harlem, which she cofounded with Arthur Mitchell.

Cicely Tyson never stopped looking for challenging parts in compelling stories, and at the age of eighty, she returned to the Broadway stage to take the lead in an all-black revival of *The Trip to Bountiful* (2013). A highly respected actress in television, on the silver screen, and on stage, Tyson has made it clear that she has no intention of resting on her laurels: "I think of myself as a work-in-progress to this day. . . . The day I ever feel I have attained greatness, I will be finished."

Cicely Tyson's stage career began in 1959 in an off-Broadway revival of Vinnette ▶
Carroll's *The Dark of the Moon*. Although she would become best known
through her work in television and film, in 2013, Tyson returned to the stage to
star in an all-black revival of *The Trip to Bountiful*. Her portrayal of character
Carrie Watts garnered a Tony Award for Best Performance by an Actress.

## *A Streetcar Named Desire*

In 2012, *A Streetcar Named Desire* became the second play produced by the team of Stephen Byrd and Alia Jones-Harvey. Like *Cat on a Hot Tin Roof*, Byrd and Jones-Harvey's first effort, *Streetcar* had already been revived many times, both on and off Broadway, and there had even been African-American versions of the Tennessee Williams' classic. However, the 2012 revival was the first major Broadway production to use unconventional casting.

When Byrd and Jones-Harvey had sought investors for *Cat*, they had faced challenges because so many people believed that a black version of the Williams play would not draw an audience. This time around, investors seemed to have a different concern; they felt that the *Streetcar* cast suffered from a lack of stars. Certainly, the lead actors—Blair Underwood, Nicole Ari Parker, Daphne Rubin-Vega, and Wood Harris—did not include James

In addition to the cast, this opening-night photo of *A Streetcar Named Desire* features the show's producers—Stephen Byrd (in the blue suit) and Alia Jones-Harvey (in the red dress). This second Byrd-Jones-Harvey production, like the first, helped draw more black theatergoers to the Great White Way by making them feel "included in this slice of American pie."

Earl Jones. Both Underwood and Parker were appearing on Broadway for the first time. But Byrd and Jones-Harvey pointed out that stars can bring their own problems, such as the expectation of Hollywood paychecks. By contrast, the *Streetcar* cast was excited by the opportunity to perform one of the greatest works ever produced by an American playwright. Moreover, the actors strongly felt that they could bring unique insights to the characters. Nicole Ari Parker, who played Blanche, explained that the concept of "characters who press on despite despair, heartbreak, and disillusionment is something that parallels the history of African-Americans."

After opening at the Broadhurst Theatre in April 2012, *Streetcar* received mixed reviews. While Ben Brantley of *The New York Times* panned the production, other critics, like Howard Shapiro of *The Philadelphia Inquirer,* praised the show for having "both life and heart." *Streetcar* ran for 105 performances.

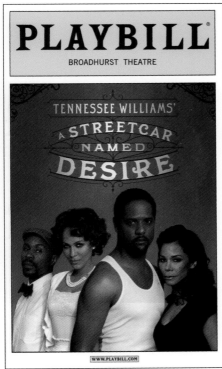

The 2012 revival of *A Streetcar Named Desire* was the first Broadway production of this drama to cast African-American actors in roles originally created for white performers. Shown on this *Playbill* are (left to right) Wood Harris, Nicole Ari Parker, Blair Underwood, and Daphne Rubin-Vega.

## *The Trip to Bountiful*

Through their revivals of *Cat on a Hot Tin Roof* and *A Streetcar Named Desire*, black producers Stephen Byrd and Alia Jones-Harvey had proven to be game changers. They had succeeded in bringing all-black versions of "white" plays to Broadway, and they had attracted a black audience, which, for many years, had been elusive. In 2013, Byrd and Jones-Harvey added another unconventionally cast play to their list of achievements. This time, they chose Horton Foote's *The Trip to Bountiful,* a work that had premiered on Broadway in 1953.

*The Trip to Bountiful* tells the story of Carrie Watts, an elderly woman who lives in a cramped Houston apartment with her son, Ludi, and his unsympathetic wife, Jessie May. Miserable in her current situation, Carrie dreams of returning to her beloved hometown of Bountiful, Texas—which is exactly what she does. Grabbing her pension check, Carrie embarks by bus to Bountiful. On the way, she meets several other travelers, including Thelma, a warm-hearted soldier's wife who becomes Carrie's traveling companion.

Aiming for star power as well as top-notch acting, Byrd and Jones-Harvey signed on Cicely Tyson to play Carrie, Cuba Gooding, Jr. to play her son, and Vanessa Williams to play Jessie May. Condola Rashad won the part of Thelma. Tyson, who was returning to Broadway after a thirty-year absence, was eighty years of age.

The drama opened in March 2013 at the Stephen Sondheim Theatre, the same theater at which it had debuted in 1953. (At that time, it was known as Henry Miller's Theatre.) Mark Kennedy of the Associated Press called the play "a first-rate revival," and even *The New York Times'* Ben Brantley—who found the play "sluggish"—praised Cicely Tyson's astounding performance. Condola Rashad, too, was singled out for her superb acting. Although the play had been written for white actors—Carrie was originally played by Lillian Gish—no one thought that the all-black cast was an issue because Foote's themes of intergenerational conflict and the desire to return home were universal. Certainly, the audience's response was warm and powerful . . . and audible. In one of the most memorable scenes, Carrie delivers a lively rendition of the hymn "Blessed Assurance." Tyson's performance was so moving that at virtually every performance, the audience would sing and clap along.

*The Trip to Bountiful* ran for nearly 200 performances before closing in October 2013. It was nominated for four Tony Awards, and Cicely Tyson took home the Tony for Best Performance by an Actress in a Leading Role in a Play. (See the inset on page 254 for more about Cicely Tyson.)

Cicely Tyson may have been in her eighties when she starred in 2013's *The Trip to Bountiful*, but according to Ben Brantley of *The New York Times*, she seemed far younger. "Once Carrie is Bountiful-bound," wrote Brantley, "she sheds years as a cat sheds fur in the summertime." Tyson's dazzling performance earned her the Tony Award for Best Performance by an Actress in a Leading Role in a Play.

On October 9, 2009, President Barack Obama was awarded the Nobel Peace Prize for "extraordinary efforts to strengthen international diplomacy and cooperation between peoples." The Norwegian Nobel Committee placed emphasis on Obama's vision of a world without nuclear weapons, which was seen as creating a climate conducive to disarmament and arms control negotiations.

The Matthew Shepard and James Byrd, Jr. Hate Crimes Prevention Act, also known as the Matthew Shepard Act, was signed into law by President Barack Obama on October 28, 2009. The act expanded the 1969 federal hate-crimes law to include crimes motivated by the victim's race, religion, ethnicity, nationality, gender, sexual orientation, and disability.

Horton Foote's *The Trip to Bountiful* explores timeless themes such as the desire to return home and intergenerational conflict. For the 2013 all-black revival of the play, producers Stephen Byrd and Alia Jones-Harvey assembled a first-rate cast, including (left to right) Vanessa Williams, Cicely Tyson, and Cuba Gooding, Jr.

# LOOKING AHEAD

The growth of black audiences is one of the most important changes that has taken place since the turn of the twenty-first century. Shows like *The Color Purple* (2005) and all-black revivals of American classics such as *Cat on a Hot Tin Roof* (2008) have given African Americans a reason to attend Broadway productions.

Struggling black actors of the early twentieth century could not have imagined the opportunities that now exist on Broadway for their twenty-first-century counterparts. Black artists are found in musicals and dramas, in starring and supporting roles. They are performing in plays written by African Americans about the black experience, and in works that were originally penned by white playwrights for white performers (and a white audience) but are now being produced with all-black or multiracial casts.

One of the most important changes that have taken place in the last few years is the growth of black audiences. Carole Shorenstein Hays, who produced August Wilson's *Fences* in 1987, once stated that in the eighties, there was no black audience because people of color didn't feel that they had a place on Broadway. That is no longer true, and the financial success of several productions—including *The Color Purple* (2005) and the 2008 revival of *Cat on a Hot Tin Roof*—has been attributed to the rising interest of black theatergoers. In a business in which less than one in four shows is able to recoup its investments, these shows are proof of the potential power of black audiences.

As more black playwrights, choreographers, composers, lyricists, producers, and other artists contribute to the theater, it will become increasingly hospitable to both African-American performers and audiences. In the words of Stephen Byrd, one of the few full-time black Broadway producers, "The heavy lifting has been done." As the twenty-first century unfolds, people of color are sure to play a growing role on the Great White Way, providing a richer experience for all theatergoers.

In 2010, Geoffrey Fletcher, writer of the screenplay *Precious*, became the first African-American screenwriter to win an Academy Award in the Best Adapted Screenplay category. A Harvard University graduate, Fletcher had attended NYU's Tisch Graduate Film Program and apprenticed under Martin Scorsese. He had also been an adjunct film professor at Columbia University.

On February 27, 2013, a statue of Rosa Parks was unveiled in National Statuary Hall in the United States Capitol. An icon of the civil rights movement, Parks is known for disobeying a Montgomery, Alabama ordinance that forced African Americans to ride in the back of local buses—a regulation that was later found to be unconstitutional by the US Supreme Court.

# Conclusion

For decades, the bright lights of the theater have lit up countless stages. They have spotlighted the talents of so many skilled people—actors and actresses, writers and producers, musicians and choreographers. Audiences have left theaters mesmerized by an extraordinary performance or humming the melodies of songs that would soon become standards. What most did not know was that for many decades, there were great performances that never reached the stage and great songs that never filled the air—simply because the barriers of racism kept talented artists separate and apart from the Great White Way.

In this book, I have tried to shine a light on the struggles of those early African-American performers who tried to gain a foothold in the world of theater; on those black men and women whose talents could not be ignored by a white establishment; and on the long road that people of color have taken to win equal access to the stage. It is my hope that the words and images found in these pages help us understand the many sacrifices that were made so that future generations would find a less difficult path to Broadway. Perhaps the spirits of those who came before can help light the way for those who continue the fight.

If there is a lesson to be learned, it is that equality can be achieved, but that the fight is long and exacts a significant toll on those on the front lines. Through the efforts of both black people and white people, tremendous strides have already been made toward achieving racial parity in every facet of American life, including the theater. Great plays featuring exceptional African-American performers are being staged even as this book goes to press. It is my hope that more change is yet to come, and that Broadway will continue to be enriched by the contribution of talented African Americans.

# Permissions

Every effort has been made to contact the photographers/copyright holders of the images used in this book. We appreciate the assistance provided by the New York Public Library in our search.

The publisher would like to offer his thanks to Wikipedia, whose image collection was the source of most of the images that appear along the bottom of many pages throughout the book.

**Foreword**
Photo on page vii reprinted by permission of Kenny Leon.

**Chapter 1**
Playbill on page 7 reprinted by permission of the Folger Shakespeare Library.

Photos on pages 8, 9, 10, 11 (right), 13, 15, 17, 20, 21, 22 (right), 23, 24, 25, and 26 from the Billy Rose Theatre Division, The New York Public Library for the Performing Arts.

Photo of Thomas Rice as Jim Crow, page 11 (left): TCS 82 (T.D. Rice). Harvard Theatre Collection, Houghton Library, Harvard University.

Poster on page 16 reprinted courtesy of Poster House, Inc.

Playbills on pages 18 and 19 reprinted by permission of the Harriet Beecher Stowe Center, Hartford, CT.

Postcard on page 22 (left) reprinted courtesy of Susan Lane of the Taconic Postcard Club.

**Chapter 2**
Photos on pages 31, 32, and 33 from *Postcards from Times Square* by George J. Lankevich. Reprinted by permission of Square One Publishers.

Photos on pages 45 and 46 by White Studio/©Billy Rose Theatre Division, The New York Public Library for the Performing Arts.

Photos on pages 36, 37, 39, 41, 42, 43, 44, 47, 53, and 54 from the Billy Rose Theatre Division, The New York Public Library for the Performing Arts.

Photo on page 55 from *Postcards from Manhattan* by George J. Lankevich. Reprinted by permission of Square One Publishers.

**Chapter 3**
Archibald John Motley's paintings "Getting Religion" (page 60) and "Black Belt" (page 86) reprinted courtesy of the Harmon Foundation of the National Archives.

Photo on page 61 from the Billy Rose Theatre Division, The New York Public Library for the Performing Arts. Photo by Paul Poole.

Photos on pages 63 (bottom), 73, 77, 79, and 83 by White Studio/©Billy Rose Theatre Division, The New York Public Library for the Performing Arts.

Photos on pages 63 (top), 64, 66, 71, 72, 74, 78, 80, and 82 from the Billy Rose Theatre Division, The New York Public Library for the Performing Arts.

Photos on pages 65, 67, 68, 69, and 81 by Vandamm Studio/©Billy Rose Theatre Division, the New York Public Library for the Performing Arts.

Photo on page 70 from the Billy Rose Theatre Division, The New York Public Library for the Performing Arts. Photo by J.W. Debenham.

Photo on page 75 from the Billy Rose Theatre Division, The New York Public Library for the Performing Arts. Photo by Lewis-Smith.

Photos on pages 84 and 85 from the Photos and Prints Division, Schomburg Center for Research in Black Culture, The New York Public Library.

**Chapter 4**
Photos on pages 91 and 92 by White Studio/©Billy Rose Theatre Division, The New York Public Library for the Performing Arts.

Photos on pages 93, 95, 98, 103 (top), 104 to 105, 113, and 114 from the Billy Rose Theatre Division, The New York Public Library for the Performing Arts.

Photos on pages 94, 106, 107, 108, 109, 110, 115, 119, and 120 by Vandamm Studio/©Billy Rose Theatre Division, the New York Public Library for the Performing Arts.

Photos on pages 96 to 97 and 99 reprinted courtesy of Special Collections and Archives, George Mason University.

Photo on page 101 from the Photos and Prints Division, Schomburg Center for Research in Black Culture, The New York Public Library. Photograph by Fred Fehl, courtesy of Gabriel Pinski.

Poster on page 102 from the Art and Artifacts Division, Schomburg Center for Research in Black Culture, The New York Public Library.

Photos on pages 103 (bottom), 116, and 117 from the Billy Rose Theatre Division, The New York Public Library for the Performing Arts. Photograph by Fred Fehl, courtesy of Gabriel Pinski.

**Chapter 5**
Photos on page 126 from the Billy Rose Theatre Division, The New York Public Library for the Performing Arts. Photographs by Fred Fehl, courtesy of Gabriel Pinski.

Photos on pages 127, 131, 132, 133 (left), and 142 by Friedman-Abeles/© Billy Rose Theatre Division, The New York Public Library for the Performing Arts.

Posters on pages 129 and 140 courtesy of Poster House, Inc.

Photos on pages 130 and 136 from the Billy Rose Theatre Division, The New York Public Library for the Performing Arts. Photographs by James J. Kriegsmann, reprinted courtesy of James Kriegsmann, Jr.

Photo on page 134 by Kenn Duncan/©Billy Rose Theatre Division, The New York Public Library for the Performing Arts.

Photos on pages 135, 137, and 143 from the Billy Rose Theatre Division, The New York Public Library for the Performing Arts.

*Playbill* cover images on pages 125, 133, and 141 used by permission. All rights reserved, Playbill Inc.

**Chapter 6**
Photos on pages 149, 150, 152 (bottom), 153 (top), 156, 157, 161, 162, 164 (bottom), 170, 171, 173, and 174 by Friedman-Abeles/© Billy Rose Theatre Division, The New York Public Library for the Performing Arts.

Photo on page 151 from the Billy Rose Theatre Division, The New York Public Library for the Performing Arts. Reprinted courtesy of Marsha Hudson, Executrix, Estate of Bert Andrews.

Photo on page 155 from the Billy Rose Theatre Division, The New York Public Library for the Performing Arts. Photograph by Fred Fehl, courtesy of Gabriel Pinski.

Photo on page 159 by Joan Marcus.

Photos on pages 163 and 167 from the Billy Rose Theatre Division, The New York Public Library for the Performing Arts.

Photo on page 165 by Kenn Duncan/©Billy Rose Theatre Division, The New York Public Library for the Performing Arts.

Photo on page 166 from the Photos and Prints Division,

Schomburg Center for Research in Black Culture, The New York Public Library. Reprinted Courtesy of Marsha Hudson, Executrix, Estate of Bert Andrews.

Photo on page 169 from the Billy Rose Theatre Division, The New York Public Library for the Performing Arts. Photo by Leroy McLucas.

*Playbill* cover images on pages 149, 152, 153, 160, and 164 used by permission. All rights reserved, Playbill Inc.

**Chapter 7**
Photos on pages 180, 181, and 190 by Friedman-Abeles/© Billy Rose Theatre Division, The New York Public Library for the Performing Arts.

Photos on pages 182, 183, 185, 188, 189, 191, 193, 194, 197, 200, 201, 204, 205, 206, 207, and 209 by Martha Swope/©Billy Rose Theatre Division, The New York Public Library for the Performing Arts.

Photos on pages 186 and 187 by Kenn Duncan/©Billy Rose Theatre Division, The New York Public Library for the Performing Arts.

Photos on pages 199 and 203 from the Billy Rose Theatre Division, The New York Public Library for the Performing Arts. Reprinted courtesy of Marsha Hudson, Executrix, Estate of Bert Andrews.

Poster on page 208 reprinted courtesy of Poster House, Inc.

Photo on page 210 from the Photos and Prints Division, Schomburg Center for Research in Black Culture, The New York Public Library. Reprinted courtesy of Marsha Hudson, Executrix, Estate of Bert Andrews.

Photo on page 211 from the Billy Rose Theatre Division,

The New York Public Library for the Performing Arts.

Photo on page 213 reprinted courtesy of Yale School of Drama/Yale Repertory Theatre.

Poster on page 214 from the Art and Artifacts Division, Schomburg Center for Research in Black Culture, The New York Public Library.

*Playbill* cover images on pages 180, 182, 186, 198, 200, and 215 used by permission. All rights reserved, Playbill Inc.

**Chapter 8**
Photos on pages 219, 223, and 249 by Martha Swope/©Billy Rose Theatre Division, The New York Public Library for the Performing Arts.

Photos on pages 221 and 234 from the Billy Rose Theatre Division, the New York Public Library for the Performing Arts. Photo by Joan Marcus.

Poster on page 222 reprinted courtesy of Poster House, Inc.

Photos on pages 224, 252, 255, 256 to 257, and 259 by Lisa Pacino, Under The Duvet Productions.

Photos on pages 226, 227, 239, and 246 by Michal Daniel.

Posters on pages 231, 232, and 236 from the Art and Artifacts Division, Schomburg Center for Research in Black Culture, The New York Public Library.

Photo on page 245 reprinted courtesy of Yale School of Drama/Yale Repertory Theatre.

*Playbill* cover images on pages 225, 228, 229, 233, 235, 238, 240, 242, 244, 247, 250, 253, and 257 used by permission. All rights reserved, Playbill Inc.

# About the Author

*Stewart Lane* fell in love with the theater when he was ten years old and saw his first Broadway show. Since then, he has devoted his life to the theater and went on to graduate from Boston University with a Bachelor of Fine Arts degree. He has acted, published two plays, and directed across the country. He is a six-time Tony Award-winning producer for *La Cage Aux Folles* (1983), *The Will Rogers Follies* (1991), *Thoroughly Modern Millie* (2002), *The Two and Only* (2006), *War Horse* (2011), and *A Gentleman's Guide to Love & Murder* (2014). He has won a 2013 Laurence Olivier Award for *Top Hat* on London's West End. In addition, he has been the recipient of four Drama Desk Awards, two New York Drama Critics' Circle Awards, and two Outer Critics Circle Awards. During his career, he has had the good fortune to work with many of the great actors of the American stage, including James Earl Jones (*The Best Man*, 2012) Leslie Uggams (*Thoroughly Modern Millie*, 2002), Blair Underwood (*Streetcar Named Desire*, 2012), and Deborah Cox (*Jekyll & Hyde*, 2013), among others.

Mr. Lane is co-owner and co-operator of the Palace Theatre on Broadway with the Nederlander Organization. Lane co-founded Broadway HD.com as a production and distribution company for stage-to-screen projects that expand the reach of live theater to audiences worldwide through digital platforms. Representing Former Mayor Rudolph Giuliani, he served on the Board of Directors at the New York State Theater at Lincoln Center and the Transitional Committee, where he appointed both the Commissioner for Cultural Affairs and the Commissioner of Film, Theater, and Broadcasting. He is both a founding member and Chairman of the Board of Directors for the Theater Museum, and he sat on the Board of Governors of the Broadway League. Currently, he serves on the Board of Governors for the Actors Fund of America, and on the Board of Advisors for the American Theatre Wing.

Stewart Lane is the author of the critically acclaimed books *Let's Put on a Show!* and *Jews on Broadway,* and is a highly sought-after speaker. He lives in Manhattan with his family. Visit him at www.mrbroadway.com.

# Index

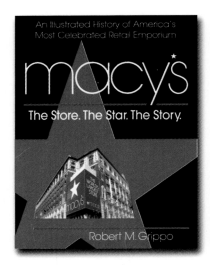
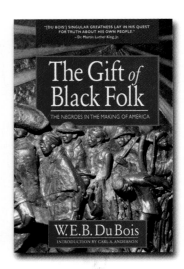

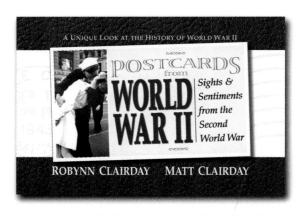
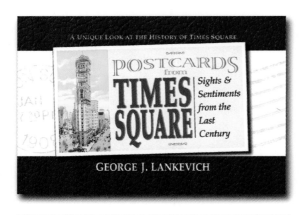